Armstrong's Handbook of Strategic Human Resource Management

FIFTH EDITION

Armstrong's Handbook of Strategic Human Resource Management

Michael Armstrong

KoganPage

LONDON PHILADELPHIA NEW DELHI

First published in Great Britain and the United States in 1992 as *Human Resource Management: Strategy and Action*
Second edition published as *Strategic Human Resource Management: A Guide to Action* 2000
Third edition 2006
Reprinted 2006
Fourth edition 2008
This edition published as *Armstrong's Handbook of Strategic Human Resource Management* 2011

120 Pentonville Road
London N1 9JN
United Kingdom
www.koganpage.com

1518 Walnut Street, Suite 1100
Philadelphia PA 19102
USA

4737/23 Ansari Road
Daryaganj
New Delhi 110002
India

© Michael Armstrong, 1992, 2000, 2006, 2008, 2011

ISBN   978 0 7494 6394 6
E-ISBN   978 0 7494 6359 3

British Library Cataloguing-in-Publication Data

A CIP record for this book is available from the British Library.

Library of Congress Cataloging-in-Publication Data

Armstrong, Michael, 1928-
   Armstrong's handbook of strategic human resource management / Michael Armstrong. – 5th ed.
      p. cm.
   Rev. ed. of: Strategic human resource management : a guide to action / Michael Armstrong. 4th ed. 2008.
      ISBN 978-0-7494-6394-6 – ISBN 978-0-7494-6395-3   1. Personnel management.
I. Armstrong, Michael, 1928- Strategic human resource management.   II. Title.
III. Title: Strategic human resource management.
   HF5549.A89784 2011
   658.3'01–dc22   2011009257

Typeset by Graphicraft Limited, Hong Kong

CONTENTS

20   Employee relations strategy 271

PART FOUR The strategic HRM toolkit   279

Introduction

Strategic human resource management (SHRM) is an approach to the development and implementation of HR strategies that are integrated with business strategies and enable the organization to achieve its goals. In essence, strategic HRM is conceptual; it is a general notion of how integration or 'fit' between HR and business strategies is achieved, the benefits of taking a longer-term view of where HR should be going and how to get there, and how coherent and mutually supporting HR strategies should be developed and implemented. Importantly, it is also about how members of HR function should adopt a strategic approach on a day-to-day basis. This means that they operate as part of the management team, ensure that HR activities support the achievement of business strategies on a continuous basis, and are consciously concerned with seeing that their activities add value.

To understand strategic HRM it is first necessary to appreciate the concepts of human resource management and strategy as covered in Chapters 1 and 2 in Part 1 (The conceptual framework of strategic HRM) respectively. The concept of strategic human resource management (strategic HRM) is then examined in detail in Chapter 3.

Part 2 of the book is concerned with the impact of strategic HRM on performance, the roles of management and HR in strategic HRM, and the processes of developing and implementing HR strategies. Part 3 covers each of the main areas of HR in which strategies are developed. The book concludes with a toolkit providing guidance on developing HR strategy through a strategic review.

PART ONE
The conceptual framework of strategic HRM

The concept of HRM

KEY CONCEPTS AND TERMS

Agency theory
AMO theory
Centre of expertise
Commitment
Contingency theory
Engagement
Hard HRM
HR architecture
HR delivery model
HR philosophy
HR policies
HR practices
HR processes
HR programmes
HR strategies
HR system

Human capital theory
Human resource management (HRM)
Institutional theory
Motivation
Organizational behaviour theory
Organizational capability
Resource-based theory
Resource dependence theory
Shared service centre
Soft HRM
Strategic business partner
Strategic human resource management
    (SHRM)
Strategic integration
Strategy
Transaction costs theory

LEARNING OUTCOMES

On completing this chapter you should be able to define the above key concepts. You should also understand:

- the nature and goals of human resource management (HRM);
- that HRM in practice is highly diverse;
- how HRM functions as a system;
- the ethical dimension of HRM;
- the critical evaluation points that can be made about HRM.

Introduction

The concepts of human resource management (HRM) and strategy (strategic management) provide the basis for strategic human resource management (SHRM). Wright and McMahan (1992: 295) explained that the field of human resource management has 'sought to become integrated with the strategic management process through the development of a new discipline referred to as strategic human resource management'. SHRM has been described by Boxall (1996) as the interface between HRM and strategic management.

Before considering SHRM it is therefore necessary to examine the processes of HRM and strategy and these will be covered in this chapter and Chapter 2 respectively. In the first part of this chapter HRM is defined and its meaning is examined in terms of its philosophy and underpinning theories. In the second part, the concept of HRM is further explored by reference to its goals, characteristics, diversity and ethical dimension. The criticisms the concept has generated – mainly from academics in the 1980s and 1990s – are summarized in the third part. The final part describes how HRM is delivered and the contexts within which delivery takes place.

The next chapter will deal with strategy – defining its nature as a means of developing a course of action for achieving an organization's purpose and discussing the major concepts associated with strategy that play an important part in SHRM, especially those relating to strategic management, strategic fit and the resource-based view. Against this background, the concept of SHRM will be explored in Chapter 3.

HRM defined

Human resource management (HRM) was defined by Boxall and Purcell (2003: 1) as 'all those activities associated with the management of employment relationships in the firm' and by Boxall et al (2007: 7) as: 'The management of work and people in organizations'. Boxall and Purcell (2010: 29) described HRM as 'an inevitable process that accompanies the growth of organizations'. HRM covers activities such as human capital management, knowledge management, organization design and development, resourcing (workforce planning, recruitment and selection, and talent management), performance management, learning and development, reward management, employee relations and employee well-being.

The notion of HRM as developed primarily by academics has a strong conceptual basis drawn from the behavioural sciences and from human capital and industrial relations theories. This chapter focuses on the concepts that underpin the HRM model, as these contribute significantly to the concept of SHRM.

The philosophy of human resource management

As conceived by the pioneers in the 1980s, the notion of human resource management is based on a philosophy that is fundamentally different from the personnel management practices of the time. Beer et al (1984: 1) started with the proposition that: 'Human resource management (HRM) involves all management decisions and actions that affect the nature of the relationship between the organization and employees – its human resources'. They believed that: 'Today... many pressures are demanding a broader, more comprehensive and more strategic perspective with regard to the organization's human resources' (ibid: 4). They also stressed that it was necessary to adopt 'a longer-term perspective in managing people and consideration of people as a potential asset rather than merely a variable cost' (ibid: 6). Beer and his colleagues (the 'Harvard school') were the first to underline the HRM tenet that it belongs to line managers. They suggested that HRM had two characteristic features: (1) line managers accept more responsibility for ensuring the alignment of competitive strategy and HR policies; (2) HR has the mission of setting policies that govern how HR activities are developed and implemented in ways that make them more mutually reinforcing.

The other major early contributors to the development of the philosophy of HRM – Fombrun et al (1984) – developed what has been termed their 'matching model', which indicated that HR systems and the organization structure should be managed in a way that is congruent with organizational strategy. This point was made in their classic statement that: 'The critical management task is to align the formal structure and human resource systems so that they drive the strategic objectives of the organization' (ibid: 37). They therefore took the first steps towards the concept of SHRM.

Following these US pioneers, as Legge (2005: 101) noted, the old term 'personnel management' increasingly gave way to human resource management (HRM). She commented that 'the term [HRM] was taken up by both UK managers (for example, Armstrong, 1987; Fowler, 1987) and UK academics'. Hendry and Pettigrew (1990: 20) observed that: 'What HRM did at this point was to provide a label to wrap around some of the observable changes, while providing a focus for challenging deficiencies – in attitudes, scope, coherence, and direction – of existing personnel management'.

The following full explanation of HRM philosophy was made by Legge (1989: 25), whose analysis of a number of HRM models identified the following common themes:

> That human resource policies should be integrated with strategic business
> planning and used to reinforce an appropriate (or change an inappropriate)
> organizational culture, that human resources are valuable and a source of
> competitive advantage, that they may be tapped most effectively by mutually

consistent policies that promote commitment and which, as a consequence, foster a willingness in employees to act flexibly in the interests of the 'adaptive organization's' pursuit of excellence.

Storey (2001: 7) noted that the beliefs of HRM included the assumptions that it is the human resource that gives competitive edge, that the aim should be to enhance employee commitment, that HR decisions are of strategic importance and that therefore HR policies should be integrated into the business strategy.

The philosophy underpinning this notion of HRM provided a new vision that was strongly criticized by many commentators during the 1990s (see the critical evaluation of HRM later in this chapter). It was supposed to be substantially different from old-fashioned personnel management, a term that has virtually disappeared since then, although in some quarters the term 'people management' has been adopted, possibly by those who dislike the connotations of 'human resources' with its apparent emphasis on exploitation and treating people as factors of production. However, whether it is called human resource management, people management or employment management, the essential nature of the ways in which organizations manage and relate to their employees has not always changed significantly from that of personnel management. New techniques and approaches (some of them 'flavours of the month') may have been introduced. But they have been treated as aspects of people management, not offspring of the human resource management philosophy.

Underpinning theories of HRM

However, the original concept of HRM had a strong theoretical base that still has relevance to the practice of people management. As David Guest (1987: 505) commented at the time: 'Human resource management appears to lean heavily on theories of commitment and motivation and other ideas derived from the field of organizational behaviour'. These theories are summarized below.

Commitment

The significance in HRM theory of organizational commitment (the strength of an individual's identification with, and involvement in, a particular organization) was highlighted in a seminal *Harvard Business Review* article by Richard Walton (Walton, 1985).

SOURCE REVIEW   From control to commitment – Walton
(1985: 77)

Workers respond best – and most creatively – not when they are tightly controlled by management, placed in narrowly defined jobs and treated as an unwelcome necessity, but, instead, when they are given broader responsibilities, encouraged to contribute and helped to take satisfaction in their work. It should come as no surprise that eliciting commitment – and providing the environment in which it can flourish – pays tangible dividends for the individual and for the company.

The traditional concept of organizational commitment is very similar to the more recent notion of organizational engagement (see Chapter 14).

Organizational behaviour theory

Organizational behaviour theory describes how people within their organizations act individually or in groups and how organizations function in terms of their structure, processes and culture. It therefore influences HRM approaches to organization design and development and enhancing organizational capability (the capacity of an organization to function effectively in order to achieve desired results). The following are the characteristics of organizational behaviour theory.

SOURCE REVIEW   Characteristics of organizational behaviour
– Ivancevich et al (2008: 11)

- It is a way of thinking about individuals, groups and organizations.

- It is multidisciplinary – it uses principles, models, theories and methods from other disciplines.

- There is a distinctly humanistic orientation – people and their attitudes, perceptions, learning capacities, feelings and goals are of major importance.

- It is performance-orientated – it deals with the factors affecting performance and how it can be improved.

- The use of scientific method is important in studying variables and relationships.

- It is applications-orientated in the sense of being concerned with providing useful answers to questions that arise when managing organizations.

Motivation

Motivation theory explains the factors that affect goal-directed behaviour and therefore influences the approaches used in human resource management to enhance engagement (the situation in which people are committed to their work and the organization and motivated to achieve high levels of performance). The two most influential motivation theories are those relating to intrinsic motivation and expectancy theory.

Intrinsic motivation refers to the self-generated factors affecting people's behaviour, which may arise from the work itself. Deci and Ryan (1985) suggested that intrinsic motivation is based on the needs to be competent and self-determining (that is, to have a choice). Intrinsic motivation can by enhanced by job or role design. In their job characteristics model, Hackman and Oldham (1974) emphasized the importance of the core job dimensions as motivators, namely: skill variety, task identity, task significance, autonomy and feedback. This links with the proposal by Walton (1985: 79) that: 'In this new commitment-based approach to the work force, jobs are designed to be broader than before, to combine planning and implementation, and to include efforts to upgrade operations, not just maintain them'.

Expectancy theory explains that motivation will be high when people know what they have to do to get a reward (which may be financial or non-financial), expect that they will be able to get the reward, and expect that the reward will be worthwhile. The theory recognizes that people have different types of needs, wants and goals and that this must be taken into account in devising HR policies and practices, especially those concerned with motivation and reward.

Expectancy theory was pioneered by Vroom (1964) and developed by Porter and Lawler (1968), who proposed that high individual performance depends on high motivation plus possession of the necessary skills and abilities, and an appropriate role and understanding of that role. From this, as Guest (1997: 268) declared: 'It is a short step to specify the HR practices that encourage high skills and abilities, for example careful selection and high investment in training; high motivation, for example employee involvement and possibly performance-related pay; and an appropriate role structure and role perception, for example job design and extensive communication and feedback'.

AMO theory

The 'AMO' formula as set out by Boxall and Purcell (2003) states that performance is a function of Ability + Motivation + Opportunity to participate. HRM practices therefore impact on individual performance if they encourage discretionary effort, develop skills and provide people with the opportunity to perform. The formula provides the basis for developing HR systems that attend to employees' interests, namely their skill requirements, motivations and the quality of their job.

Human capital theory

Human capital theory is concerned with how people in an organization contribute their knowledge, skills and abilities to enhancing organizational capability and the significance of that contribution. As Jackson and Schuler (2007: 25) stated: 'Organizations can use HRM in a variety of ways to increase their human capital... For example, they can "buy" human capital in the market (eg by offering desirable compensation packages) or "make" it internally (eg by offering extensive training and development opportunities)'.

Resource dependence theory

Resource dependence theory groups and organizations gain power over each other by controlling valued resources. HRM activities are assumed to reflect the distribution of power in the system.

Resource-based theory

Resource-based theory, often referred to as the resource-based view, blends concepts from organizational economics (Penrose, 1959) and strategic management (Barney, 1991). The theory states that competitive advantage is achieved if a firm's resources are valuable, rare and costly to imitate. HRM can play a major part in ensuring that the firm's human resources meet those criteria.

Institutional theory

Organizations conform to internal and external environmental pressures in order to gain legitimacy and acceptance.

Transaction costs theory

Transaction costs economics assumes that businesses develop organizational structures and systems that economize the costs of the transactions (interrelated exchange activities) that take place during the course of their operations. The approach used will take account of the phenomenon of bounded rationality (the extent to which people behave rationally is limited by their capacity to understand the complexities of the situation they are in and their emotional reactions to it) and the tendency toward opportunism (satisfying self-interest). To take advantage of bounded rationality and minimize opportunism, implicit and explicit contracts are made and HRM practices are set up to manage these contracts.

Agency theory

Agency theory, also known as principal-agent theory, explains that in most firms there is a separation between the owners (the principals) and the agents (the managers). The principals may not have complete control over their agents. The latter can therefore act in ways that are not fully revealed to their principals and that may not be in accordance with the wishes of those principals. Agency theory indicates that it is desirable to operate a system of incentives for agents, ie directors or managers, to motivate and reward acceptable behaviour.

Contingency theory

Contingency theory states that HRM practices are dependent on the organization's environment and circumstances. This means that, as Paauwe (2004: 36) explained: 'the relationship between the relevant independent variables (eg HRM policies and practices) and the dependent variable (performance) will vary according to the influences such as company size, age and technology, capital intensity, degree of unionization, industry/sector ownership and location'.

Contingency theory is associated with the concept of fit – the need to achieve congruence between an organization's HR strategies, policies and practices and its business strategies within the context of its external and internal environment.

Karen Legge (1978: 97) exercised a major influence on the acceptance of the relevance of contingency theory. She observed that: 'Contingency theory in its positive sense just makes the theoretical point that it is "contingencies" in an organization's environment that, acting as both constraints and opportunities, influence the organization's structure and processes'. She also produced the following suggestions on applying contingency theory.

SOURCE REVIEW   Contingent approach to managerial problem solving – Legge (1978: 99)

- An objective-setting exercise, based on a diagnosis of what specific objectives are appropriate to the organizational context involved.

- An analytical classification of the alternatives (whether payment systems or management styles or different approaches to reorganizing work) that are the subject of the design exercise.

- An analysis, preferably involving the construction of a dynamic processual model, of the context in which such an alternative is to apply.

- The selection of one of the alternatives on the basis that it 'fits' the context in which it is to operate in such a way as to facilitate the achievement of the specified objectives.

- A recognition of the need to evaluate systematically not only the basis for selecting a specific alternative in the first instance, but its degree of success following implementation.

The goals of HRM

The overall purpose of human resource management (or people management) is to ensure that the organization is able to achieve success through people. Ulrich and Lake (1990: 96) remarked that: 'HRM systems can be the source of organizational capabilities that allow firms to learn and capitalize on new opportunities'. The following policy goals for HRM were suggested by David Guest (1991: 154–59):

- Commitment: behavioural commitment to pursue agreed goals and attitudinal commitment reflected in a strong identification with the enterprise.
- Flexibility: functional flexibility and the existence of an adaptable organization structure with the capacity to manage innovation.
- Quality: this refers to all aspects of managerial behaviour that bear directly on the quality of goods and services provided, including the management of employees and investment in high-quality employees.
- Strategic integration: the ability of the organization to integrate HRM issues into its strategic plans, ensure that the various aspects of HRM cohere, and provide for line managers to incorporate a HRM perspective into their decision making.

Commitment, as defined by Guest, is similar to the more recent concept of engagement (see Chapter 14).

The policy goals for HRM identified by Caldwell (2001) included managing people as assets that are fundamental to the competitive advantage of the organization, aligning HRM policies with business policies and corporate strategy, and developing a close fit of HR policies, procedures and systems with one another. Boxall and Purcell (2003, p 11) stated that the economic goals of HRM are 'cost effectiveness, organizational flexibility, short-run responsiveness and long-run agility'.

Characteristics of HRM

Conceptually, the characteristics of HRM are that it is:

- strategic with an emphasis on integration;
- commitment-orientated;
- based on the belief that people should be treated as assets (human capital);
- unitarist rather than pluralist, ie based on the belief that management and employees share the same concerns and it is therefore in both their interests to work together, rather than the belief that the interests of employees will not necessarily coincide with their employers;

- individualistic rather than collective in its approach to employee relations;
- a management-driven activity – the delivery of HRM is a line management responsibility;
- focused on business values, although this emphasis is being modified in some quarters and more recognition is being given to the importance of moral and social values.

But HRM also has an ethical dimension, which means that it expresses its concern for the rights and needs of people in organizations through the exercise of social responsibility.

The diversity of HRM

Although HRM can be described generally in terms of the characteristics listed above, many HRM models exist, and practices within different organizations are diverse, often only corresponding to the conceptual version of HRM in a few respects. Dyer and Holder (1998) have pointed out that HRM goals vary according to competitive choices, technologies, characteristics of employees (eg could be different for managers) and the state of the labour market. Boxall (2007: 48) remarked that: 'Human resource management covers a vast array of activities and shows a huge range of variations across occupations, organizational levels, business units, firms, industries and societies'.

Hard and soft HRM

As an illustration of this diversity, a distinction was made by Storey (1989: 8) between the 'hard' and 'soft' versions of HRM. He wrote that: 'The hard one emphasizes the quantitative, calculative and business-strategic aspects of managing human resources in as "rational" a way as for any other economic factor. By contrast, the soft version traces its roots to the human-relations school; it emphasizes communication, motivation and leadership.' The human relations school referred to by John Storey was founded by Elton Mayo (1933) but its leading exponent was Douglas McGregor (1960). His 'theory Y' stressed the importance of recognizing the needs of both the organization and the individual and creating conditions that would reconcile these needs so that members of the organization could work together for its success and share in its rewards.

However, it was pointed out by Keenoy (1997: 838) that 'hard and soft HRM are complementary rather than mutually exclusive practices', and research in eight UK organizations by Truss et al (1997) indicated that the distinction between hard and soft HRM was not as precise as some commentators have implied. Their conclusions are set out below.

SOURCE REVIEW   Conclusions on hard and soft models of HRM – Truss et al (1997: 70)

Even if the rhetoric of HRM is 'soft', the reality is almost always 'hard', with the interests of the organization prevailing over those of the individual. In all the organizations, we found a mixture of both hard and soft approaches. The precise ingredients of this mixture were unique to each organization, which implies that factors such as the external and internal environment of the organization, its strategy, culture and structure all have a vital role to play in the way in which HRM operates.

The ethical dimension

HRM has an ethical dimension; that of exercising concern for the interests (well-being) of employees, bearing in mind Schneider's (1987: 450) view that 'organizations are the people in them: ... people make the place'. Beer et al (1984: 13) emphasized that: 'It is not enough to ask how well the management of human resources serves the interests of the enterprise. One should ask how well the enterprise's HRM policies serve the well-being of the *individual employee*' (original emphasis). Ulrich (1997: 5) argued that HR professionals should 'represent both employee needs and implement management agendas'. Boxall et al (2007: 5) pointed out that: 'While HRM does need to support commercial outcomes (often called "the business case"), it also exists to serve organizational needs for social legitimacy'.

Ideally an ethical approach would involve:

- treating people equally in terms of the opportunities for employment, learning and development provided for them;
- treating people according to the principles of procedural justice (Adams, 1965 and Leventhal, 1980), ie the ways in which people are managed are fair, consistent and transparent;
- treating people according to the principles of distributive justice (Adams, 1965 and Leventhal, 1980), ie rewards are distributed to them according to their contribution and they receive what was promised to them;
- treating people according to the principles of natural justice, ie individuals should know the standards they are expected to achieve and the rules to which they are expected to conform, they should be given a clear indication of where they are failing or what rules have been broken and, except in cases of gross misconduct, they should be given a chance to improve before disciplinary action is taken;

- taking account of the views of employees on matters that affect them;
- being concerned with the well-being of employees as well as the pursuit of commercial gain;
- offering as much security of employment as possible;
- providing a working environment that protects the health and safety of employees and minimizes stress;
- acting in the interests of providing a reasonable balance for employees between their life and their work;
- protecting employees against harmful practices at work, eg bullying, harassment and discrimination.

But ethical behaviour on the part of employers may not be regarded as important and certainly does not necessarily happen. It was asserted by Winstanley and Woodall (2000: 6) that 'the ethical dimension of HR policy and practice has been almost ignored in recent texts on HRM, where the focus has shifted to "strategic fit" and "best practice" approaches'. Grant and Shields (2002) stated that the emphasis typically placed on the business case for HRM suggests a one-sided focus on organizational outcomes at the expense of employees. It is interesting to note that overall ethical considerations are not mentioned in the 2009 version of the Chartered Institute of Personnel and Development's Profession Map – does this mean that the professional institute for HR practitioners in the UK attaches no importance to ethics?

Critical evaluation of the concept of HRM

On the face of it, the original concept of HRM had much to offer, at least to management. But the following reservations have been expressed about it:

- Even if HRM does exist as a distinct process, which many doubt, it is full of contradictions (Blyton and Turnbull, 1992).
- HRM is simplistic – as Fowler (1987: 3) wrote: 'The HRM message to top management tends to be beguilingly simple. Don't bother too much about the content or techniques of personnel management, it says. Just manage the context. Get out from behind your desk, bypass the hierarchy, and go and talk to people. That way you will unlock an enormous potential for improved performance.'
- The HRM rhetoric presents it as an all or nothing process that is ideal for any organization, despite the evidence that different business environments require different approaches.
- The unitarist/managerialist approach to industrial relations implicit in HRM prompted Fowler (1987: 3) to write: 'At the heart of the concept is the complete identification of employees with the aims and values of the business – employee involvement but on the company's

terms. Power in the HRM system remains very firmly in the hands of the employer. Is it really possible to claim full mutuality when at the end of the day the employer can decide unilaterally to close the company or sell it to someone else?'

- HRM appears torn between preaching the virtues of individualism (concentration on the individual) and collectivism in the shape of teamwork (Legge, 1989).

- There is a potential tension between the development of a strong corporate culture and employees' ability to respond flexibly and adaptively (Legge, 1989).

- HRM is 'macho-management dressed up as benevolent paternalism' (Legge, 2005: 48).

- HRM is manipulative. The forces of internal persuasion and propaganda may be deployed to get people to accept values with which they may not be in accord and that in any case may be against their interests. Willmott (1993: 534) asserted that: 'any (corporate) practice/value is as good as any other so long as it secures the compliance of employees'.

- 'The more we study HRMism, the more we find out about it and the more we elaborate it, the more elusive and obscure it becomes.' (Keenoy, 1997: 825).

- Guest (1991: 149) referred to the 'optimistic but ambiguous label of human resource management'.

There may be something in these criticisms but the fact remains that as a description of people management activities in organizations, HRM is here to stay, even if it is applied diversely or only used as a label to describe traditional personnel management practices. There is much talk now about such things as HR strategy, human capital management, engagement, talent management and partnership, as well as plenty of developments in people management practices such as competency-based HRM, e-HRM, high performance work systems, performance management and reward management. But with the possible exception of HR strategy, these have not been introduced under the banner of the HRM concept as originally defined.

In the words of John Storey (2001: 5), HRM has to a degree become 'a generic term simply denoting any approach to employment management'. The ways in which it is delivered as described below take place irrespective of the degree to which what is done corresponds with the conceptual HRM model.

How HRM is delivered

HRM is delivered through the HR architecture of an organization, which includes the HR system and the HR delivery model adopted by the HR function.

HR architecture

Purcell (1999: 38) suggested that the focus should be on 'appropriate HR architecture and the processes that contribute to organizational performance'. HR architecture is much more than just the structure of the HR function; it also includes the HR systems and processes and employee behaviours. As explained by Becker et al (2001: 12): 'We use the term HR architecture to broadly describe the continuum from the HR professionals within the HR function, to the system of HR related policies and practices, through the competencies, motivation and associated behaviours of the firm's employees'. Becker and Huselid (2006: 899) stated that: 'It is the fit between the HR architecture and the strategic capabilities and business processes that implement strategy that is the basis of HR's contribution to competitive advantage'. It was noted by Hird et al (2010: 25) that: '... this architecture is seen as a unique combination of the HR function's structure and delivery model, the HR practices and system, and the strategic employee behaviours that these create'.

The HR system

The HR system consists of the interrelated and jointly supportive HR practices that together enable HRM goals to be achieved. The HR structure and method of delivery are important but as Becker and Huselid (2006) argue, it is the HR system that is the key HR asset. Boselie et al (2005: 73) pointed out that in its traditional form HRM can be viewed as 'a collection of multiple discrete practices with no explicit or discernible link between them. The more strategically minded system approach views HRM as an integrated and coherent bundle of mutually reinforcing practices.' Kepes and Delery (2007: 385) comment that 'One of the defining characteristics of SHRM has been the proposition that HRM systems and not individual HRM practices are the source of competitive advantage: specifically, it is proposed that coherent and internally aligned systems form "powerful connections" that create positive synergistic effects on organizational outcomes'.

As illustrated in Figure 1.1, a HRM system brings together HR philosophies that describe the overarching values and guiding principles adopted in managing people. Taking account of the internal and external contexts in which the organization operates, a HRM system also develops:

- HR strategies that define the direction in which HRM intends to go;
- HR policies that provide guidelines defining how these values, principles and strategies should be applied and implemented in specific areas of HRM;
- HR processes that comprise the formal procedures and methods used to put HR strategic plans and policies into effect;

FIGURE 1.1   An HRM system

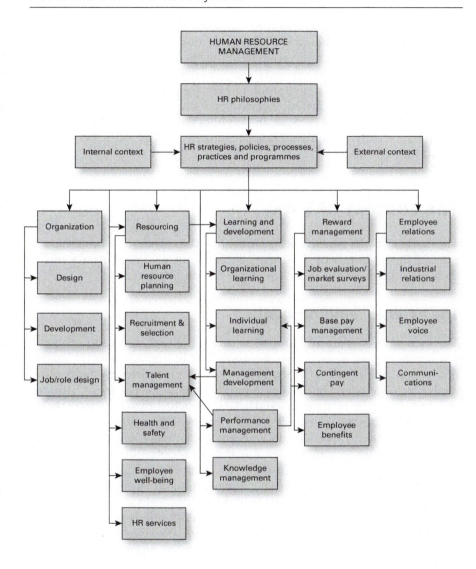

- linked HR practices that consist of the approaches used in managing people;
- HR programmes that enable HR strategies, policies and practices to be implemented according to plan.

The HR delivery model

The HR delivery model is the approach used by HR to make a strategic contribution to the achievement of organizational goals, provide specialist expertise, and carry out the transaction elements of HR's work such as recruitment, training and administration. This may or may not be translated into the so-called 'three-legged stool' of HR structure consisting of strategic business partners, a centre of expertise and shared services. This is based broadly on Ulrich's (1997) ideas, although, as reported by Hird et al (2010), Ulrich has recently stated that this is not actually 'his idea' at all, but an interpretation of his writing.

The context of HRM

The design of a HR system takes place within the context of the internal and external environments of the organization. In line with contingency theory, these exert considerable influence on the HR architecture.

The external environment

The external environment consists of social, political, legal and economic developments and competitive pressures. Global competition in mature production and service sectors is increasing. This is assisted by easily transferable technology and reductions in international trade barriers. Customers are demanding more as new standards are reached through international competition. Organizations are reacting to this competition by becoming 'customer focused', speeding up response times, emphasizing quality and continuous improvement, accelerating the introduction of new technology, operating more flexibly and 'losing cost'. The pressure has been for businesses to become 'lean and mean', downsizing and cutting out layers of management and supervision. They reduce permanent staff to a core of essential workers, increase the use of peripheral workers (sub-contractors, temporary staff) and 'outsource' work to external service providers. These pressures can be considerable in an economic downturn such as the one that began in 2008.

The internal environment

The following aspects of the internal environment will affect HR policy and practice:

- the type of business or organization – private, public or voluntary sector; manufacturing or service;
- the size of the organization;
- the age or maturity of the organization;

- the technology or key activities of the business (this will determine how work is organized, managed and carried out);
- the type of people employed, eg professional staff, knowledge workers, technicians, administrators, production workers, sales and customer service staff;
- the financial circumstances of the organization, especially in economic downturns;
- the organization's culture – the established pattern of values, norms, beliefs, attitudes and assumptions that shapes the ways in which people behave and things get done;
- the political and social climate within the organization.

KEY LEARNING POINTS

HRM defined

Human resource management (HRM) is concerned with how people are employed and managed in organizations.

Philosophy of HRM

The beliefs of HRM include the assumptions that it is the human resource that gives competitive edge, that the aim should be to enhance employee commitment, that HR decisions are of strategic importance, and that therefore HR policies should be integrated into the business strategy.

Underpinning theories

'Human resource management appears to lean heavily on theories of commitment and motivation and other ideas derived from the field of organizational behaviour' (Guest, 1987: 505).

Goal of HRM

The goal of HRM is to ensure that the organization is able to achieve success through people.

Characteristics of HRM

The characteristics of HRM are that it is:

- strategic with an emphasis on integration;
- commitment-orientated;
- based on the belief that people should be treated as assets (human capital);

- unitarist rather than pluralist, ie based on the belief that management and employees share the same concerns and it is therefore in both their interests to work together, rather than the belief that the interests of employees will not necessarily coincide with those of their employers;
- individualistic rather than collective in its approach to employee relations;
- a management-driven activity – the delivery of HRM is a line management responsibility;
- focused on business values, although this emphasis is being modified in some quarters and more recognition is being given to the importance of moral and social values.

The diversity of HRM

Although HRM can be described generally in terms of the characteristics listed above, many HRM models exist and practices within different organizations are diverse, often only corresponding to the conceptual version of HRM in a few respects.

The ethical dimension of HRM

HRM has an ethical dimension; that of exercising social responsibility, ie being concerned for the interests (well-being) of employees and acting ethically with regard to the needs of people in the organization.

Reservations about HRM

On the face of it, the concept of HRM has much to offer, at least to management. But reservations have been expressed about it. There may be something in these criticisms but the fact remains that as a description of people management activities in organizations, HRM is here to stay, even if it is applied diversely or only used as a label to describe traditional personnel management practices.

Delivery of HRM

HRM is delivered through the HR architecture of an organization, which includes the HR system and the HR delivery model adopted by the HR function.

The context of HRM

The design of a HR system takes place within the context of the internal and external environments of the organization. In line with contingency theory, these exert considerable influence on the HR architecture.

References

Adams, J S (1965) Injustice in social exchange, in *Advances in Experimental Psychology*, (ed) L Berkowitz, Academic Press, New York

Armstrong, M (1987) Human resource management: a case of the emperor's new clothes, *Personnel Management*, August, pp 30–35

Barney, J B (1991) Firm resources and sustained competitive advantage, *Journal of Management*, 17 (1), pp 99–120

Becker, B E and Huselid, M A (2006) Strategic human resource management: where do we go from here? *Journal of Management*, 32 (6), pp 898–925

Becker, B E, Huselid, M A and Ulrich, D (2001) *The HR Score Card: Linking people, strategy, and performance*, Harvard Business School Press, Boston, MA

Beer, M et al (1984) *Managing Human Assets*, The Free Press, New York

Blyton, P and Turnbull, P (eds) (1992) *Reassessing Human Resource Management*, Sage Publications, London

Boselie, P, Dietz, G and Boon, C (2005) Commonalities and contradictions in HRM and performance research, *Human Resource Management Journal*, 15 (3), pp 67–94

Boxall, P F (1996) The strategic HRM debate and the resource-based view of the firm, *Human Resource Management Journal*, 6 (3), pp 59–75

Boxall, P F (2007) The goals of HRM, in *Oxford Handbook of Human Resource Management*, (eds) P Boxall, J Purcell and P Wright, pp 48–67, Oxford University Press, Oxford

Boxall, P F and Purcell, J (2003) *Strategy and Human Resource Management*, Palgrave Macmillan, Basingstoke

Boxall, P F and Purcell, J (2010) An HRM perspective on employee participation, in *The Oxford Handbook of Participation in Organizations*, (eds) A Wilkinson, P J Gollan, M Marchington and D Lewins, I29–51, Oxford University Press, Oxford

Boxall, P F, Purcell, J and Wright, P (2007) The goals of HRM, in *The Oxford Handbook of Human Resource Management*, (eds) P Boxall, J Purcell and P Wright, pp 1–18, Oxford University Press, Oxford

Caldwell, R (2001) Champions, adapters, consultants and synergists: the new change agents in HRM, *Human Resource Management Journal*, 11 (3), pp 39–52

Deci, E L and Ryan, R M (1985) *Intrinsic Motivation and Self-determination in Human Behaviour*, Plenum, New York

Dyer, L and Holder, G W (1998) Strategic human resource management and planning, in *Human Resource Management: Evolving roles and responsibilities*, (ed) L Dyer, Bureau of National Affairs, Washington DC

Fombrun, C J, Tichy, N M and Devanna, M A (1984) *Strategic Human Resource Management*, Wiley, New York

Fowler, A (1987) When chief executives discover HRM, *Personnel Management*, January, p 3

Grant, D and Shields, J (2002) In search of the subject: researching employee reactions to human resource management, *Journal of Industrial Relations*, 44 (3), pp 313–34

Guest, D E (1987) Human resource management and industrial relations, *Journal of Management Studies*, 24 (5), pp 503–21

Guest, D E (1991) Personnel management: the end of orthodoxy, *British Journal of Industrial Relations*, **29** (2), pp 149–76

Guest, D E (1997) Human resource management and performance: a review of the research agenda, *The International Journal of Human Resource Management*, **8** (3), 263–76

Hackman, J R and Oldham, G R (1974) Motivation through the design of work: test of a theory, *Organizational Behaviour and Human Performance*, **16** (2), pp 250–79

Hendry, C and Pettigrew, A (1990) Human resource management: an agenda for the 1990s, *International Journal of Human Resource Management*, **1** (1), pp 17–44

Hird, M, Sparrow, P and Marsh, C (2010) HR structures: are they working? in *Leading HR*, (eds) P Sparrow, A Hesketh, M Hird and C Cooper, pp 23–45, Palgrave Macmillan, Basingstoke

Ivancevich, J M, Konopaske, R and Matteson, M T (2008) *Organizational Behaviour and Management*, 8th edn, McGraw-Hill/Irwin, New York

Jackson, S E and Schuler, R S (2007) Understanding human resource management in the context of organizations and their environments, in *Strategic Human Resource Management*, (eds) R S Schuler and S E Jackson, pp 23–48, Blackwell, Oxford

Keenoy, T (1997) HRMism and the images of re-presentation, *Journal of Management Studies*, **34** (5), pp 825–41

Kepes, S and Delery, J E (2007) HRM systems and the problem of internal fit, in *Oxford Handbook of Human Resource Management*, (eds) P Boxall, J Purcell and P Wright, pp 385–404, Oxford University Press, Oxford

Legge, K (1978) *Power, Innovation and Problem Solving in Personnel Management*, McGraw-Hill, Maidenhead

Legge, K (1989) Human resource management: a critical analysis, in *New Perspectives in Human Resource Management*, (ed) J Storey, Routledge, London

Legge, K (2005) *Human Resource Management: Rhetorics and realities*, Macmillan, Basingstoke

Leventhal, G S (1980) What should be done with equity theory? in *Social Exchange: Advances in theory and research*, (ed) G K Gergen, M S Greenberg and R H Willis, pp 27–55, Plenum, New York

Mayo, E (1933) *Human Problems of an Industrial Civilization*, Macmillan, London

McGregor, D (1960) *The Human Side of Enterprise*, McGraw-Hill, New York

Paauwe, J (2004) *HRM and Performance: Achieving long term viability*, Oxford University Press, Oxford

Penrose, E (1959) *The Theory of the Growth of the Firm*, Blackwell, Oxford

Porter, L W and Lawler, E E (1968) *Managerial Attitudes and Performance*, Irwin-Dorsey, Homewood, IL

Purcell, J (1999) Best practice or best fit: chimera or cul-de-sac, *Human Resource Management Journal*, **9** (3), pp 26–41

Schneider, B (1987) The people make the place, *Personnel Psychology*, **40** (3), pp 437–53

Storey, J (1989) From personnel management to human resource management, in *New Perspectives on Human Resource Management*, (ed) J Storey, pp 1–18, Routledge, London

Storey, J (2001) Human resource management today: an assessment, in *Human Resource Management: A critical text*, (ed) J Storey, pp 3–20, Thompson Learning, London

Truss, C et al (1997) Soft and hard models of human resource management: a re-appraisal, *Journal of Management Studies*, **34** (1), pp 53–73

Ulrich, D (1997) *Human Resource Champions*, Harvard Business School Press, Boston, MA

Ulrich, D and Lake, D (1990) *Organizational Capability: Competing from the inside out*, Wiley, New York

Vroom, V (1964) *Work and Motivation*, Wiley, New York

Walton, R E (1985) From control to commitment in the workplace, *Harvard Business Review*, March/April, pp 77–84

Willmott, H (1993) Strength is ignorance, slavery is freedom: managing culture in modern organizations, *Journal of Management Studies*, **30** (4), pp 515–52

Winstanley, D and Woodall, J (2000) The ethical dimension of human resource management, *Human Resource Management Journal*, **10** (2), pp 5–20

Wright, P M and McMahan, G C (1992) Theoretical perspectives for SHRM, *Journal of Management*, **18** (2), pp 295–320

02 The concept of strategy

Introduction

As defined by Johnson et al (2005: 9), business strategy '... is the direction and scope of an organization over the longer term, which achieves advantage in a changing environment through its configuration of resources and competences with the aim of fulfilling stakeholder expectations'. The word strategy derives from the Greek '*strategus*', a general. Strategy was originally a broad, rather vaguely defined description of the art used by a commander-in-chief when conducting a military campaign and projecting and directing large movements against an enemy. Commanders-in-chief and military campaigns do not exist in business, public sector or voluntary organizations, but at least this definition conveys the messages that strategy is the ultimate responsibility of the head of the organization, is an art, and is concerned with projecting and directing large movements.

The aim of this chapter is to provide a basis for understanding the concept of strategic human resource management (SHRM) by describing the fundamental nature of business strategy, bearing in mind the role of SHRM as described in the next chapter – that of enabling the organization to achieve its strategic goals. One of the purposes of this chapter is to counter the belief that business strategy is a highly rational affair that provides a firm basis for HR strategy. Strategy is in fact a far more intuitive, evolutionary and reactive process than most people believe.

The chapter starts with a brief description of the development of the concept of strategy and then defines the concept in more detail. It goes on to describe the nature of strategy in terms of its various elements. This is followed by a review of the processes of strategy formulation and implementation and the chapter ends with comments on the reality of the notion of strategy.

Development of the concept of strategy

The foundations of the study of strategy were laid by Peter Drucker (1955: 311) who stated in his seminal work, *The Practice of Management*, that 'the important decisions, the decisions that really matter, are strategic'. The first major contribution to the study of strategy was made by Alfred Chandler, whose most famous pronouncement was that structure follows strategy. But he also produced the following comprehensive definition of strategy (one of the first): 'Strategy can be defined as the determination of the basic long-term goals and objectives of an enterprise, and the adoption of courses of action and the allocation of resources necessary for carrying out these goals' (Chandler, 1962: 13).

The concept of business strategy was developed by another of the pioneers, Igor Ansoff (1965: 6), who wrote that strategy is about 'deciding what sort of business the firm is in and what kinds of business it will seek to enter'. He stated that the term strategic means 'pertaining to the relation between the firm and its environment' (ibid: 5) and described strategy as 'a rule for making decisions' (ibid: 119). In 1972 Kenneth Andrews explored in greater depth the concept of corporate strategy. He defined it comprehensively in a later edition as:

> ... the pattern of decisions in a company that determines and reveals its objectives, purposes or goals, produces the principal policies and plans for achieving these goals, and defines the range of business the company is to pursue, the kind of economic and human organization it is or intends to be, and the nature of the economic or non-economic contribution it intends to make to its shareholders, employees, customers and communities.
>
> (Andrews, 1987: 13)

He suggested that '... the word strategy still retains a close connection to a conscious purpose and implies a time dimension reaching into the future. At its simplest, a strategy can be a very specific plan of action directed at a specified result within a specified period of time' (ibid: xi).

The overall concept having been defined by the pioneers, subsequent writers explored more specific aspects of strategy. Porter (1985) was perhaps the most influential. He developed the notion of competitive advantage, although this term was introduced 20 years earlier by Ansoff (1965: 110), who noted that it arises when a firm 'seeks to identify particular properties of individual product markets which will give [it] a strong competitive position'. Importantly, Porter also introduced the idea of the value chain. Mintzberg (1978, 1987, 1994) distinguished between deliberate or intended strategies and emergent strategies and analysed the process of strategy formulation. Wernerfelt (1984) and Barney (1991, 1995) built on the ideas of Penrose (1959) to develop the highly influential 'resource-based view'. Prahalad and Hamel (1990) argued that competitive advantage results in the long term when a firm builds 'core competencies' that are superior to those of its rivals, and when it learns faster and applies its learning more effectively than its competitors do. More recently, Johnson et al (2008) popularized business model innovation as a strategic approach to developing a business.

Strategy defined

Strategy was defined by Thompson and Strickland (1996: 20) as: 'The pattern of actions managers employ to achieve organizational objectives'. Strategy has two fundamental meanings. First, it is forward looking. It is about deciding where you want to go and how you mean to get there. It is concerned with both ends and means. In this sense a strategy is a declaration of intent: 'This is what we want to do and this is how we intend to do it'. Strategies define longer-term goals but they also cover how those goals will be attained (strategic planning). They guide purposeful action to deliver the required result. As defined by Quinn (1980: 7): 'A strategy is the pattern or plan that integrates an organization's goals into a cohesive whole'. A good strategy is one that works, one that, as Abell (1993: 1) expressed it, enables organizations to adapt by 'mastering the present and pre-empting the future'.

The second meaning of strategy is conveyed by the concept of strategic fit. The focus is upon the organization and the world around it. To maximize competitive advantage a firm must match its capabilities and resources to the opportunities available in the external environment. As Hofer and Schendel (1986: 4) concluded: 'A critical aspect of top management's work today involves matching organizational competences (internal resources and skills) with the opportunities and risks created by environmental change in ways that will be both effective and efficient over the time such resources will be deployed.'

Strategy has been defined in other ways by the many writers on this subject, for example:

- A strategy 'is a sequence of united events which amounts to a coherent pattern of business behaviour.' (Kay, 1993: 9)

- 'The emphasis [in strategy] is on focused actions that differentiate the firm from its competitors.' (Purcell, 1999: 35)

- 'Strategy, then, is a set of strategic choices, some of which may be formally planned. It is inevitable that much, if not most, of a firm's strategy emerges in a stream of action over time.' (Boxall and Purcell, 2003: 15)

- 'Strategy is about building sustainable competitive advantage that in turn creates above-average financial performance.' (Becker and Huselid, 2006: 899)

The nature of strategy

The nature of strategy can be described in terms of a number of related elements that define and elaborate on what it involves – its purpose, the factors to be taken into account in developing and implementing it, and the concepts that guide our understanding of its function. They can be categorized as follows:

- The basic concept of competitive advantage, which describes what the strategy is there to achieve and how it will do this.

- A tool for analysing the factors affecting the attainment of the aims of the strategy – the value chain.

- The notion of core competencies or distinctive capabilities as the basis for attaining competitive advantage.

- An explanation of a key factor associated with gaining competitive advantage through distinctive capabilities – the resource-based view.

- Analyses of strategic notions and processes such as strategic management.
- The process of business model innovation.

Competitive advantage

The concept of competitive advantage was popularized by Porter (1985). Competitive advantage, Porter explained, arises out of a firm creating value for its customers. To achieve it, firms select markets in which they can excel and present a moving target to their competitors by continually improving their position.

Porter emphasized the importance of differentiation, which consists of offering a unique product or service, and focus – concentrating on particular buyers or product markets more effectively than competitors. He also developed his framework of three generic strategies that organizations can use to gain competitive advantage: innovation, quality and cost leadership. He posed (1996: 76) the following questions on competitive positioning:

- Which of our product or service varieties are the most distinctive?
- Which of our product or service varieties are the most profitable?
- Which of our customers are the most satisfied?
- Which customers, channels, or purchase occasions are the most profitable?
- Which of the activities in our value chain are the most different and effective?

Porter's concept of the value chain is described below.

A distinction has been made by Barney (1991) between the competitive advantage that a firm presently enjoys but others will be able to copy, and sustained competitive advantage, which competitors cannot imitate.

The value chain

The concept of the value chain was also introduced by Porter (1985). As he described it, a value chain is a chain of activities for a firm operating in a specific industry. It identifies those activities in a firm that are strategically relevant and underlie its key capabilities. The ultimate aim of the exercise is to perform these activities better than competitors.

The value chain is 'a breakdown of the production process into segments and functional activities' (Kay (1993: 19)). Products pass through all activities of the chain in order, and at each activity the product gains some value. The chain of activities gives the products more added value than the sum of added values of all activities. A value system includes the value chains of a firm's supplier (and their suppliers all the way back), the firm itself, the firm's distribution channels, and the firm's buyers (and presumably extends to the buyers of their products, and so on). Sparrow et al (2010) refer to the existence of a value web that recognizes the existence of multiple stakeholders and partners at each stage of the value chain. This web extends beyond the internal chain of activities to a broad range of external partnerships or other key relationships.

Value chain analysis identifies the activities of a firm and then studies the economic implications of those activities. It includes four steps: (1) defining the strategic business unit; (2) identifying critical activities; (3) defining products; and (4) determining the value of an activity. This leads to addressing two key questions: (1) what activities should a firm perform and how? and (2) what is the configuration of the firm's activities that would enable it to add value to the product and to compete in its industry?

The significance of the concept is that it provides a useful analytical tool in strategic planning.

Core competencies and distinctive capabilities

Core competencies or distinctive capabilities – as Wright et al (2007: 86) comment, 'the distinction between them seems blurred' – describe what the organization is specially or uniquely capable of doing. A special competence was described by Quinn (1980: 179) as a feature that 'makes the organization unique and better able to perform its functions than its competitors'. Distinctive capabilities can exist in such areas as technology, innovation, marketing, delivering quality, and making good use of human and financial resources. The concept of core competencies was originated by Pralahad and Hamel (1990: 82) who described them as a company's critical resource that 'represented the collective learning in the organization'.

Kay (1999) commented that the opportunity for companies to sustain competitive advantage is determined by their capabilities. He noted that there is a difference between distinctive capabilities and reproducible capabilities. Distinctive capabilities are those characteristics that cannot be replicated by competitors, or that can only be imitated with great difficulty. Reproducible capabilities are those that can be bought or created by any company with reasonable management skills, diligence and financial resources. Most technical capabilities are reproducible. As Kamoche (1996: 215) pointed out: 'The capability-based view is concerned with actions, processes and related behavioural efforts to attain a competitive posture'. Teece et al (2002) emphasized that competitive advantage rests on dynamic capabilities.

Four criteria have been proposed by Barney (1991) for deciding whether a resource can be regarded as a distinctive capability or competency: value creation for the customer, rarity compared to the competition, non-imitability and non-substitutability. Eisenhardt and Martin (2000: 1106) noted that capabilities are a 'set of specific and identifiable processes, such as product development, strategic decision making, and alliancing'. Ulrich (2007: 127) stated that: 'Capabilities represent the skills, abilities and expertise of the organization. They describe what organizations are able to do and how they do it... Capabilities represent the ability of the organization to use resources, get things done and behave to reach goals.'

Capability requirements can change as the organization changes. They need to be dynamic – to be developed over time in response to changing demands. Teece et al (2002) emphasize that competitive advantage rests on distinctive processes. And Teece (2007: 1319–20) commented that: 'Dynamic capabilities enable business enterprises to create, deploy, and protect the intangible assets that support superior long-run business performance... These capabilities can be harnessed to continuously create, extend, upgrade, protect, and keep relevant the enterprise's unique asset base.'

The concept of capabilities forms the foundation of the resource-based view of strategy as described below.

The resource-based view

The resource-based view of strategy is that the firm is a bundle of distinctive resources that are the keys to developing competitive advantage – the strategic capability of a firm depends on its resource capability. It is based on the ideas of Penrose (1959: 24–25), who wrote that the firm is 'an administrative organization and a collection of productive resources' and saw resources as 'a bundle of potential services'. It was expanded by Wernerfelt (1984: 172), who explained that strategy 'is a balance between the exploitation of existing resources and the development of new ones'. Resources were defined by Hunt (1991: 322) as 'anything that has an enabling capacity'.

The concept was developed by Barney (1991: 102) who stated that 'a firm is said to have a competitive advantage when it is implementing a value creating strategy not simultaneously being implemented by any current or potential competitors and when these other firms are unable to duplicate the benefits of this strategy'. This will happen if their resources are valuable, rare, inimitable and non-substitutable. He noted later (Barney 1995: 49) that an environmental (SWOT) analysis of strengths, weaknesses, opportunities and threats was only half the story: 'A complete understanding of sources of a firm's competitive advantage requires the analysis of a firm's internal strengths and weaknesses as well'. He emphasized that: 'Creating sustained competitive advantage depends on the unique resources and capabilities that a firm brings to competition in its environment. To discover these resources and capabilities, managers must look inside their firm for valuable, rare and costly-to-imitate resources, and then exploit these resources through their organization' (ibid: 60). The following rationale for resource-based strategy was produced by Grant:

SOURCE REVIEW   Rationale for resource-based strategy
– Grant (1991: 133)

The resources and capabilities of a firm are the central considerations in formulating its strategy: they are the primary constants upon which a firm can establish its identity and frame its strategy, and they are the primary sources of the firm's profitability. The key to a resource-based approach to strategy formulation is understanding the relationships between resources, capabilities, competitive advantage, and profitability – in particular, an understanding of the mechanisms through which competitive advantage can be sustained over time. This requires the design of strategies which exploit to maximum effect each firm's unique characteristics.

The resource-based view makes an important contribution to the concept of strategic HRM as explained in Chapter 3.

Strategic processes

Commentators on the sometimes elusive concept of strategy have tried to explain how it works through the notions and processes of strategic management, strategic intent, strategic goals, strategic plans and strategic decisions.

Strategic management

According to Boxall and Purcell (2003: 44): 'Strategic management is best defined as a process. It is a process of strategy making, of forming and, if the firm survives, reforming its strategy over time.' Strategic management was defined by Johnson et al (2005: 6) as the process of 'understanding the strategic position of an organization, making strategic choices for the future, and turning strategy into action'. The purpose of strategic management has been expressed by Rosabeth Moss Kanter (1984: 288) as being to 'elicit the present actions for the future' and become 'action vehicles – integrating and institutionalizing mechanisms for change' (ibid: 301).

The key strategic management activity as identified by Thompson and Strickland (1996: 3) is 'deciding what business the company will be in and forming a strategic vision of where the organization needs to be headed – in effect, infusing the organization with a sense of purpose, providing long-term direction, and establishing a clear mission to be accomplished'.

The focus is on identifying the organization's mission and strategies, but attention is also given to the resource base required to make it succeed. Managers who think strategically will have a broad and long-term view of where they are going. But they will also be aware that they are responsible first for planning how to allocate resources to opportunities that contribute

FIGURE 2.1 Strategic management model

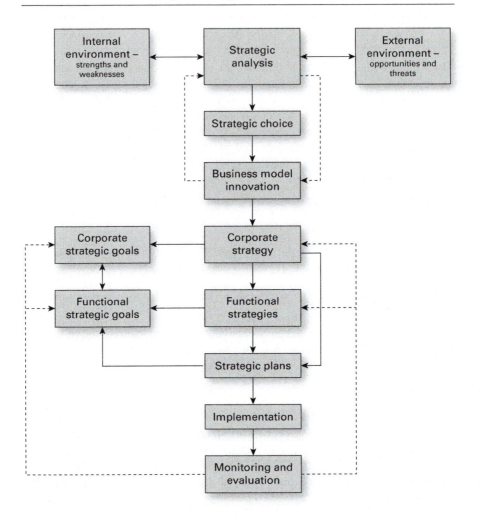

to the implementation of strategy, and secondly for managing these opportunities in ways that will add value to the results achieved by the firm.

The process of strategic management is modelled in Figure 2.1. It involves analysing the internal and external environment, exercising strategic choice (there is always choice), formulating corporate and functional strategies and goals, implementing strategies, and monitoring and evaluating progress in achieving goals. But in practice, it is not as simple and linear as that.

Strategic intent

In its simplest form, strategy could be described as an expression of the intentions of the organization – what it means to do and how the business means to 'get from here to there'. As defined by Hamel and Pralahad (1989), strategic intent refers to the expression of the leadership position the organization wants to attain and establishes a clear criterion on how progress towards its achievement will be measured. They emphasized that 'strategic intent is clear about ends, it is flexible as to means' and that: 'The goal of strategic intent is to fold the future back into the present. The important question is not "How will next year be different from this year?" but "What must we do differently next year to get closer to our strategic intent?"' (ibid: 66).

According to Johnson et al (2005: 13) strategic intent is an expression of 'the desired future state of an organization'. Strategic intent could be a very broad statement of vision or mission and/or it could more specifically spell out the goals and objectives to be attained over the longer term.

The strategic intent sequence has been defined by Miller and Dess (1996) as a broad vision of what the organization should be.

Strategic capability

Strategic capability refers to the ability of an organization to develop and implement strategies that will achieve sustained competitive advantage. It is therefore about the capacity to select the most appropriate vision, to define realistic intentions, to match resources to opportunities and to prepare and implement strategic plans.

The strategic capability of an organization depends on the strategic capabilities of its managers. People who display high levels of strategic capability know where they are going and know how they are going to get there. They recognize that although they must be successful now to succeed in the future, it is always necessary to create and sustain a sense of purpose and direction.

Strategic goals

Strategic goals define where the organization wants to be. They were described by Quinn (1980:7) as 'those that affect the organization's overall direction and viability'. They may be specified in terms of actions, quantified in terms of growth, or expressed in general terms as aspirations rather than specifics.

Strategic plans

Strategic plans are formal expressions of how an organization intends to attain its strategic goals over a defined period of time. Boxall and Purcell (2003: 34) make the point that: 'We should not make the mistake of equating the strategies of a firm with formal strategic plans... It is better if we understand the strategies of firms as sets of strategic choices, some of which may stem from planning exercises and set piece debates in senior management, and some of which emerge in a stream of action.' Mintzberg (1987: 73) suggested that: 'So-called strategic planning must be recognized for what it is: a means, not to create strategy, but to program a strategy already created – to work out its implications formally'.

Strategic decisions

As described by Johnson et al (2005: 10), strategic decisions are about:

- the long-term direction of an organization;
- the scope of an organization's activities;
- gaining advantage over competitors;
- addressing changes in the business environment;
- building resources and competences (capability);
- the values and expectations of stakeholders.

They are therefore likely to be complex, be made in circumstances of uncertainty, affect operational decisions, require an integrated approach and involve considerable changes.

Business model innovation

Business model innovation is a recently formulated approach to strategy that focuses on how the firm creates value. The aim is to change the ways in which companies view their business operations and to provide guidance on mapping their future strategy. Business model innovation is concerned with the development or even re-creation of a business through a review of all the elements of its business model in order to identify opportunities to increase its competitiveness and prosperity. A business model can be defined simplistically as a description of how a company makes money, but as Johnson et al (2008) claim, it is more complicated than that (their views are summarized in Chapter 9, which deals with the process in detail).

The formulation of strategy

Developing strategy is a matter of creating a sense of direction and purpose and ensuring strategic fit. It used to be regarded as a logical, step-by-step affair that was described by Whittington (1993) as the classical approach – strategy formulation as a rational process of deliberate calculation. Conceptually this involves the following:

1 Define the mission.
2 Set objectives.
3 Conduct internal and external environmental scans to assess internal strengths and weaknesses and external opportunities and threats (a SWOT analysis).
4 Analyse existing strategies and the business model to determine their relevance in the light of the internal and external appraisal. This may include gap analysis, which will establish the extent to which

environmental factors might lead to gaps between what could be achieved if no changes were made and what needs to be achieved. The analysis would also cover resource capability, answering the question: 'Have we sufficient human or financial resources available now or that can readily be made available in the future to enable us to achieve our objectives?'

5 Define in the light of this analysis the distinctive capabilities of the organization.

6 Define the key strategic issues emerging from the previous analysis. These will be concerned with such matters as product-market scope, delivering value to customers, enhancing shareholder value and resource capability, and the need to change the business model.

7 Determine corporate and functional strategies for achieving goals and competitive advantage, taking into account the key strategic issues. These may include business strategies for growth or diversification, business model innovation, or broad generic strategies for innovation, quality or cost leadership; or they could take the form of specific corporate/functional strategies concerned with product-market scope, technological development or human resource development.

8 Prepare integrated strategic plans for implementing strategies.

9 Implement the strategies.

10 Monitor implementation and revise existing strategies or develop new strategies as necessary.

This model of the process of strategy formulation should allow scope for iteration and feedback, and the activities incorporated in the model are all appropriate in any process of strategy formulation. But the model is essentially linear and deterministic – each step logically follows the earlier one and is conditioned entirely by the preceding sequence of events. This is a misrepresentation of reality. In practice the formulation of strategy can never be as rational and linear an affair as some writers describe it or as some managers attempt to carry it out. As Quinn (1980: 15) pointed out, this formal planning approach 'tends to focus unduly on measurable quantitative forces and to underestimate the vital qualitative, organizational and power-behavioural factors that so often determine strategic success in one situation versus another'. He also noted that organizations typically construct their strategies with processes that are 'fragmented, evolutionary, and largely intuitive' (ibid: 15).

It is also necessary to bear in mind that, as described by Mintzberg and Lampel (1999: 27), the formulation of strategy is a highly complex process: 'Strategy formation is judgemental designing, intuitive reasoning, and emergent learning; it is about transformation as well as perpetuation; it must involve individual cognition and social interaction, cooperative as well as conflictive; it has to include analyzing before and after as well as negotiating during;

and all this may be in response to a demanding environment. Try to omit any of this, and watch what happens!'

The reality of strategy

Sparrow et al (2010: 4) asserted succinctly that: 'Strategy is not rational and never has been'. It has been said (Bower, 1982: 631) that 'strategy is everything not well defined or understood'. This may be going too far, but in reality, strategy formulation can best be described as 'problem solving in unstructured situations' (Digman, 1990: 53) and strategies will always be formed under conditions of partial ignorance. Quinn (1980: 9) pointed out that a strategy may simply be 'a widely held understanding resulting from a stream of decisions'. He believed that strategy formulation takes place by means of 'logical incrementalism', ie it evolves in several steps rather than being conceived as a whole. The following are his views on the strategy process.

SOURCE REVIEW   The evolutionary nature of strategy – Quinn (1980: 14–15)

Although the formal planning approach is excellent for some purposes, it tends to focus unduly on measurable quantitative forces and to under-emphasize the vital qualitative, organizational and power-behavioural factors that so often determine strategic success... The processes used to arrive at the total strategy are typically fragmented, evolutionary, and largely intuitive... The real strategy tends to evolve as internal decisions and external events flow together to create a new, widely shared consensus for action among key members of the top management team.

Pettigrew and Whipp (1991: 26) pointed out that: '... strategy does not move forward in a direct linear way, nor through easily discernible sequential phases. Quite the reverse, the pattern is much more appropriately seen as continuous, iterative and uncertain.'

Another difficulty is that strategies are often based on the questionable assumption that the future will resemble the past. Some years ago, Robert Heller (1972: 150) had a go at the cult of long-range planning: 'What goes wrong', he wrote, 'is that sensible anticipation gets converted into foolish numbers: and their validity always hinges on large loose assumptions'. More recently, Faulkner and Johnson (1992: 17–18) have said of long-term planning that it:

> ... was inclined to take a definitive view of the future, and to extrapolate trend lines for the key business variables in order to arrive at this view. Economic

turbulence was insufficiently considered, and the reality that much strategy is formulated and implemented in the act of managing the enterprise was ignored. Precise forecasts ending with derived financials were constructed, the only weakness of which was that the future almost invariably turned out differently.

Strategy formulation is not necessarily a deterministic, rational and continuous process, as was pointed out by Mintzberg (1987). He believes that, rather than being consciously and systematically developed, strategy reorientation happens in what he calls brief 'quantum loops'. A strategy, according to Mintzberg, can be deliberate – it can realize the intentions of senior management, for example to attack and conquer a new market. But this is not always the case. In theory, he says, strategy is a systematic process: first we think, then we act; we formulate then we implement. But we also 'act in order to think'. In practice, 'a realized strategy can emerge in response to an evolving situation' (ibid: 68) and the strategic planner is often 'a pattern organizer, a learner if you like, who manages a process in which strategies and visions can emerge as well as be deliberately conceived' (ibid: 73). This concept of 'emergent strategy' conveys the essence of how in practice organizations develop their business and HR strategies.

Mintzberg was even more scathing about the weaknesses of strategic planning in his 1994 article in the *Harvard Business Review* on 'The rise and fall of strategic planning'. He contends that 'the failure of systematic planning is the failure of systems to do better than, or nearly as well as, human beings'. He went on to say that: 'Far from providing strategies, planning could not proceed without their prior existence... real strategists get their hands dirty digging for ideas, and real strategies are built from the nuggets they discover.' And 'sometimes strategies must be left as broad visions, not precisely articulated, to adapt to a changing environment'. He emphasized that strategic management is a learning process as managers of firms find out what works well in practice for them.

Following up on the Mintzberg thesis, Digman (1990: 11) commented that the most effective decision-makers are usually creative, intuitive people 'employing an adaptive, flexible process'. Moreover, since most strategic decisions are event-driven rather than pre-programmed, they are unplanned. And Boxall and Purcell (2003: 34) suggested that '... it is better if we understand the strategies of firms as sets of strategic choices, some of which may stem from planning exercises and set-piece debates in senior management, and some of which may emerge in a stream of action'.

Implementation of strategy

'Implementation entails converting the strategic plan into action and then into results' (Thompson and Strickland, 1996: 20). Dreaming up a strategy is fairly easy; getting it to work is hard. Rosabeth Moss Kanter (1984: 305) noted that: 'Many companies, even very sophisticated ones, are much better at generating impressive plans on paper than they are at getting "owner-ship" of the plans so that they actually guide operational decisions'. It was emphasized by Linda Gratton (2000: 30) that 'there is no great strategy, only great execution'.

Some writers on strategy focus more on the formulation process than on how it can be made to work. There have been exceptions. Kenneth Andrews (1987) devoted a whole chapter in his book *The Concept of Corporate Strategy* (1987: 81–96) to implementation. He commented that goal-directed implementation is 'the essence of strategic management' and noted that 'because of the neglect of implementation as integral to strategy, the concept [of strategy] has been battered by distortion over the past 20 years'. He also remarked that 'the belief that strategy formulation, under the name of strategic planning, is primarily a staff activity, assisted by consulting firms, is a related distortion made possible by ignoring the problems of implementation'. This, he claimed, was because plans were formulated 'without reference to company capability, personal values and entrenched personal values'. He recommended that 'strategy formulation and implementation should be allowed to interact'. Karl Weick (1987: 230) stated that 'execution *is* analysis and implementa-tion *is* formulation' (original emphasis). In their chapter on implementation, Thompson and Strickland (1996: 241) observed that:

> What makes strategy implementation a tougher, more time-consuming challenge than crafting strategy is the wide array of managerial activities that have to be attended to, the many ways managers can proceed, the demanding people-management skills required, the perseverance it takes to get a variety of initiatives launched and moving, the number of bedevilling issues that must be worked out, and the resistance to change that must be overcome.

It was pointed out by Quinn (1980: 168) that many strategies fail because 'they could not be adequately coordinated for implementation'. An effective strategy is a living process described by Rosabeth Moss Kanter (1984) as an action vehicle. John Purcell (1999) believes that the focus of strategy should be on implementation.

The aim of implementation is to make the strategy an operating reality by building the capacity of the organization to put into practice the intentions worked out in the planning stage. Strategy should be implementation orien-tated – it should be designed with implementation in mind. All too frequently there is a say/do gap between the strategy as designed and the strategy as implemented. Even where there is a 'grand design' and much rhetoric, the reality is different – the links are difficult to maintain, line managers are indifferent or incapable of playing their part, and employees are suspicious of or hostile to the newly linked initiatives. Problems are caused by poor project management, inadequate attention to managing change, and a failure to ensure that supporting processes are in place.

The following reward strategy questions need to be asked and answered at the design stage:

- How will it add value?
- How is it going to be put into effect?
- What supporting processes will be needed and can they be made available?
- Who is going to be involved in implementation?
- How are we going to make sure that those involved know what they have to, know why they are expected to do it, believe that it is worthwhile and have the skills to do it?
- Are people likely to react negatively to the proposed strategy and, if so, how do we deal with their concerns?
- How much time will be needed; how much time have we got?
- Will any additional resources be required and can they be made available?
- Are there any likely implementation problems and how will they be dealt with?

The reality of strategy

The classical view of the strategy process as described by Rosemary Harrison (2009: 331) rests on two assumptions:

- that decision-makers have a common purpose and are driven by a shared economic logic when making strategic decisions: all seek to maximize economic rewards and minimize costs for the business;
- that decision-makers systematically 'collect and sort information about alternative potential solutions, compare each solution against premeditated criteria to assess degree of fit, arrange solutions in order of preference, and make an optimizing choice which they then equally systematically draw up plans to implement' (Miller et al, 1999: 44).

In practice, decisions are not necessarily 'arrived at by a step-by-step process which is both logical and linear' (Miller et al, 1999: 44). People are constrained by 'human frailties and demands from both within and outside the organization' (ibid: 45). All decision-making is limited by the bounded rationality of the people involved – their capacity to understand the complexities of the situation they are in and their emotional reactions to it. Harrison (2009: 331) pointed out that: 'Some of the factors that pull players away from a purely rational approach include confused, excessive, incomplete or unreliable data, incompetent processing or communicating of information, pressures of time, human emotions and differences in individuals' cognitive processes, mental maps and reasoning capacity'.

It was asserted by Quinn (1980: 33) that it is possible 'to predict the broad direction but not the precise nature of the ultimate strategy'. He believed that 'strategy deals not just with the unpredictable but also with the unknowable' (ibid: 163). Shaun Tyson (1997: 280) pointed out that, realistically, strategy:

- has always been emergent and flexible – it is always about to be, it never exists at the present time;
- is not only realized by formal statements but also comes about by actions and reactions;
- is a description of a future-orientated action that is always directed towards change;
- is conditioned by the management process itself.

But while the limitations of formal strategic planning should be recognized, strategic management still has an important role to play. A systematic approach still has its uses as a means of providing an analytical framework for strategic decision making and as a reference point for monitoring the implementation of strategy. Mintzberg may have expressed doubts about strategic planning but he did not minimize the significance of strategy when he wrote: 'Strategy making is a process interwoven with all that it takes to manage an organization' (Mintzberg, 1994: 114).

KEY LEARNING POINTS

Strategy defined

'The pattern of actions managers employ to achieve organizational objectives; a company's actual strategy is partly planned and partly reactive to changing circumstances' (Thompson and Strickland, 1996: 20).

The meaning of strategy

Strategy has two fundamental meanings. First, it is forward looking. It is about deciding where you want to go and how you mean to get there. It is concerned with both ends and means. In this sense a strategy is a declaration of intent.

The fundamental characteristics of strategy

- Forward looking.
- The organizational capability of a firm depends on its resource capability.
- Strategic fit – the need when developing HR strategies to achieve congruence between them and the organization's business strategies within the context of its external and internal environment.

The key concepts of strategy

- The value chain identifies those activities in a firm that are strategically relevant and underlie its key capabilities.
- Core competencies or distinctive capabilities describe what the organization is specially or uniquely capable of doing.
- The resource-based view of strategy is that the strategic capability of a firm depends on its resource capability. Competitive advantage is achieved if the resources are valuable, rare, inimitable and non-substitutable.
- Strategic management is the process of understanding the strategic position of an organization, making strategic choices for the future, and turning strategy into action.
- Strategic intent is an expression of the desired future state of an organization.
- Strategic capability refers to the ability of an organization to develop and implement strategies that will achieve sustained competitive advantage.
- Strategic goals define where the organization wants to be.
- Strategic plans are formal expressions of how an organization intends to attain its strategic goals.
- Strategic decisions are about the long-term direction of an organization and the scope of its activities.
- Business model innovation focuses on how the firm creates value. The aim is to change the ways in which companies view their business operations and provide guidance on mapping their future strategy.

Developing strategy

Developing strategy is a matter of creating a sense of direction and purpose and ensuring strategic fit. Strategy formulation is not necessarily a deterministic, rational and continuous process.

Implementing strategy

The aim of implementation is to make the reward strategy an operating reality by building the capacity of the organization to put into practice the proposals worked out in the development stage. Strategy should be implementation orientated – it should be designed with implementation in mind.

> Role of strategic management
>
> While the limitations of formal strategic planning should be recognized, strategic management still has an important role to play. A systematic approach still has its uses as a means of providing an analytical framework for strategic decision making and as a reference point for monitoring the implementation of strategy.

References

Abell, D F (1993) *Managing with Dual Strategies: Mastering the present, pre-empting the future*, Free Press, New York

Andrews, K R (1987) *The Concept of Corporate Strategy*, 3rd edn, Irwin, Homewood

Ansoff, H I (1965) *Corporate Strategy*, McGraw-Hill, New York

Barney, J B (1991) Firm resources and sustained competitive advantage, *Journal of Management*, **17** (1), pp 99–120

Barney, J B (1995) Looking inside for competitive advantage, *Academy of Management Executive*, **9** (4), pp 49–61

Becker, B E and Huselid, M A (2006) Strategic human resources management: where do we go from here? *Journal of Management*, **32** (6), pp 898–925

Bower, J L (1982) Business policy in the 1980s, *Academy of Management Review*, 7 (4), pp 630–38

Boxall, P F and Purcell, J (2003) *Strategy and Human Resource Management*, Palgrave Macmillan, Basingstoke

Chandler, A D (1962) *Strategy and Structure*, MIT Press, Boston, MA

Digman, L A (1990) *Strategic Management: Concepts, decisions, cases*, Irwin, Homewood, IL

Drucker, P E (1955) *The Practice of Management*, Heinemann, London

Eisenhardt, K M and Martin, J A (2000) Dynamic capabilities: what are they? *Strategic Management Journal*, **21** (10/11), pp 1105–21

Faulkner, D and Johnson, G (1992) *The Challenge of Strategic Management*, Kogan Page, London

Grant, R M (1991) The resource-based theory of competitive advantage: implications for strategy formulation, *California Management Review*, **33** (3), pp 114–35

Gratton, L A (2000) Real step change, *People Management*, 16 March, pp 27–30

Hamel, G and Pralahad, C K (1989) Strategic intent, *The Harvard Business Review*, May/June, pp 63–76

Harrison, R (2009) *Learning and Development*, 5th edn, CIPD, London

Heller, R (1972) *The Naked Manager*, Barrie & Jenkins, London

Hofer, C W and Schendel, D (1986) *Strategy Formulation: Analytical Concepts*, West Publishing, New York

Hunt, S (1991) The resource-advantage theory of competition, *Journal of Management Inquiry*, **4** (4), pp 317–22

Johnson, G, Scholes, K and Whittington, R (2005) *Explaining Corporate Strategy*, 7th edn, FTPrentice Hall, Harlow

Johnson, M, Christensen, C and Kagermann, H (2008) Reinventing your business model, *Harvard Business Review*, December, pp 52–59

Kamoche, K (1996) Strategic human resource management within a resource capability view of the firm, *Journal of Management Studies*, 33 (2), pp 213–33

Kanter, R M (1984) *The Change Masters*, Allen & Unwin, London

Kay, J (1993) *Foundations of Corporate Success*, Oxford University Press, Oxford

Kay, J (1999) Strategy and the illusions of grand designs, *Mastering Strategy, Financial Times*, pp 2–4

Miller, A and Dess, G G (1996) *Strategic Management*, 2nd edn, McGraw Hill, New York

Miller, S, Hickson, D J and Wilson, D C (1999) Decision-making in organizations, in *Managing Organizations: Current issues*, (eds) S R Clegg, C Hardy and W R Nord, Sage, London

Mintzberg, H T (1978) Patterns in strategy formation, *Management Science*, May, pp 934–48

Mintzberg, H T (1987) Crafting strategy, *Harvard Business Review*, July/August, pp 66–74

Mintzberg, H T (1994) The rise and fall of strategic planning, *Harvard Business Review*, January/February, pp 107–14

Mintzberg, H and Lampel, J (1999) Reflecting on the strategy process, *Sloan Management Review*, Spring, pp 21–30

Penrose, E (1959) *The Theory of the Growth of the Firm*, Blackwell, Oxford

Pettigrew, A and Whipp, R (1991) *Managing Change for Competitive Success*, Blackwell, Oxford

Porter, M E (1985) *Competitive Advantage: Creating and sustaining superior performance*, New York, The Free Press

Porter, M E (1996) What is strategy? *Harvard Business Review*, November/December, pp 61–78

Prahalad, C K and Hamel, G (1990) The core competence of the organization, *Harvard Business Review*, May/June, pp 79–93

Purcell, J (1999) Best practice or best fit: chimera or cul-de-sac, *Human Resource Management Journal*, 9 (3), pp 26–41

Quinn, J B (1980) *Strategies for Change: Logical Incrementalism*, Irwin, Georgetown, Ontario

Sparrow, P et al (2010) Introduction: performance-led HR, in *Leading HR*, (eds) P Sparrow, A Hesketh, M Hird and C Cooper, pp 1–22, Palgrave Macmillan, Basingstoke

Teece, D J (2007) Explicating dynamic capabilities: the nature and microfoundations of (sustainable) enterprise performance, *Strategic Management Journal*, 28 (13), 1319–50

Teece, D J, Pisano, G and Shuen, A (2002) Dynamic capabilities and strategic management, in *Strategy in Business*, (ed) M Mazzucato, Sage, London

Thompson, A A and Strickland, A J (1996) *Strategic Management, Concepts and cases*, 9th edn, Irwin, Chicago

Tyson, S (1997) Human resource strategy: a process for managing the contribution of HRM to organizational performance, *The International Journal of Human Resource Management*, 8 (3), pp 277–90

Ulrich, D (2007) Alignment of HR strategies and the impact on firm performance, in *Strategic Human Resource Management*, (eds) R S Schuler and S E Jackson, pp 124–37, Blackwell, Oxford

Weick, K E (1987) Substitutes for corporate strategy, in *The Competitive Challenge: Strategies for industrial innovation and renewal*, (ed) D J Teece, Ballinger, Cambridge, MA

Wernerfelt, B (1984) A resource-based view of the firm, *Strategic Management Journal*, 5 (2), pp 171–80

Whittington, R (1993) *What is Strategy and Does it Matter?* Routledge, London

Wright, P M, Dunford, B B and Snell, S A (2007) Human resources and the resource-based view of the firm, in *Strategic Human Resource Management*, 2nd edn, (eds) R S Schuler and S E Jackson, pp 76–97, Blackwell, Oxford

The concept of strategic human resource management

Introduction

Strategic human resource management 'focuses on the overall HR strategies adopted by business units and companies' (Boxall et al, 2007: 3). The aim of this chapter is to develop this basic idea by examining in detail the nature of SHRM and analysing the framework for SHRM provided by the concepts of strategic fit and the resource-based view, and the notions of best practice, best fit and 'bundling'. The reality of SHRM – the relevance to HR practitioners of what can sometimes appear to be a somewhat academic or nebulous affair – is considered at the end of the chapter.

SHRM defined

SHRM is an approach to managing people that deals with how the organization's goals will be achieved through its human resources by means of integrated HR strategies, policies and practices. It is based on the following propositions:

- the human resources of an organization play a strategic role in its success;
- HR strategies and plans should be integrated with business strategies and plans;
- human capital is a major source of competitive advantage;
- it is people who implement the business strategy;
- a systematic approach should be adopted to planning and implementing HR strategies.

There are many definitions of SHRM. For example, SHRM has been described in general terms by Schuler (1992: 30) as 'all those activities affecting the behaviour of individuals in their efforts to formulate and implement the strategic needs of the business'. Mabey et al (1998: 25) introduced the key notion of capability when they defined SHRM as the process of 'developing corporate capability to deliver new organizational strategies'. The HR activities aspect of SHRM was emphasized by Wright and McMahan (1992: 298) when they defined it as: 'The pattern of planned human resource deployments and activities intended to enable an organization to achieve its goals'. Alvesson (2009: 52) also focused on goal achievement but incorporated the role of employment relationships when he wrote that SHRM is concerned with 'how the employment relationships for all employees can be managed in such a way as to contribute optimally to the organization's goal achievement'. Schuler and Jackson (2007: 5) concentrated on integration when they stated that SHRM is about 'systematically linking people with the firm'.

The nature of SHRM

The concept of SHRM is complex and somewhat amorphous. To understand SHRM it is necessary to analyse its elements, define its aims and examine its meaning.

The elements of SHRM

Three key elements of SHRM have been described by Mabey et al (1998: 24–25):

1 Internal processes of organizational change are caused or necessitated by processes of external environmental change.
2 Under these new environmental pressures (competition, technology, clients' demands and so on) management must develop new and appropriate strategies to defend or advance corporate interests.
3 This strategic response in turn requires organizational responses. 'If the organization is to be capable of achieving or delivering the new strategy it will be necessary to design and implement changes in any or all aspects of human resource structures and systems.'

This analysis was extended by Colbert (2007: 98–99) who suggested that:

SHRM is predicated on two fundamental assertions. First is the idea that an organization's human resources are of critical strategic importance – that the skills, behaviours and interactions of employees have the potential to provide both the foundation for strategy formulation and the means for strategy implementation. Second is the belief that a firm's HRM practices are instrumental in developing the strategic capability of its pool of human resources.

Becker and Huselid (2006: 899) commented that SHRM focuses on organizational performance rather than individual performance. It also emphasizes the role of HR management systems as solutions for businesses as a whole rather than individual HR management practices in isolation.

Aims of SHRM

SHRM supplies a perspective on the way in which critical issues or success factors related to people can be addressed and strategic decisions can be made that have a major and long-term impact on the behaviour and success of the organization. As Lengnick-Hall and Lengnick-Hall (1988: 454) argued: 'Achieving competitive advantage through human resources requires that these activities be managed from a strategic perspective'.

The fundamental aim of strategic HRM is to generate strategic capability by ensuring that the organization has the skilled, committed and well-motivated employees it needs to achieve sustained competitive advantage. It has two main objectives. The first is to achieve fit or integration – fitting or aligning HR strategies vertically with business strategies and integrating HR strategies with one another. The second objective is to provide a sense of direction in an often turbulent environment so that the business needs of the organization, and the individual and collective needs of its employees, can be met by the development and implementation of coherent and practical HR policies and programmes.

As Dyer and Holder (1998: 13) remarked, SHRM should provide 'unifying frameworks which are at once broad, contingency based and integrative'. The rationale for SHRM is the perceived advantage of having an agreed and understood basis for developing and implementing approaches to people management that takes into account the changing context in which the firm operates and its business plans and priorities. They also advocated 'consistency between HR goals... and the underlying business strategy and relevant environmental conditions' (ibid: 10). It has been suggested by Lengnick-Hall and Lengnick-Hall (1990) that underlying this rationale in a business is the concept of achieving competitive advantage through HRM.

When considering the aims of SHRM, account should be taken of ethical considerations – the interests of all the stakeholders in the organization, employees in general as well as owners and management, and the responsibilities of the organization to the wider community. In Storey's (1989) terms, soft strategic HRM will place greater emphasis on the human relations aspect of people management, stressing continuous development, communication, involvement, security of employment, the quality of working life and work–life balance. On the other hand, hard strategic HRM will emphasize the yield to be obtained by investing in human resources in the interests of the business. SHRM should attempt to achieve a proper balance between the hard and soft elements. All organizations exist to achieve a purpose and they must ensure that they have the resources required to do so, and that they use them effectively. But they should also take into account the human factors contained in the concept of soft strategic HRM. In the words of Quinn Mills (1983) they should plan with people in mind, taking into account the needs and aspirations of all the members of the organization. The problem is that hard considerations in many businesses will come first, leaving soft ones some way behind.

Organizations must also consider their responsibilities to society in general on the grounds that because they draw resources from society, they must give something back to society. The exercise of corporate social responsibility (CSR), defined by McWilliams et al (2006: 1) as 'actions that appear to further some social good beyond the interests of the firm and that which is required by law', may be regarded as outside the scope of human resource management. But because CSR relates to ethical actions in the interests of people, there is a strong link, and it is therefore an aspect of organizational behaviour that can legitimately be included in the strategic portfolio of HR specialists.

The meaning of strategic HRM

It was suggested by Hendry and Pettigrew (1986) that strategic HRM has four meanings:

1 The use of planning.
2 A coherent approach to the design and management of HR systems based on an employment policy and manpower strategy and often underpinned by a 'philosophy'.
3 Matching HRM activities and policies to some explicit business strategy.
4 Seeing the people of the organization as a 'strategic resource' for the achievement of 'competitive advantage'.

Strategic HRM addresses broad organizational concerns relating to changes in structure and culture, organizational effectiveness and performance, matching resources to future requirements, the development of distinctive capabilities, knowledge management, and the management of change. It is concerned with both human capital requirements and the development of process capabilities, that is, the ability to get things done effectively. Overall, it will address any major people issues that affect or are affected by the strategic plans of the organization. As Boxall (1996: 61) remarked: 'The critical concerns of HRM, such as choice of executive leadership and formation of positive patterns of labour relations, are strategic in any firm'.

A defining characteristic of strategic HRM is its concern with the vertical integration of HR strategies with the business strategy, and with the horizontal integration of individual HR strategies with one another – the concept of strategic fit as discussed below.

Strategic fit

The notion of strategic fit is fundamental to SHRM, as was stressed by the following commentators:

● 'The primary role of strategic HRM should be to promote a fit with the demands of the competitive environment' (Wright and Snell, 1998: 758).
● 'By strategic we mean that HR activities should be systematically designed and intentionally linked to an analysis of the business and its context' (Schuler et al, 2001: 127).
● 'The skills and behaviours of employees must fit the strategic needs of the firm in order for the workforce to be a source of competitive advantage' (Allen and Wright, 2007: 95).
● 'The central premise of strategic human resource management theory is that successful organizational performance depends on

a close fit or alignment between business and human resource strategy' (Batt, 2007: 429).

In more detail, Schuler (1992: 18) stated that: 'Strategic human resource management is largely about integration and adaptation. Its concern is to ensure that: (1) human resources (HR) management is fully integrated with the strategy and strategic needs of the firm (vertical fit); (2) HR policies cohere both across policy areas and across hierarchies (horizontal fit); and (3) HR practices are adjusted, accepted and used by line managers and employees as part of their everyday work.'

However, Wright and McMahan (1992) pointed out that maximizing fit could be counterproductive when the organization has to manage change and cope with conflicting competitive goals in a complex environment. Purcell et al (2003: 4) thought that 'the need is not just to find the right fit now but to have the flexibility to meet future challenges'. Similarly, Allen and Wright (2007: 96) commented that 'a tight fit between HRM and strategy may inhibit the ability of the firm to remain flexible enough to adapt to changing circumstances'. A conflict exists between the concepts of fit and flexibility.

Strategic flexibility and fit

Strategic flexibility is defined as the ability of the firm to respond and adapt to changes in its competitive environment. Fit is concerned with aligning business and HR strategy, and functional HR strategies with one another. It has been argued that these concepts of flexibility and fit are incompatible: fit implies a fixed relationship between the HR strategy and business strategy, but the latter has got to be flexible, so how can good fit be maintained? But Wright and Snell (1998) have suggested that the concepts of fit and flexibility are complementary – fit exists at a point in time while flexibility has to exist over a period of time. At first sight, the goals of fit and flexibility may appear to be incompatible but, as they argue: 'The strategic management challenge is to cope with change (requiring flexibility) by continually adapting to achieve fit between a firm and its external circumstances' (ibid: 537). This comment draws attention to the importance of the time element in strategic HRM. The formulation and implementation of strategy is an evolutionary process. Indeed, strategy may well be developed as it is being implemented because of the new demands arising from a changing environment.

Environmental differences will affect a flexibility/fit strategy. As indicated by Wright and Snell (1998), in a stable, predictable environment, the strategy could be to develop people with a narrow range of skills (or not to develop multiskilled people) and to elicit a narrow range of behaviour (eg tight job descriptions). In a dynamic, unpredictable environment, however, organizations might develop organic HR systems that produce a human capital pool with people possessing a wide range of skills who can engage in a wide variety of behaviours. The need is to achieve resource flexibility by developing a variety of 'behavioural scripts' and encouraging employees to apply them in different situations, bearing in mind the increased amount of discretionary behaviour that may be appropriate in different roles.

The tension between fit and flexibility can be resolved, at least in part, by making the distinction between present fit and future flexibility, and by introducing the notion that the latter is a process that takes place over time. Another perspective was provided by Mintzberg (1994: 107) who distinguished 'strategic programming' from 'strategic thinking'. The former involves deciding on a series of action steps to achieve a strategic goal, formalizing those steps for implementation, and articulating the results expected from those steps. The latter entails taking information from numerous sources and integrating that information into a vision of what direction the business should take. Wright and Snell (1998: 768) suggested that: 'Strategic programming seems quite consistent with an emphasis on achieving strategic fit, whereas strategic thinking is consistent with an emphasis on building flexibility'.

The resource-based view of strategic HRM

The resource-based view (RBV) expresses the belief that it is the range of resources in an organization, including its human resources, that produces its unique character and creates competitive advantage. As described in Chapter 2, it is based on the ideas of Penrose (1959), which were expanded by Wernerfelt (1984). Barney (1991) suggested that resources that are valuable, rare, inimitable and non-substitutable will lead to competitive advantage. He later defined human resources as including 'all the experience, knowledge, judgement, risk taking propensity and wisdom of individuals associated with a firm' (Barney, 1995: 50). Hamel and Prahalad (1989) declared that competitive advantage is obtained if a firm can obtain and develop human resources that enable it to learn faster and apply its learning more effectively than its rivals.

Unique talents among employees – including superior performance, productivity, flexibility, innovation, and the ability to deliver high levels of personal customer service – are ways in which people provide a critical ingredient in developing an organization's competitive position. People also provide the key to managing the pivotal interdependencies across functional activities and the important external relationships. It can be argued that one of the clear benefits arising from competitive advantage based on the effective management of people is that such an advantage is hard to imitate. An organization's HR strategies, policies and practices are a distinctive blend of processes, procedures, personalities, styles, capabilities and organizational culture. These provide what Boxall (1996: 67) refers to as 'human process advantage'.

The resource-based view provides a practical justification for key aspects of a firm's HR policies and practices such as human capital management, talent management, knowledge management, and learning and development. Kamoche (1996: 214–15) stated that: 'In the resource-based view, the firm is seen as a bundle of tangible and intangible resources and capabilities required for product/market competition'. In his opinion, the RBV builds on and provides a unifying framework for the field of strategic human resource management. Boxall (1996: 66) pointed out that: 'The resource-based view of the firm provides a conceptual basis, if we needed one, for asserting that key human resources are sources of competitive advantage.'

The strategic goal emerging from the resource-based view will be to 'create firms which are more intelligent and flexible than their competitors' (Boxall, 1996: 66) by hiring and developing more talented staff and by extending their skills base. Resource-based strategy is therefore concerned with the enhancement of the human or intellectual capital of the firm. As Ulrich (1998: 126) commented: 'Knowledge has become a direct competitive advantage for companies selling ideas and relationships. The challenge to organizations is to ensure that they have the capability to find, assimilate, compensate and retain the talented individuals they need.'

It was asserted by Becker et al (1997: 47) that there are 'two features of organizational systems that increase their inimitability and would apply to high performance work systems: path dependency and causal ambiguity. Path dependency refers to policies that are developed over time and cannot be easily purchased in the market by competitors. Causal ambiguity focuses on the numerous and subtle interrelationships in such a system that are not easily observed from outside the firm.'

Allen and Wright (2007: 98) also noted that: 'Labelled as path dependency by Becker and Gerhart (1996), the unique historical conditions under which HRM is formed in individual firms may make its understanding and replication very difficult'.

The significance of the resource-based view of the firm is that it highlights the importance of a human capital management approach to HRM. This provides the justification for investing in people through resourcing, talent management, and learning and development programmes as a means of enhancing competitive advantage with an emphasis on building flexibility and developing the integrative linkage.

Perspectives on strategic HRM

It was contended by Delery and Doty (1996: 802–03) that 'organizations adopting a particular strategy require HR practices that are different from those required by organizations adopting different strategies' and that organizations with 'greater congruence between their HR strategies and their (business) strategies should enjoy superior performance'. They identify three HRM perspectives:

1 The universalistic perspective – some HR practices are better than others and all organizations should adopt these best practices. There is a universal relationship between individual 'best' practices and firm performance.

2 The contingency perspective – in order to be effective, an organization's HR policies must be consistent with other aspects of the organization. The primary contingency factor is the organization's strategy. This can be described as 'vertical fit'.

3 The configurational perspective – Delery and Doty (1996: 804) state that: 'In order to be effective, an organization must develop an HR system that achieves both horizontal and vertical fit. Horizontal fit refers to the internal consistency of the organization's HR policies or practices, and vertical fit refers to the congruence of the HR system with other organizational characteristics such as firm strategy. An ideal configuration would be one with the highest degree of horizontal fit.'

An alternative way of presenting these perspectives was suggested by Richardson and Thompson (1999). They proposed adopting the commonly used terms of best practice and best fit approaches for the universalistic and contingency perspectives and 'bundling' as the third approach. This followed the classification made by Guest (1997) of fit as an ideal set of practices, fit as contingency and fit as bundles. The best practice, best fit and bundling approaches are discussed below.

The best practice approach

This 'universalist' approach is based on the assumption that there is a set of best HRM practices and that adopting them will lead to superior organizational performance. They are universal in the sense that they are best in any situation.

Lists of best practices

A number of lists of 'best practices' have been produced, the best known of which was produced by Pfeffer (1994), namely:

1 employment security;
2 selective hiring;
3 self-managed teams;
4 high compensation contingent on performance;
5 training to provide a skilled and motivated workforce;
6 reduction of status differentials;
7 sharing information.

The following list was drawn up by Guest (1999):

1 Selection and the careful use of selection tests to identify those with the potential to make a contribution.

2 Training, and in particular a recognition that training is an ongoing activity.

3 Job design to ensure flexibility, commitment and motivation, including steps to ensure that employees have the responsibility and autonomy to use their knowledge and skills fully.

4 Communication to ensure that a two-way process keeps everyone fully informed.

5 Employee share ownership programmes to increase employees' awareness of the implications of their actions for the financial performance of the firm.

The notions of a high-performance, high commitment or high involvement management as described in Chapter 8 can incorporate best practice characteristics.

Problems with the best practice model

The 'best practice' rubric has been attacked by a number of commentators. Cappelli and Crocker-Hefter (1996: 7) comment that the notion of a single set of best practices has been overstated: 'There are examples in virtually every industry of highly successful firms that have very distinctive management practices. We argue that these distinctive human resource practices help to create unique competencies that differentiate products and services and, in turn, drive competitiveness.' Becker et al (1997: 41) believe that 'an inordinate focus on "best practices" is misguided and may even be counterproductive'. Purcell (1999: 26) noted that 'the search for best practice tends to take on the flavour of a moral crusade'. He has also criticized the best-practice or universalist view by pointing out the inconsistency between a belief in best practice and the resource-based view that focuses on the intangible assets, including HR, that allow the firm to do better than its competitors. He asks how can 'the universalism of best practice be squared with the view that only some resources and routines are important and valuable by being rare and imperfectly imitable?' and states that: 'The claim that the bundle of best practice HRM is universally applicable leads us into a utopian cul-de-sac' (ibid: 36). And Boxall et al (2007: 5) remain 'deeply sceptical about claims for universal applicability for particular HRM practices or clusters of practices [but] this does not rule out the search for general principles in the management of work and people'.

In accordance with contingency theory, which emphasizes the importance of interactions between organizations and their environments so that what organizations do is dependent on the context in which they operate, it is difficult to accept that there is any such thing as universal best practice.

What works well in one organization will not necessarily work well in another because it may not fit its strategy, culture, management style, technology or working practices. Becker et al (1997: 41) remark that: 'Organizational high-performance work systems are highly idiosyncratic and must be tailored carefully to each firm's individual situation to achieve optimum results'.

However, a knowledge of what is assumed to be best practice can be used to inform decisions on what practices are most likely to fit the needs of the organization, as long as it is understood why a particular practice should be regarded as a best practice and what needs to be done to ensure that it will work in the context of the organization. Becker and Gerhart (1996) argue that the idea of best practice might be more appropriate for identifying the principles underlying the choice of practices, as opposed to the practices themselves. Perhaps it is best to think of 'good practice' rather than 'best practice'.

The best fit approach

The best fit approach emphasizes that HR strategies should be contingent on the context; the circumstances of the organization and its type. Best fit can be perceived in terms of vertical integration or alignment between the organization's business and HR strategies. There is a choice of models, namely: life-cycle, competitive strategy, and strategic configuration.

The life-cycle model

The life-cycle model is based on the theory that the development of a firm takes place in four stages: start-up, growth, maturity and decline. This is in line with product life-cycle theory. The basic premise of this model was expressed by Baird and Meshoulam (1988: 117) as follows:

> Human resource management's effectiveness depends on its fit with the organization's stage of development. As the organization grows and develops, human resource management programmes, practices and procedures must change to meet its needs. Consistent with growth and development models it can be suggested that human resource management develops through a series of stages as the organization becomes more complex.

Buller and Napier (1993) explain that in a start-up phase, management of the HR function may be loose and informal; it may even be performed by the founder/owner. As the organization experiences high growth in sales, products and markets, the demand for new employees increases. This demand is beyond the capacity of the founder and line managers to handle. The organization typically responds to this pressure by adding more formal structure and functional specialists, including HR. The role of HR in this high-growth stage is to attract the right kinds and numbers of people, but it is also the time for innovation and the development of talent management, performance management, learning and development and reward policies and practices. As the organization matures, HR may become less innovative and more inclined to consolidate and develop existing practices rather than create new ones. In the decline stage HR may not have the scope to engage so wholeheartedly with the programmes operating in maturity. HR might well be involved in the difficult decisions that follow downsizing and being taken over.

This is a plausible picture of what may happen and it is backed up by some empirical research. For example, a study by Schuler and Jackson (1987) found evidence that firms with products in the growth stage placed higher priorities on HR management innovation and planning than firms with products in the mature phase. But it is a model of what might happen rather than what should happen. There seems to be no good reason why the HR function in a mature firm should rest on its laurels; quite the opposite. Perhaps the model can serve most usefully as an analytical tool that can be used to alert HR planners to what is happening in the firm and what they might do about it.

Lengnick-Hall and Lengnick-Hall (1988: 460) believe that the whole issue of fit deserves reassessment: 'Research has shown that achieving fit is not always desirable. Further, a focus on maximizing fit can be counter-productive if organization change is needed or if the firm has adopted conflicting competitive goals to correspond to a complex competitive environment.'

Best fit and competitive strategies

Three strategies aimed at achieving competitive advantage have been identified by Porter (1985):

1 Innovation – being the unique producer.
2 Quality – delivering high quality goods and services to customers.
3 Cost leadership – the planned result of policies aimed at 'managing away expense'.

It was contended by Schuler and Jackson (1987) that to achieve the maximum effect it is necessary to match the role characteristics of people in an organization with the preferred strategy.

Strategic configuration

Another approach to best fit is the proposition that organizations will be more effective if they match one of the ideal types defined by theories such as those produced by Mintzberg (1979) and Miles and Snow (1978). This increased effectiveness is attributed to the internal consistency or fit between the patterns of relevant contextual, structural and strategic factors.

The typology of organizations produced by Mintzberg (1979) classified them into five categories: simple structure, machine bureaucracy, professional bureaucracy, divisionalized form, and adhocracy. Miles and Snow (1978) identified four types of organizations, classifying the first three types as 'ideal' organizations:

1 Prospectors, which operate in an environment characterized by rapid and unpredictable changes.

2 Defenders, which operate in a more stable and predictable environment than prospectors and engage in more long-term planning.

3 Analysers, which are a combination of the prospector and defender types. They operate in stable environments like defenders and also in markets where new products are constantly required like prospectors.

4 Reactors, which are unstable organizations existing in what they believe to be an unpredictable environment. They lack consistent, well-articulated strategies and do not undertake long-range planning.

Research conducted by Doty et al (1993) established that the Miles and Snow theory had a high level of predictive validity. In other words, it indicated a reasonably powerful link between the extent to which there was fit in terms of context, structure and strategy and organizational effectiveness. The same research failed to establish any significant link between organizational effectiveness and the Mintzberg typology.

Comments on the concept of best fit

The best fit model seems to be more realistic than the best practice model. As Dyer and Holder (1998: 31) pointed out: 'The inescapable conclusion is that what is best depends'. It can therefore be claimed that best fit is more important than best practice. But there are limitations to the concept of best fit. Paauwe (2004: 37) argued that: 'It is necessary to avoid falling into the trap of contingent determinism' [ie acting as if the context absolutely determines the strategy]. There is, or should be, room for making strategic choices'.

There is a danger of mechanistically matching HR policies and practices with strategy. It is not credible to claim that there are single contextual factors that determine HR strategy, and internal fit cannot therefore be complete. As Boxall (2007: 61) pointed out: 'It is clearly impossible to make all HR policies reflective of a chosen competitive or economic mission'.

Purcell (1999: 35) refers to the concept of 'idiosyncratic contingency', which 'shows that each firm has to make choices not just on business and operational strategies but on what type of HR system is best for its purposes'. He also commented that: 'The search for a contingency or matching model of HRM is also limited by the impossibility of modelling all the contingent variables, the difficulty of showing their interconnection, and the way in which changes in one variable have an impact on others, let alone the need to model idiosyncratic and path dependent contingencies' (ibid: 37).

Bundling

'Bundling' or 'configuration' is the development and implementation of several HR practices together so that they are interrelated and mutually supportive and therefore complement and reinforce each other. This is the process of horizontal integration or internal fit, which is also referred to as the use of 'complementarities'. Richardson and Thompson (1999) believe that a strategy's success turns on combining vertical or external fit and horizontal or internal fit. They concluded that a firm with bundles of associated HR practices should have a higher level of performance, providing it also achieves high levels of fit with its competitive strategy.

MacDuffie (1995: 204) explained the concept of bundling as follows: 'Implicit in the notion of a "bundle" is the idea that practices within bundles are interrelated and internally consistent, and that "more is better" with respect to the impact on performance, because of the overlapping and mutually reinforcing effect of multiple practices'. His research in US automotive assembly plants established that 'innovative HR practices affect performance not individually but as interrelated elements in an internally consistent HR bundle' (ibid: 197).

Dyer and Reeves (1995: 656–57) note that 'bundles of or configurations of activities are more important in enhancing labour productivity than any single activity... The logic in favour of bundling is straightforward... Since employee performance is a function of both ability and motivation, it makes sense to have practices aimed at enhancing both.' They explained that there are several ways in which employees can acquire needed skills (such as careful selection and training) and multiple incentives to enhance motivation (different forms of financial and non-financial rewards). Their study of various models listing HR practices that create a link between HRM and business performance found that the activities appearing in most of the models were involvement, careful selection, extensive training and contingent compensation. Following research in 43 automobile processing plants in the United States, Pil and MacDuffie (1996) established that when a high-involvement work practice is introduced in the presence of complementary HR practices, not only does the new work practice produce an incremental improvement in performance, but so do the complementary practices.

The aim of bundling is to achieve coherence, which is one of the four 'meanings' of strategic HRM defined by Hendry and Pettigrew (1986). Coherence exists when a mutually reinforcing set of HR policies and practices has been developed, which jointly contribute to the attainment of the organization's strategies for matching resources to organizational needs, improving performance and quality and, in commercial enterprises, achieving competitive advantage. David Guest (1989: 42) includes in his set of propositions about HRM the point that strategic integration is about, inter alia, the ability of the organization 'to ensure that the various aspects of HRM cohere'.

The process of bundling HR strategies is an important aspect of the concept of strategic HRM. In a sense, strategic HRM is holistic; it is concerned with the organization as a total entity and addresses what needs to be done across the organization as a whole. It is not interested in isolated programmes and techniques, or in the ad hoc development of HR practices. In their discussion of the four policy areas of HRM (employee influence, human resource management flow, reward systems, and work systems), Beer et al (1984: 10) suggested that this framework can stimulate managers to plan how to accomplish the major HRM tasks 'in a unified, coherent manner rather than in a disjointed approach based on some combination of past practice, accident and ad hoc response to outside pressures'.

One way of looking at the concept of bundling is to say that some measure of coherence will be achieved if there is an overriding strategic imperative or driving force such as performance, customer service, quality, increasing levels of engagement, talent management, or the need to develop skills and competences that initiates various processes and policies designed to link together and operate in concert to deliver results. The development of high-performance, high-commitment or high-involvement systems (see Chapters 8 and 10) is in effect bundling because it groups a number of HR practices together to produce synergy and thus make a greater impact.

Bundling can take place in a number of other ways. For example, competency frameworks can be devised that are used in assessment and development centres and to specify recruitment standards, identify learning and development needs, indicate the standards of behaviour or performance required, and serve as the basis for human resource planning. They could also be incorporated into performance management processes in which the aims are primarily developmental and competencies are used as criteria for reviewing behaviour and assessing learning and development needs. Job evaluation could be based on levels of competency, and competency-based pay systems could be introduced. Grade structures could define career ladders in terms of competency requirements (career family structures) and thus provide the basis for learning and development programmes. They can serve the dual purpose of defining career paths and pay progression opportunities. A high performance work system (see Chapter 10) bundles a number of HR practices together, as does talent management (see Chapter 17).

The problem with the bundling approach is that of deciding which is the best way to relate different practices together. There is no evidence that one bundle is generally better than another.

The reality of strategic HRM

Strategic HRM, as this chapter has shown, has been a happy hunting ground for academics over many years. But what does all this conceptualizing mean in real life? What can practitioners learn from it as they go about their business? Hendry and Pettigrew (1990) in a series of publications presented cases that demonstrated the importance of studying the emerging process of strategy formulation and implementation. They show that this is a complex interactive process, heavily influenced by a variety of contextual historical factors. As a result, there is no straightforward flow from business strategy to HRM.

Before answering these questions it is worth recalling the rationale for strategic HRM – that it is the basis for developing and implementing approaches to people management that enable the organization to achieve its objectives and take into account the changing context in which the firm operates and its longer-term requirements. It should also be borne in mind that strategic HRM is a mindset that only becomes real when it produces actions and reactions that can be regarded as strategic, either in the form of overall or specific HR strategies or strategic behaviour on the part of HR professionals working alongside line managers. Perkins and Shortland (2006) have highlighted the merits of what they call 'informed premeditation'.

As modelled in Figure 3.1, strategic HRM is about both HR strategies and the strategic management activities of HR professionals. There is always choice about those strategies and the strategic role of HR and this choice is based on strategic analysis as conducted in strategic reviews (see the strategic toolkit in Part 4 of this book).

FIGURE 3.1

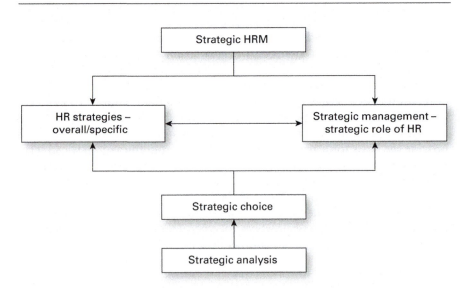

KEY LEARNING POINTS

Strategic HRM (SHRM) defined

SHRM is an approach to managing people that deals with how the organization's goals will be achieved through its human resources by means of integrated HR strategies, policies and practices. It is based on the fundamental proposition that the human resources of an organization play a strategic role in its success.

The conceptual basis of strategic HRM

- 'Strategic HRM is the interface between HRM and strategic management'. It takes the notion of HRM as a strategic, integrated and coherent approach and develops that in line with the concept of strategic management (Boxall, 1996).
- An organization's human resources are of critical strategic importance.
- A firm's HRM practices are instrumental in developing the strategic capability of its pool of human resources.

The aim of strategic HRM

To generate organizational capability by ensuring that the organization has the skilled, engaged, committed and well-motivated employees it needs to achieve sustained competitive advantage.

Implications of the resource-based view

The creation of firms that are 'more intelligent and flexible than their competitors' (Boxall, 1996) by hiring and developing more talented staff and by extending the skills base.

The three HRM 'perspectives' of Delery and Doty (1996)

- Universalistic perspective – some HR practices are better than others and all organizations should adopt these best practices.
- Contingency – in order to be effective, an organization's HR policies must be consistent with other aspects of the organization.
- Configurational – relating HRM to the 'configuration' of the organization in terms of its structures and processes.

The concepts of 'best practice' and 'best fit'

- The concept of best practice is based on the assumption that there is a set of best HRM practices that are universal in the sense that they are best in any situation, and that adopting them will lead to superior organizational performance. This concept of universality is criticized because it takes no account of the local context.

- The concept of best fit emphasizes that HR strategies should be congruent with the context and circumstances of the organization. 'Best fit' can be perceived in terms of vertical integration or alignment between the organization's business and HR strategies.
- It is generally accepted that best fit is more important than best practice.

The significance of bundling

The process of bundling HR strategies is an important aspect of the concept of strategic HRM, which is concerned with the organization as a total system or entity and addresses what needs to be done across the organization as a whole.

The practical implications of strategic HRM theory

The theory addresses major people issues that affect or are affected by the strategic plans of the organization. It provides the rationale for HR practitioners acting as strategic partners on an everyday basis.

References

Allen, M R and Wright, P (2007) Strategic management and HRM, in *Oxford Handbook of Human Resource Management*, (eds) P Boxall, J Purcell and P Wright, pp 88–107, Oxford University Press, Oxford

Alvesson, M (2009) Critical perspectives on strategic HRM, in *The Routledge Companion to Strategic Human Resource Management*, (eds) J Storey, P M Wright and D Ulrich, pp 52–67, Routledge, Abingdon

Baird, L and Meshoulam, I (1988) Managing two fits of strategic human resource management, *Academy of Management Review*, **13** (1), pp 116–28

Barney, J B (1991) Firm resources and sustained competitive advantage, *Journal of Management*, **17** (1), pp 99–120

Barney, J B (1995) Looking inside for competitive advantage, *Academy of Management Executive*, **9** (4), pp 49–61

Batt, R (2007) Service strategies, in *The Oxford Handbook of Human Resource Management*, (eds) P Boxall, J Purcell and P Wright, pp 428–49, Oxford University Press, Oxford

Becker, B E and Gerhart, B (1996) The impact of human resource management on organisational performance, progress and prospects, *Academy of Management Journal*, **39** (4), pp 779–801

Becker, B E and Huselid, M (2006) Strategic human resource management: where do we go from here? *Journal of Management*, **32** (6), pp 898–925

Becker et al (1997) HR as a source of shareholder value: research and recommendations, *Human Resource Management*, **36** (1), pp 39–47

Beer, M et al (1984) *Managing Human Assets*, The Free Press, New York

Boxall, P F (1996) The strategic HRM debate and the resource-based view of the firm, *Human Resource Management Journal*, **6** (3), pp 59–75

Boxall, P F (2007) The goals of HRM, in *The Oxford Handbook of Human Resource Management*, (eds) P Boxall, J Purcell and P Wright, pp 48–67, Oxford University Press, Oxford

Boxall, P F, Purcell, J and Wright, P (2007) Human resource management: scope, analysis and significance, in *The Oxford Handbook of Human Resource Management*, (eds) P Boxall, J Purcell and P Wright, pp 1–18, Oxford University Press, Oxford

Buller, P F and Napier, N K (1993) Strategy and human resource management: integration in fast growth versus other mid-sized firms, *British Journal of Management*, **4** (1), 77–90

Cappelli, P and Crocker-Hefter, A (1996) Distinctive human resources are firms' core competencies, *Organizational Dynamics*, **24** (3), pp 7–22

Colbert, B A (2007) The complex resource-based view: implications for theory and practice in strategic human resource management, in *Strategic Human Resource Management*, (eds) R S Schuler and S E Jackson, pp 98–123, Blackwell, Oxford

Delery, J E and Doty, H D (1996) Modes of theorizing in strategic human resource management: tests of universality, contingency and configurational performance predictions, *Academy of Management Journal*, **39** (4), pp 802–35

Doty, D H, Glick, W H and Huber, G P (1993) Fit, equifinality, and organizational effectiveness: a test of two configurational theories, *Academy of Management Journal*, **36** (6), pp 1195–250

Dyer, L and Holder, G W (1998) Strategic human resource management and planning, in *Human Resource Management: Evolving roles and responsibilities*, (ed) L Dyer, pp 1–46, Bureau of National Affairs, Washington DC

Dyer, L and Reeves, T (1995) Human resource strategies and firm performance: what do we know and where do we need to go? *The International Journal of Human Resource Management*, **6** (3), pp 656–70

Guest, D E (1989) Human resource management: its implications for industrial relations and trade unions, in *New Perspectives in Human Resource Management*, (ed) J Storey, pp 41–55, Routledge, London

Guest, D E (1997) Human resource management and performance: a review of the research agenda, *The International Journal of Human Resource Management*, **8** (3), pp 263–76

Guest, D E (1999) Human resource management: the workers' verdict, *Human Resource Management Journal*, **9** (2), pp 5–25

Hamel, G and Prahalad, C K (1989) Strategic intent, *The Harvard Business Review*, May/June, pp 63–76

Hendry, C and Pettigrew, A (1986) The practice of strategic human resource management, *Personnel Review*, **15** (5), pp 2–8

Hendry, C and Pettigrew, A (1990) Human resource management: an agenda for the 1990s, *International Journal of Human Resource Management*, **1** (1), pp 17–44

Kamoche, K (1996) Strategic human resource management within a resource capability view of the firm, *Journal of Management Studies*, **33** (2), pp 213–33

Lengnick-Hall, C A and Lengnick-Hall, M L (1988) Strategic human resource management: a review of the literature and a proposed typology, *Academy of Management Review*, **13**, pp 454–70

Lengnick-Hall, C A and Lengnick-Hall, M L (1990) *Interactive Human Resource Management and Strategic Planning*, Quorum Books, Westport

Mabey, C, Salaman, G and Storey, J (1998) *Human Resource Management: A strategic introduction*, Blackwell, Oxford

MacDuffie, J P (1995) Human resource bundles and manufacturing performance, *Industrial Relations Review*, **48** (2), pp 199–221

McWilliams, A, Siegal, D S and Wright, P M (2006) Corporate social responsibility: strategic implications, *Journal of Management Studies*, **43** (1), pp 1–12

Miles, R E and Snow, C C (1978) *Organizational Strategy: Structure and process*, McGraw Hill, New York

Mintzberg, H T (1979) *The Structuring of Organizations*, Prentice-Hall, Englewood Cliffs, NJ

Mintzberg, H T (1994) The rise and fall of strategic planning, *Harvard Business Review*, January/February, pp 107–14

Paauwe, J (2004) *HRM and performance: Achieving long term viability*, Oxford University Press, Oxford

Penrose, E (1959) *The Theory of the Growth of the Firm*, Blackwell, Oxford

Perkins, S J and Shortland, S M (2006) *Strategic International Human Resource Management*, Kogan Page, London

Pfeffer, J (1994) *Competitive Advantage Through People*, Harvard Business School Press, Boston

Pil, F K and MacDuffie, J P (1996) The adoption of high-involvement work practices, *Industrial Relations*, **35** (3), pp 423–55

Porter, M E (1985) *Competitive Advantage: Creating and sustaining superior performance*, The Free Press, New York

Purcell, J (1999) Best practice or best fit: chimera or cul-de-sac, *Human Resource Management Journal*, **9** (3), pp 26–41

Purcell, J et al (2003) *People and Performance: How people management impacts on organisational performance*, CIPD, London

Quinn Mills, D (1983) Planning with people in mind, *Harvard Business Review*, November/December, pp 97–105

Richardson, R and Thompson, M (1999) *The Impact of People Management Practices on Business Performance: A literature review*, Institute of Personnel and Development, London

Schuler, R S (1992) Strategic human resource management: linking people with the strategic needs of the business, *Organizational Dynamics*, **21** (1), pp 18–32

Schuler, R S and Jackson, S E (1987) Linking competitive strategies with human resource management practices, *Academy of Management Executive*, **9** (3), pp 207–19

Schuler, R S and Jackson, S E (2007) *Overview of SHRM, Strategic Human Resource Management*, 2nd edn, Blackwell, Oxford

Schuler, R S, Jackson, S E and Storey, J (2001) HRM and its link with strategic management, in *Human Resource Management: A critical text*, 2nd edn, (ed) J Storey, pp 114–30, Thompson Learning, London

Storey, J (1989) From personnel management to human resource management, in *New Perspectives on Human Resource Management*, (ed) J Storey, pp 1–18, Routledge, London

Ulrich, D (1998) A new mandate for human resources, *Harvard Business Review*, January/February, pp 124–34

Wernerfelt, B (1984) A resource-based view of the firm, *Strategic Management Journal*, **5** (2), pp 171–80

Wright, P and McMahan, G (1992) Theoretical perspectives for human resource management, *Journal of Management*, **18** (2), pp 295–320

Wright, P M and Snell, S A (1998) Towards a unifying framework for exploring fit and flexibility in strategic human resource management, *Academy of Management Review*, **23** (4), pp 756–72

PART TWO
The practice of strategic HRM

The strategic role of HR

04

Introduction

Strategic HRM (SHRM) is not just about strategic planning. It is equally if not more concerned with the implementation of strategy. It is also concerned with the strategic behaviour of HR specialists working with their line management colleagues on an everyday basis to ensure that the business goals of the organization are achieved and its values are put into practice. The strategic role of HR professionals is examined in this chapter. It starts with an overview of the strategic nature of HR and continues with a review of the strategic business partner model. The chapter concludes with analyses of the strategic roles of HR directors, HR business partners and HR advisors or assistants.

The strategic role of HR practitioners

The role of HR practitioners can be divided into two main areas: transactional activities and strategic activities. Transactional activities consist of the service delivery aspects of HR – recruitment, training, dealing with people issues, legal compliance and employee services. HR strategic activities support the achievement of the organization's goals and values and involve the development and implementation of forward-looking HR strategies that are integrated with one another and aligned to business objectives. Importantly they work with their line management colleagues in the continuous formulation and execution of the business strategy. But HR practitioners must not pursue business objectives at the expense of the ethical considerations spelt out in Chapter 1.

It is important to get the balance between strategic and transactional activities right. In its anxiety to enhance the standing of the HR profession, the Chartered Institute of Personnel and Development (the CIPD) sometimes gives the impression that the only thing that counts is 'being strategic'. Forget about the boring transactional activities. Rosabeth Moss Kanter (1984: 294) thought that '"strategic" is clearly an overused word'. Alvesson (2009: 57) noted that 'HR people are redefining themselves from being administrators and managers to becoming "strategists"'. He felt that: 'Sometimes one gets the impression that there is very little "non-strategic" HRM going on' (ibid: 57).

HR must also get its transactional service delivery activities right – that's what it's there to do, day-by-day, and its reputation with line managers largely depends on this. As an HR specialist commented to Caldwell (2004: 203): 'My credibility depends on running an extremely efficient and cost effective administrative machine... If I don't get that right, and consistently, then you can forget about any big ideas.' Another person interviewed during Caldwell's research referred to personnel people as 'reactive pragmatists', a view that in many organizations is in accord with reality. And Syrett (2006: 63) commented that: 'Whatever strategic aspirations senior HR practitioners have, they will amount to nothing if the function they represent cannot deliver the essential transactional services their internal line clients require'.

But in accordance with the resource-based view, which emphasizes the importance of human capital in achieving competitive advantage, the credibility of HR professionals, especially at the highest level, also depends on their ability to make a strategic contribution which ensures that the organization has the quality of skilled and engaged people it needs. Sparrow et al (2010: 88) observed that 'HR must be fully responsive to the strategy and business model of the business. HR is not a rule to itself. It is not "HR for HR", but HR (as broadly defined across the competing stakeholders whom HR has to satisfy) for the business.' The strategic nature of HR has been expressed in the strategic partner model as described below.

The strategic business partner model

HR practitioners share responsibility with their line management colleagues for the success of the enterprise. In 1985, Shaun Tyson, anticipating Dave Ulrich by 13 years, described them as business managers who have the capacity to identify business opportunities, to see the broad picture and to understand how their role can help to achieve the company's business objectives. They integrate their activities closely with top management and ensure that they serve a long-term strategic purpose. They anticipate needs, act flexibly and are proactive.

The notion of strategic partner was introduced by Dyer and Holder (1988), not Dave Ulrich as is generally assumed. They described the role as follows.

SOURCE REVIEW   The strategic partner role for HR – Dyer and Holder (1988: 31–32)

The recommended role for the HR function is that of 'strategic partner'. This role typically has four aspects: (1) top HR executives cooperate with their line counterparts in formulating HR strategies, (2) top HR executives fully participate in all business strategy sessions as equals to CFOs and other top executives thus permitting early evaluation of proposals from an HR perspective, (3) HR executives work closely with line managers on an ongoing basis to ensure that all components of the business strategies are adequately implemented and (4) the HR function itself is managed strategically.

Ulrich and Lake (1990) popularized the idea of the HR strategic business partner and this was taken up enthusiastically within the HR profession and its professional body – the CIPD – as the concept of business partnering. The Chartered Institute of Personnel and Development (2007) explained that the task of strategic business partners was to work closely with business leaders, influencing strategy and steering its implementation.

Ulrich and Lake (1990: 95–96) argued that:

> To ensure that management practices become a means for gaining a sustained competitive advantage, human resource professionals need to become strategic business partners and gear their activities to improving business performance. To do this they require a good working knowledge of the organization and its strategies. In assessing the role of human resources in an organization, management needs to determine the extent to which these professionals meet the following criteria:
>
> 1 Spend time with customers and clients – diagnosing, discussing and responding to needs.
> 2 Actively participate in business planning meetings and offer informed insights on strategic, technological and financial capabilities.
> 3 Understand business conditions.
> 4 Demonstrate competence in business knowledge, particularly customer relations, delivery of world-class management practices and management of change'.

Schuler and Jackson (2007: xiv) made a similar point when they wrote: 'Today, human resource professionals are being challenged to learn more about the business, its strategy, its environment, its customers, and its competitors'.

Note that none of these comments indicated any awareness that HR should be aware of ethical as well as business considerations and act accordingly. However, to do Dave Ulrich justice, he did write later that HR professionals should 'represent both employee needs and implement management agendas' (Ulrich, 1997: 5).

The Ulrich term 'strategic business partner' has been shortened in common parlance to 'business partner'. Conceptually, HR business partners work closely with line managers and are probably embedded in a business unit or a line function. They fully understand the strategies and activities of their unit or function and appreciate the role they can play as partners to the line managers with whom they work in ensuring that business goals are achieved. Business partners are there to enable those line managers to achieve their objectives through their people.

The strategic role of HR directors

The strategic role of HR directors is to promote the achievement of the organization's goals and values by: (1) developing and implementing HR strategies that are integrated with the business strategy and are coherent and mutually supportive; (2) ensuring that a strategic approach is adopted which ensures that HR activities support the business and add value; and (3) taking into account the ethical dimension of HRM. To carry out this role HR directors need to:

- understand the strategic goals of the organization;
- appreciate the business imperatives and performance drivers relative to these goals;
- understand the business model of the organization (how it makes money) and play a part in business model innovation;
- comprehend how sustainable competitive advantage can be obtained through the human capital of the organization and know how HR practices can contribute to the achievement of strategic goals;
- contribute to the development of the business strategy on an 'outside-in' basis (Wright et al, 2004), starting from an analysis of the customer, competitor and business issues the organization faces: the HR strategy then derives directly from these challenges to create solutions, add value and ensure that the organization has the distinctive human capital required to make an impact;
- contribute to the development for the business of a clear vision and a set of integrated values;
- ensure that senior management understands the HR implications of its business strategy;
- see the big picture including the broader context (the competitive environment and the business, economic, social and legal factors that affect it) in which the organization operates;
- think in the longer term of where HR should go and how to get there;
- understand the kinds of employee behaviour required to execute the business strategy successfully;
- believe in and practise evidence-based management;
- be capable of making a powerful business case for any proposals on the development of HR strategies;
- fully embrace ethical considerations when developing and implementing HR strategy.

The strategic role of heads of HR functions

The strategic role of heads of HR functions is fundamentally the same for their function as that of HR directors for the whole organization. They promote the achievement of the organization's business goals by developing and implementing functional strategies that are aligned with the business strategy and integrated with the strategies for other HR functions, and adopt a strategic approach in the sense of ensuring that HR activities support the business, add value and are ethical. To carry out this role, heads of HR functions should:

- understand the strategic goals of the organization as they affect their function;
- appreciate the business imperatives and performance drivers relative to these goals;
- help senior management to understand the implications of its strategy for the HR function;
- know how HR practices in the function can contribute to the achievement of the strategic goals;
- ensure that their activities provide added value for the organization;
- be aware of the broader context (the competitive environment and the business, economic, social and legal factors that affect it) in which the function operates;
- think in terms of the bigger and longer-term picture of where HR strategies for the function should go and how to get there;
- believe in and practise evidence-based management;
- be capable of making a powerful business case for any proposals on the development of HR strategies for the function;
- fully embrace ethical considerations when developing and implementing HR strategy for their function.

The strategic role of HR business partners

The strategic role of HR business partners is to promote the achievement of the business goals of the organizational unit or function in which they operate. In doing so, they need to take account of ethical considerations. To carry out this role they should:

- understand the business and its competitive environment;
- understand the goals of their part of the business and its plans to attain them;
- ensure that their activities provide added value for the unit or function;
- build relationships founded on trust with their line management clients;
- provide support to the strategic activities of their colleagues;
- align their activities with business requirements;
- believe in and practise evidence-based management;
- be proactive, anticipating requirements, identifying problems and producing innovative and evidence-based solutions to them;
- see the broad picture and rise above the day-to-day detail;
- fully take into account ethical considerations when performing their business partner role.

The strategic contribution of HR advisors or assistants

The role of HR advisors or assistants is primarily that of delivering effective HR services within their function or as a member of an HR service centre. While they will not be responsible for the formulation of HR strategies, they may contribute to them within their own speciality. They will need to understand the business goals of the departments or managers for whom they provide services in order to ensure that these services support the achievement of those goals. They should also fully take into account ethical considerations when performing their role.

KEY LEARNING POINTS

- The work of HR practitioners is divided into two main areas: transactional activities and strategic activities.

- The credibility of HR professionals, especially at the highest level, also depends on their ability to make a strategic contribution that ensures that the organization has the quality of skilled and engaged people it needs. But HR must also get its transactional service delivery activities right.

- Human resource professionals need to become strategic business partners concerned with improving business performance. But they should not pursue business objectives at the expense of ethical considerations.

- The strategic role of HR directors is to promote the achievement of the organization's goals and values by: (1) developing and implementing HR strategies that are integrated with the business strategy and are coherent and mutually supportive; (2) ensuring that a strategic approach in the sense of making sure HR activities support the business and add value is adopted throughout the HR function; and (3) taking into account the ethical dimension of HRM.

- The strategic role of heads of HR functions is fundamentally the same for their function as that of HR directors for the whole organization.

- The role of HR advisors or assistants is primarily that of delivering effective HR services within their function or as a member of an HR service centre. While they will not be responsible for the formulation of HR strategies, they may contribute to them within their own speciality.

References

Alvesson, M (2009) Critical perspectives on strategic HRM, in *The Routledge Companion to Strategic Human Resource Management*, (eds) J Storey, P M Wright and D Ulrich, pp 52–67, Routledge, Abingdon

Caldwell, R (2004) Rhetoric, facts and self-fulfilling prophesies: exploring practitioners' perceptions of progress in implementing HRM, *Industrial Relations Journal*, 35 (3), pp 196–215

Chartered Institute of Personnel and Development (2007) *HR Business Partnering*, CIPD, London

Dyer, L and Holder, G W (1988) Strategic human resource management and planning, in *Human Resource Management: Evolving roles and responsibilities*, (ed) L Dyer, pp 1–46, Bureau of National Affairs, Washington DC

Kanter, R M (1984) *The Change Masters*, Allen & Unwin, London

Schuler, R S and Jackson, S E (2007) *Strategic Human Resource Management*, Blackwell, Oxford

Sparrow, P et al (2010) Using business model change to tie HR into strategy: reversing the arrow, in *Leading HR*, (eds) P Sparrow, A Hesketh, M Hird and C Cooper, pp 68–89, Palgrave Macmillan, Basingstoke

Syrett, M (2006) Four reflections on developing a human capital measurement capability, in *What's the Future for Human Capital?*, CIPD, London

Tyson, S (1985) Is this the very model of a modern personnel manager? *Personnel Management*, May, pp 22–25

Ulrich, D (1997) *Human Resource Champions*, Harvard Business School Press, Boston, MA

Ulrich, D and Lake, D (1990) *Organizational Capability: Competing from the inside out*, Wiley, New York

Wright, P M, Snell, S A and Jacobsen, H H (2004) Current approaches to HR strategies: inside-out versus outside-in, *Human Resource Planning*, 27 (4), pp 36–46

The impact of strategic HRM

05

KEY CONCEPTS AND TERMS

The 'black box'
Contingency theory
Expectancy theory
Key performance indicators
Performance
Reverse causation

LEARNING OUTCOMES

On completing this chapter you should be able to define the key concepts above. You should be aware of:

- the meaning of performance;
- the outcomes of research into the link between HRM and firm performance;
- the explanations for any impact HRM does make on performance;
- the specific areas where HRM can make an impact.

Introduction

The aims of this chapter are to describe how SHRM makes an impact on organizational performance and to look at what actions can be taken to achieve that impact, bearing in mind the view expressed by Delery (1998) that firms gain a competitive advantage from the human resources that they attract and retain rather than from their HR practices per se. As Guest (1997: 269) argued: 'The distinctive feature of HRM is its assumption that improved performance is achieved through the people in the organization'. If, therefore, appropriate HR policies and processes are introduced, it may also be assumed that HRM will improve firm performance. To back up these assumptions, three questions need to be answered: (1) what is performance? (2) what impact does HRM make on performance? and (3) how does HRM make that impact?

It is first necessary to understand what is meant by performance in order to establish appropriate measures for assessing the impact of HRM. What impact HRM makes is good to know, if only to demonstrate to dubious chief executives and line managers that HRM is a good thing. A considerable amount of research has been conducted recently on the impact of HRM, which is discussed in the second section of this chapter. Ulrich (1997a) commented that managers and HR professionals need to be able to explain how and why HR practices lead to their outcomes. So it is also necessary to understand as far as possible how that impact is made in order to justify, develop and implement effective HR policies and practices, and this is dealt with in the third section. Finally, in the light of the research, consideration is given to how strategic HRM can make a contribution to improving business performance.

The concept of performance

The concept of performance covers both what has been achieved and how it has been achieved. Sheilds (2007: 20) explained that, 'we can conceptualize work and work performance as a system'. This system comprises the three elements of inputs, throughputs (the processes and activities involved in transforming inputs into outcomes) and outcomes arranged in a linear sequence.

Identifying the HRM inputs is not difficult. Outcomes can be measured, the most obvious and most used measures in research studies being in terms of key performance indicators (KPIs), which identify the results or outcomes that are assumed to be crucial to the achievement of high performance and are usually to do with financial results (profitability) or productivity. Measuring the 'how' – the throughputs – is more difficult. As Purcell et al (2003: 2) remarked: '... we do not know why or how HR policies translate into performance. This is known as the "black box" problem'.

Research on the link between HR activities and performance

There has been much research over the last decade or so that has attempted to answer the question: 'Do HR practices make a positive impact on organizational performance?' This is summarized in Table 5.1.

TABLE 5.1

Researcher(s)	Methodology	Outcomes
Arthur (1990, 1992, 1994)	Data from 30 US strip mills used to assess impact on labour efficiency and scrap rate by reference to the existence of either a high commitment strategy* or a control strategy*.	Firms with a high commitment strategy had significantly higher levels of both productivity and quality than those with a control strategy.
Huselid (1995)	Analysis of the responses of 968 US firms to a questionnaire exploring the use of high performance work practices*, the development of synergies between them and the alignment of these practices with the competitive strategy.	Productivity is influenced by employee motivation; financial performance is influenced by employee skills, motivation and organizational structures.
Huselid and Becker (1996)	An index of HR systems in 740 firms was created to indicate the degree to which each firm adopted a high performance work system.	Firms with high values on the index had economically and statistically higher levels of performance.
Becker et al (1997)	Outcomes of a number of research projects were analysed to assess the strategic impact on shareholder value of high performance work systems.	High performance systems make an impact as long as they are embedded in the management infrastructure.
Patterson et al (1997)	The research examined the link between business performance and organization culture and the use of a number of HR practices.	HR practices explained significant variations in profitability and productivity (19% and 18% respectively). Two HR practices were particularly significant: (1) the acquisition and development of employee skills; and (2) job design including flexibility, responsibility, variety and the use of formal teams.

TABLE 5.1 *Continued*

Researcher(s)	Methodology	Outcomes
The 1998 Workplace Employee Relations Survey (as analysed by Guest et al, 2000a)	An analysis of the survey, which sampled some 2,000 workplaces and obtained the views of about 28,000 employees.	A strong association exists between HRM and both employee attitudes and workplace performance.
The Future of Work Survey, Guest et al (2000b)	835 private sector organizations were surveyed and interviews were carried out with 610 HR professionals and 462 chief executives.	A greater use of HR practices is associated with higher levels of employee commitment and contribution and is in turn linked to higher levels of productivity and quality of services.
Thompson (2002)	A study of the impact of high performance work practices such as teamworking, appraisal, job rotation, broad-banded grade structures and sharing of business information in 623 UK aerospace establishments.	The number of HR practices and the proportion of the workforce covered appeared to be the key differentiating factor between more and less successful firms.
West et al (2002)	Research conducted in 61 UK hospitals obtaining information on HR strategy, policy and procedures from chief executives and HR directors and mortality rates.	An association between certain HR practices and lower mortality rates was identified. As noted by Professor West: 'If you have HR practices that focus on effort and skill; develop people's skills; encourage co-operation, collaboration, innovation and synergy in teams for most, if not all employees, the whole system functions and performs better'.

TABLE 5.1 *Continued*

Researcher(s)	Methodology	Outcomes
Purcell et al (2003)	A University of Bath longitudinal study of 12 companies to establish how people management impacts on organizational performance.	The most successful companies had what the researchers called 'the big idea'. The companies had a clear vision and a set of integrated values that were embedded, enduring, collective, measured and managed. They were concerned with sustaining performance and flexibility. Clear evidence existed between positive attitudes towards HR policies and practices, levels of satisfaction, motivation and commitment, and operational performance. Policy and practice implementation (not the number of HR practices adopted) is the vital ingredient in linking people management to business performance and this is primarily the task of line managers.
Guest et al (2003)	An exploration of the relationship between HRM and performance in 366 UK companies using objective and subjective performance data and cross-sectional and longitudinal data.	Some evidence was shown of an association between HRM, as described by the number of HR practices in use, and performance, but there was no convincing indication that the greater application of HRM is likely to result in improved corporate performance.

Comments on the research

With one exception, the studies summarized above revealed that there was a link between certain HR practices and whatever criteria were used to indicate the level of performance. But Guest (1997: 274) commented that: 'At present the studies report a promising association between HRM and outcomes, but we are not yet in a position to assert cause and effect'. If there is a significant link, how is the impact achieved? It is not enough to justify HRM by proving that it is a good thing. What counts is what can be done to ensure that it is a good thing. Ulrich (1997b: 304) pointed out that: 'HR practices seem to matter; logic says it is so; survey findings confirm it. Direct relationships between investment and attention to HR practices are often fuzzy, however, and vary according to the population sampled and the measures used.' Wood (1999: 408) analysed 15 studies of the HRM/performance link and found that they had 'concentrated on assessing the link between practices and performance, with an increasing disregard for the mechanisms linking them. This has meant that there has been no systematic link between HR outcomes and performance.' The longitudinal research by Purcell et al (2003) tried to remedy that weakness.

There are a number of problems that have been identified in other studies. Paauwe and Richardson (1997: 258) commented on 'the difficulty in establishing convincing accounts of chains of cause and effect'. This was explained by Boselie et al (2005: 75), who referred to the causal distance between an HRM input and an output such as financial performance: 'Put simply, so many variables and events, both internal and external, affect organizations that this direct linkage strains credibility'.

Another problem is the assumption some people make that correlations indicate causality – if variable A is associated with variable B then A has caused B. It might have, but again it might not. As Wall and Wood (2005) pointed out, most of the efforts to prove causal relationships have so far produced little but persuasive associations. This is linked to the issue of 'reversed causality', which is the assumption, as Purcell et al (2003: 2) put it: 'That although it is nice to believe that more HR practices leads to higher economic return, it is just as possible that it is successful firms that can afford more extensive (and expensive) HRM practices'. Although they also comment that when successful firms invest heavily in HRM they may do so to help sustain high performance.

Purcell et al (2003: 61) cast doubts on the validity of some of the attempts through research to make the connection: 'Our study has demonstrated convincingly that research which only asks about the number and extent of HR practices can never be sufficient to understand the link between HR practices and business performance. As we have noted, it is misleading to assume that simply because HR policies are present that they will be implemented as intended.'

Another methodological problem with much of the research on the HR/ performance link is that the analysis has been done the wrong way round – identifying current HR practices and measuring performance before the practices were introduced, thus making the dubious assumption that the performance of the firm was affected by the practices that were not yet in place. As Boxall et al (2007: 6) remarked: 'A huge proportion of the studies measuring HR practices of some kind and firm performance have found associations – but between the former and past performance, thus leaving us poorly placed to assert that causality runs from the selected HR practices to performance'. The best approach is the type of longitudinal study undertaken by Purcell et al (2003), which examined the impact of existing HR practices over succeeding years.

However, it must be accepted that HR practices do make a difference. It may be difficult to prove exactly how they do so in terms of the precise link between cause and effect but, as described below, it is possible to develop propositions that explain in broad terms what happens in the black box.

How strategic HRM makes an impact

An overall assessment of how SHRM impacts on performance was made by Becker and Huselid (2006) as follows:

SOURCE REVIEW   How SHRM impacts on performance – Becker and Huselid (2006: 899)

SHRM focuses on organizational performance rather than individual performance... It also emphasizes the role of HR management systems as solutions to business problems (including positive and negative complementarities) rather than individual HR management practices in isolation. But strategic means more than a systems focus or even financial performance. Strategy is about building sustainable competitive advantage that in turn creates above-average financial performance. The simplest depiction of the SHRM model is a relationship between a firm's HR architecture and firm performance. The HR architecture is composed of the systems, practices, competencies, and employee performance behaviours that reflect the development and management of the firm's strategic human capital. Above-average firm performance associated with the HR architecture reflects the quasi rents associated with that strategic resource.

This was the subject of research by Rogg et al (2001), who suggested that HRM affects performance by first influencing climate, which then determines performance. They also argued that the direct links between HRM practices and performance are relatively weak because it is not HRM practices (including reward) themselves that affect performance, but rather the extent to which they lead to a favourable climate.

David Guest (1997: 268) stated that: 'The assumption is that "appropriate" HRM practices tap the motivation and commitment of employees'. He explained how expectancy theory might help to explain the HR/performance link as follows.

SOURCE REVIEW How expectancy theory might explain the HR/performance link – Guest (1997: 268)

The expectancy theory of motivation provides one possible basis for developing a more coherent rationale about the link between HRM practices and performance. Although expectancy theory is concerned primarily with motivation, it is also a theory about the link between motivation and performance. Specifically, it proposes that high performance, at the individual level, depends on high motivation plus possession of the necessary skills and abilities and an appropriate role and understanding of that role. It is a short step to specify the HRM practices that encourage high skills and abilities, for example careful selection and high investment in training; high motivation, for example employee involvement and possibly performance-related pay; and an appropriate role structure and role perception, for example job design and extensive communication and feedback.

The conclusion reached by Purcell et al (2003) was that HR practice feeds in as an 'ingredient' in the workplace and, through various mechanisms, feeds out through the other side as improved performance. They noted that: 'There is clear evidence of a link between positive attitudes to HR policies and practices, levels of satisfaction, motivation and commitment and operational performance' (ibid: 72).

Any theory about the impact of HRM on organizational performance is based on three propositions: (1) that HR practices can enable the organization to attract and retain the skilled and engaged people it needs and make a direct impact on employee characteristics such as engagement, discretionary behaviour and cooperation; (2) that if employees have these characteristics it is probable that organizational performance in terms of productivity, quality and levels of customer satisfaction will improve; and (3) if such aspects of organizational performance improve, the business performance measured by sales, profits, market share and market value will also improve. However,

FIGURE 5.1

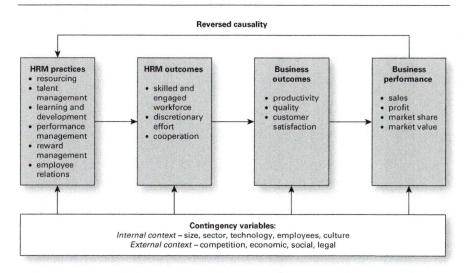

according to these propositions, HRM does not make a direct impact and, as pointed out by Paauwe and Richardson (1997), the relationship is further complicated by the possibility of reversed causality and the contingency variables arising from the context in which the organization operates. A model of the impact of HRM that takes these considerations into account, based on a model produced by Paauwe (2004), is shown in Figure 5.1.

How strategic HRM concepts impact on practice

The practice areas covered by SHRM that impact on performance are summarized in Table 5.2.

TABLE 5.2

HR practice area	How it impacts
Attracting, developing and retaining high quality people	Matches people to the strategic and operational needs of the organization. Provides for the acquisition, development and retention of talented employees who can deliver superior performance, productivity, flexibility, innovation, and high levels of personal customer service, and who 'fit' the culture and the strategic requirements of the organization.
Talent management	Ensures that the talented and well motivated people required by the organization to meet present and future needs are available.
Working environment – core values, leadership, work/life balance, managing diversity, secure employment	Develops 'the big idea' (Purcell et al, 2003), ie a clear vision and a set of integrated values. Makes the organization 'a great place to work'.
Job and work design	Provides individuals with stimulating and interesting work and gives them the autonomy and flexibility to perform these jobs well. Enhances job satisfaction and flexibility, which encourages greater performance and productivity.
Learning and development	Enlarges the skill base and develops the levels of competence required in the workforce. Encourages discretionary learning, which happens when individuals actively seek to acquire the knowledge and skills that promote the organization's objectives. Develops a climate of learning – a growth medium in which self-managed learning as well as coaching, mentoring and training flourish.

TABLE 5.2 *Continued*

HR practice area	How it impacts
Managing knowledge and intellectual capital	Focusing both on organizational and individual learning and providing learning opportunities and opportunities to share knowledge in a systematic way. Ensuring vital stocks of knowledge are retained and improving the flow of knowledge, information and learning within the organization.
Increasing engagement	Encouraging people to identify themselves with and act upon the core values of the organization and willingly contribute to the achievement of organizational goals. Developing a climate of cooperation and trust; clarifying the psychological contract.
High performance management	Developing a performance culture that encourages high performance in such areas as productivity, quality, levels of customer service, growth, profits and, ultimately, the delivery of increased shareholder value. Empowering employees to exhibit the discretionary behaviours most closely associated with higher business performance such as risk taking, innovation and knowledge sharing, and establishing trust between managers and subordinates.
Reward management	Developing motivation, commitment and job engagement by valuing people in accordance with their contribution.
Employee relations	Creating a climate of trust and cooperation.

KEY LEARNING POINTS

HRM and performance

- 'The distinctive feature of HRM is its assumption that improved performance is achieved through the people in the organization' (Guest, 1997).
- If appropriate HR policies and processes are introduced, it may also be assumed that HRM will improve firm performance.
- HR professionals need to be able to explain how and why HR practices lead to their outcomes.

Performance

The concept of performance covers both what has been achieved and how it has been achieved.

Research on the HR/performance link

A number of research studies have revealed that there is a link between certain HR practices and whatever criteria were used to indicate the level of performance. 'At present the studies report a promising association between HRM and outcomes, but we are not yet in a position to assert cause and effect' (Guest, 1997).

How HR affects performance

- 'The assumption is that "appropriate" HRM practices tap the motivation and commitment of employees' (Guest, 1997).
- The conclusion reached by Purcell et al's (2003) research was that HR practice feeds in as an 'ingredient' in the workplace and, through various mechanisms, feeds out through the other side as improved performance.
- 'There is clear evidence of a link between positive attitudes to HR policies and practices, levels of satisfaction, motivation and commitment and operational performance' (Purcell et al, 2003).

Any theory about the impact of HRM on organizational performance is based on three propositions: (1) that HR practices can enable the organization to attract and retain the skilled and engaged people it needs and make a direct impact on employee characteristics such as engagement, discretionary behaviour and cooperation; (2) that if employees have these characteristics it is probable that organizational performance in terms of productivity, quality and levels of customer satisfaction will improve; and (3) if such aspects of organizational performance improve, the business performance measured by sales, profits, market share and market value will also improve.

References

Arthur, J (1990) *Industrial Relations and Business Strategies in American Steel Minimills*, unpublished PhD dissertation, Cornell University

Arthur, J B (1992) The link between business strategy and industrial relations systems in American steel mills, *Industrial and Labor Relations Review*, 45 (3), pp 488–506

Arthur, J (1994) Effects of human resource systems on manufacturing performance and turnover, *Academy of Management Review*, 37 (4), pp 670–87

Becker, B E and Huselid, M (2006) Strategic human resource management: where do we go from here? *Journal of Management*, 32 (6), pp 898–925

Becker, B E et al (1997) HR as a source of shareholder value: research and recommendations, *Human Resource Management*, 36 (1), pp 39–47

Boselie, P, Dietz, G and Boon, C (2005) Commonalities and contradictions in HRM and performance research, *Human Resource Management Journal*, 15 (3), pp 67–94

Boxall, P F, Purcell, J and Wright, P (2007) The goals of HRM, in *Oxford Handbook of Human Resource Management*, (eds) P Boxall, J Purcell and P Wright, pp 48–67, Oxford University Press, Oxford

Delery, J E (1998) Issues of fit in strategic human resource management: implications for research, *Human Resource Management Review*, 8 (3), pp 289–309

Guest, D E (1997) Human resource management and performance: a review of the research agenda, *The International Journal of Human Resource Management*, 8 (3), pp 263–76

Guest, D E et al (2000a) *Employee Relations, HRM and Business Performance: An analysis of the 1998 Workplace Employee Relations Survey*, Chartered Institute of Personnel and Development, London

Guest, D E et al (2000b) *Effective People Management: Initial findings of Future of Work Survey*, Chartered Institute of Personnel and Development, London

Guest, D E et al (2003) Human resource management and corporate performance in the UK, *British Journal of Industrial Relations*, 41 (2), pp 291–314

Huselid, M A (1995) The impact of human resource management practices on turnover, productivity and corporate financial performance, *Academy of Management Journal*, 38 (3), pp 635–72

Huselid, M A and Becker, B E (1996) Methodological issues in cross-sectional and panel estimates of the human resource-firm performance link, *Industrial Relations*, 35 (3), pp 400–22

Paauwe, J (2004) *HRM and Performance: Achieving long term viability*, Oxford University Press, Oxford

Paauwe, J and Richardson, R (1997) Introduction, *International Journal of Human Resource Management*, 8 (3), pp 257–62

Patterson, M G et al (1997) *Impact of People Management Practices on Performance*, Institute of Personnel and Development, London

Purcell, J et al (2003) *People and Performance: How people management impacts on organisational performance*, CIPD, London

Rogg, K L et al (2001) Human resource practices, organisational climate, and customer satisfaction, *Journal of Management*, 27 (4), pp 431–49

Sheilds, J (2007) *Managing Employee Performance and Reward*, Cambridge University Press, Port Melbourne

Thompson, M (2002) *High Performance Work Organization in UK Aerospace*, The Society of British Aerospace Companies, London

Ulrich, D (1997a) *Human Resource Champions*, Harvard Business School Press, Boston, MA

Ulrich, D (1997b) Measuring human resources: an overview of practice and a prescription for results, *Human Resource Management*, **36** (3), pp 303–20

Wall, T and Wood, S (2005) The romance of human resource management and business performance and the case for big science, *Human Relations*, **58** (4), pp 429–62

West, M A et al (2002) The link between the management of employees and patient mortality in acute hospitals, *International Journal of Human Resource Management*, **13** (8), pp 1299–310

Wood, S (1999) Human resource management and performance, *International Journal of Management Reviews*, **1** (4), pp 397–413

Strategic HRM in action

Introduction

The purpose of this chapter is to illustrate the processes involved in formulating and implementing HR strategy through five case studies based on interviews conducted by the author and Phil Long of the CIPD. These cases reveal how HR directors and the other members of top management teams tackle strategic HRM issues. They reveal much diversity of practice as a result of the different purposes, environments and circumstances of the organizations concerned.

Formulating HR strategy

Taking into account Tyson and Witcher's (1994) point that you can only study HR strategy in the context of business strategies, the processes of formulating both business and HR strategies in a number of organizations are described below.

ABC Distribution

ABC Distribution distributes food products, mainly to major retailers. The critical success factors for the organization as spelt out by its Managing Director and the Finance Director are its ability to meet its profit targets and to grow the business substantially on a consistent basis by developing a reputation for providing added value services, developing business with existing customers, winning new customers, and acquisitions. The company has doubled in size in the last four years. Underpinning the development of the company are the needs to grow the infrastructure, to develop management and leadership, and to extend quality and safety programmes.

Business strategy

The Managing Director agreed that in a sense their business strategy evolved in a semi-formal way, but this evolution took place 'by the key people understanding what the total business was trying to do, and their part in it; then they went away and put their bits together; then we pulled all of it together'. He commented that: 'Our strategy is very simple and very broad... it can be put down in a few sentences. It's what lies around it that has to be developed.'

He emphasized that: 'We sought to demonstrate to the rest of the business that we (the Board) were a team. Where a team hadn't existed before, a team was now running the company.'

The Deputy Managing Director explained how he saw the formulation of the business strategy taking place: 'We put our strategy together within the framework of the financial targets we have to meet and our values for quality, integrity and management style'.

In answer to the question: 'How does your organization develop its business strategies?' the Director of Finance said that: 'It started off as being very simple in that we had an objective to grow in excess of the rate of growth demanded by our parent company... However, that process has become less naive, more detailed and more structured as the business grows... I see planning as a process that goes on and on and on and becomes more complex and more refined.'

He also made the following comment: 'Don't forget, not all strategies necessarily involve massive change... you can have a strategy to stay as you are.'

The Director of Marketing emphasized the dynamic nature of strategy in a growing business operating in a highly competitive environment: 'We have a strategy document which is concerned with developing market share and growth and is being continuously updated... The update is driven by the Board... We have to make sure that we continue to refresh the strategy.'

The Director of HR commented that: 'The longer-term strategy is developed basically by the Board getting together and working its way through... We also share that plan with the senior management team.'

HR strategy

The Managing Director described their approach to developing the HR strategy as follows: 'Our HR strategy has to respond to our business needs... So we start with a business plan; we know we are going to grow at a certain rate. Then we do a skills audit and predict how many managers we are going to need. Out of this comes our HR development policy on skills training, leadership training and recruitment.'

The Deputy Managing Director thought that the HR Director was basically responsible for developing their HR strategy: 'We all look at our business strategy and express a view on the people we need, but our HR director pulls it all together and interprets our ramblings into something coherent'.

However, in answering a question on how HR strategies were developed, the Director of Finance admitted that: 'We probably have more HR policies than strategies because the strategies are there in a simple sense but not 100 per cent well-articulated – for valid reasons; we are a growing business'.

The Director of HR referred to the way in which strategic initiatives were developed: 'First the HR people meet and we bounce ideas about and seek ideas. Then if we have a new initiative we put it to the Board for discussion.'

Loamshire Council

Loamshire Council is a District Council that is generally recognized as being a very well run and capable local authority. It is particularly good at dealing with the environment and, as the Chief Executive said: 'We tend to care so passionately about our environment that we focus an almost dispro-portionate amount of our resources on environmental issues'. He further commented that the critical success factors for the authority were meeting the perceived needs of the community, creating customer satisfaction with the services provided and, importantly: 'an overall appreciation of the effec-tiveness of members of staff and the contribution they make towards the organization as a whole'.

Corporate strategy

The following comments were made by the Chief Executive on how corporate strategy was developed:

> We do not have a single document which says 'this is the Loamshire Council corporate strategy'. What we do have are three processes which run in parallel

and together represent the corporate strategy. These comprise a general strategy for developing services, a management strategy which concentrates on the managerial processes which we need to design to bring out the best in the organization, and the key areas for achievement document which focuses on specific actions.

Strategies are developed by a top-down, bottom-up process. The members of the Council, the policy makers, debate the strategic issues from which firm strategic proposals would develop. Individual members of staff are then given opportunities to contribute... A distinguishing feature of all our corporate strategy work has been the opportunity for widespread involvement in the process.

It is incredibly important that within an organization there is somebody who has the personal responsibility for monitoring, evaluating and reviewing the effectiveness of that organization... That strategic management role lies at the heart of the Chief Executive's responsibility.

The Director of Planning commented as follows on the process of strategic planning:

The reality is you choose directions and you move in particular directions, then all sorts of things happen that you can't possibly have conceived of, and you weave these into your strategy.

Strategy is rooted in the vision and the culture... Life's very complicated, there are no easy solutions, and you don't start at Go when you throw a six and proceed from there. You pick up a very complex jigsaw and you work through it. But the vision helps.

On how the top team operates, the Director of Planning said that: 'The things we bring to the team are personal characteristics as much as the management skills we all learn at various stages... the fact that we have a spectrum of personalities strengthens the team.'

HR strategy

The Chief Executive stated that:

Human resource strategy has got to be owned by the top management body within an organization. Their commitment must be absolute otherwise it simply won't be applied in practice. Everything flows from the corporate strategies we have set down. It's about having a very strong focus on the overall effectiveness of the organization, its direction and how it's performing.

There is commitment to, and belief in, and respect for individuals, and I think that these are very important factors in an organization.

When asked how HR strategies were developed, the Director of HR replied:

Initially what I did was to list all the activities in which we were currently involved in HR and sent a questionnaire to all the directors stating 'This is what we are doing' and asking: 'Do you want us to continue doing it? If so, do you want the same, or more, or less? Are we doing it well? Could we do it better?

What are the things we are not doing that you think we ought to be doing?' The next thing I did was to have two open days in which I invited managers to come in and tell us what their perceptions of HR were. And this confirmed our eagerness to get rid of duplication and delays in HR matters. We were fast getting in the way and holding the whole process up. And that's where we got the agreement of the organization that empowerment should be our strategy.

On this strategy for empowerment, the Director of Technical Services remarked: 'The positive aspect of the devolution of responsibility for HR management is that it puts people management back where it should be'.

Megastores

Megastores is one of the country's largest and most successful high street retailers. It has a very powerful overriding commercial objective: to increase shareholders' value, and to do this by providing value-for-money products and delivering consistently high levels of customer service.

Business strategy

The Managing Director made the following observations about strategic management: 'Strategy is developing a route to better the business in the medium to long term. You cannot fully maximize the business opportunities unless you've got the proper management structure to create them. In business you have to look at the options available, make a decision and then drive that way.'

The approach to strategy formulation was described by the Director of Finance as follows:

> Our strategy tends to be based on the resolution of issues. There is a base strategy and we continue to question whether that is the right thing to be going forward with. We have a strategic planning framework throughout the group. It's called value-based management (VBM), the fundamentals of which are to make sure that whatever you do, you must maximize shareholder value...
> It provides us with a basis for looking at what we are doing and the resources we require we've never had before.

However, he also commented that: 'We're highly profitable, but in turn we invest an awful lot in our people. We spend a lot of money on the training and development of people throughout the organization. It's probably one of our key differentiators.'

The Director of Stores gave these perspectives on the strategic planning process:

> We have in place a formal business planning process in which we divide the planning into three levels. One is at business level where we identify issues that we deal with as a company, the second level is product-market planning, and the third level is local market planning.

Our business strategy is formed through value-based management, which is a discipline for pulling everything together and ensures that decisions are made on the basis of their real value to the business rather than someone's strength of personality or hunch. This in itself required the involvement of all the directors in a more formal business planning process. Three or four years ago we worked more individually and now we work more as a team.

There are elements of our business which are incredibly value creating. There are others which are incredibly value destroying. The trick is to identify the ones which are value creating and funnel resources to them.

There are a number of blocks that make up our business strategy. The first is our overall objective. Against this we spin off a number of elements we call major initiatives. These are coordinated by our Director of Corporate Planning, but it is the functional directors who are really charged with taking ownership of these objectives.

HR strategy

The comments made by the Managing Director and a number of other directors on the formulation of HR strategy are given below:

- 'The biggest challenge will be to maintain [our] competitive advantage and to do that we need to maintain and continue to attract very high calibre people' (Managing Director).

- 'All we do in terms of training and manpower planning is directly linked to business improvement' (Managing Director).

- 'The key differentiator on anything any company does is fundamentally the people, and I think that people tend to forget that they are the most important asset. Money is easy to get hold of, good people are not' (Managing Director).

- 'The influence in terms of strategic direction must always be based on the key areas of marketing and operations' (Director of Finance).

- 'We have to help the business achieve its objectives and the HR strategy has to be very much tailored towards those objectives' (Director of HR).

When questioned on his approach to the development of HR strategies, the Director of HR replied: 'I start with the top line, the four or five things which are the strategic platform for the company. I get my managers together to look at the implications. We then pull it together so that it is all derived from the original strategic platforms and then work top-down and bottom-up to get the amalgam of what we can achieve. This then feeds into the final operating plan so we can agree budgets.'

Mercia Systems

Mercia Systems is engaged in the business of precision engineering, including the development and manufacture of specialized optical, mechanical, electrical and electronic equipment primarily for defence purposes. Two major factors have affected the company: first, the contraction in the defence industry and, second, the change in government policy from cost-plus contracting to competitive tendering. This compelled the company to develop an entirely new business strategy and to carry out a comprehensive re-engineering process.

Critical success factors

The Managing Director stated unequivocally that: 'The things that are essential to an organization's success, any organization, not just this one, are the people. They are the common denominator throughout the organization.'

The critical success factors for Mercia Systems were defined as follows:

- 'The one factor that drives us is technology know-how. This means we offer solutions, not products. That is really what we have to sell and it depends on people strength' (Managing Director).

- 'We have a vision of what we want to be and are advancing more quickly than the rest of the competition. CIM [computer integrated manufacture] is at the heart of it. We have tackled MRPII [manufacturing resource planning] as the first phase of CIM and this means that we are faster than our competitors and are more likely to deliver on time than them' (General Manager).

- 'We are characterized in the marketplace as a high-tech company with specific expertise in the field of optics and particularly electro-optics. We are known for the excellence of our technical solutions and the quality of our products. In the past we have been criticized for asking a premium price for high technology products. Part of the message we are now getting across is that we can battle it out on value for money as well... People like working with us because they get straight answers to their questions, including 'we don't know' if we really don't know. So our basic competences are high technical quality and people with the skills needed to forge good relationships with customers' (Marketing Director).

Business strategy

Business strategy is stimulated and reviewed centrally by a business strategy group. The business is split into a number of sectors (three in Glasgow) and each sector submits its business plan to the strategy group. This is a simple three-page summary that describes the broad objectives of their business sector, discusses the key competitive factors affecting it and sets out specific short-to-medium-term objectives, which are then translated into an operating plan. The plans look at a horizon of 10 years but for practical purposes there is a rolling three-year budget. This means that besides looking at the immediate budget, the two key questions asked are, as the General Manager put it: 'Where are you going to be in three years' time? and What are you doing now to get better?' And this, he said, 'is a very demanding discipline'.

The Marketing Director explained the approach as follows:

The key to the business planning process is that it has to be a linked story from the top to the bottom of the company and MRPII [manufacturing resource planning] is part of the vehicle for doing that. Our Director of Strategic Planning works with the Technical Director to involve and guide the Board on the overall strategic direction of the company. This is communicated as the strategic vision. Working from that, my role is to work with the group directors to evolve strategies for each of the businesses we have chosen to be in. These are then reviewed and agreed by the executive and a strategic development group. One of the roles of that group is to check that our activities relate to and support the strategy established by the executive. If they do not, this may not be because they are wrong, and we may have to go back and review the strategy.

The formulation of business strategy is very much a team effort. As the Managing Director said: 'Tell all the top executive people, including the HR and finance directors, that they are directors first and foremost and all must make a contribution to strategic planning'.

The lead may be taken by the Managing Director and the strategic team, of which the HR Director is a member, but the heads of the business groups make a major and continuing contribution. The broad thrust of the strategy as a means of realizing the vision is quite clear, but it is in a constant state of evolution, reacting as necessary in response to changing situations but also proactively anticipating new opportunities.

HR strategies

The overall approach to the formulation of HR strategies was summarized by the Managing Director as follows: 'The main thing we have to do is to ensure that we have the right core technologies and the right competences within the company to achieve the vision and strategy'.

The General Manager commented that:

Within the Board one of the things that is constantly reviewed is human resource strategy. We have the long-term view of the type of organization we believe we need as a technology company and we have evolutionary plans of how we are going to get there. In the early stages we had a very strong functional organization; our evolution process now involves the development of problem-solving teams which are set up at a high standard to encourage getting it right first time. In manufacturing we have mixed discipline teams with a team leader and a much flatter structure than we used to have. We have two pilot projects where research and development engineers are part of the team on the shop floor with a common team leader. The eventual aim is for all engineering and manufacturing to be organized in this way. The next step is to develop product families in which business generation and sales are brought into the team as well. So the team leaders almost become general managers.

The Marketing Director pointed out that the HR strategy 'was clearly established in the planning process and it had hard objectives in the same way as the business strategy'.

The HR Director explained that business strategy defines what has to be done to achieve success and that HR strategy must complement it, bearing in mind that one of the critical success factors for the company is its ability to attract and retain the best people. HR strategy must help to ensure that Mercia Systems is a best practice company. This implies that: 'The HR strategy must be in line with what is best in industry and this may mean visiting four or five different companies, looking at what they are doing and taking a bit from one and a bit from another and moulding them together to form the strategy'.

Welland Water

Welland Water is a large water company operating, as pointed out by the Managing Director: 'in a monopolistic situation providing a service that is absolutely fundamental to life'. But he also stated that: 'we recognize that our organization must not abuse that situation and that we must implant in the company values that would be appropriate in a competitive environment'.

He went on to say:

> We can demonstrate that the services we are giving our customers are improving dramatically, year on year... We have an ongoing commitment to involve our customers – we were the first water company to actually prepare an annual report for them... We carry out frequent tracking research which shows that our customers' perceptions of us are improving, on occasions despite a contrary trend in the national water industry... But the critical success factor which allows all this to happen is the level of employee satisfaction and commitment we have, because without that, we can't achieve any of the other things. And we know about this because we get consultants to carry out periodical employee surveys which we discuss with everyone.

Business strategy

The Managing Director described the approach to formulating business strategy as follows:

> Our strategic approach is very simple. It is summarized in our vision statement: we aim to provide the level of services our customers demand at a level of charges that our customers would see as acceptable. Our business strategies are formed essentially from top-down setting of the parameters and then bottom-up preparation of business plans in which all our people are involved. They prepare all their own business plans which reflect the top-down constraints, and because they are preparing them that automatically buys their commitment to them.

> Our best ideas for policies and strategies come from the people who carry out the work. We don't have people locked into little rooms thinking: 'What's the next strategic move for the business?'
>
> What you need are people who are in tune with what's happening throughout the organization; who are listening, talking, picking up all the ideas... What we try to do is to capture all that knowledge, all those initiatives, all that expertise, and reflect that in the way we take the business forward.
>
> I like to talk about getting values in place rather than constructing strategies.

The Finance Director explained the significance of the vision statement in developing business strategies: 'The company developed a vision statement which encompasses the key forward-looking strategy over a period of time but without timescales having been set down. This has set the guidelines for future initiatives and any such initiative in the rolling five-year business plan is judged on whether it fits in with that vision.'

HR strategy

The Managing Director made the point that: 'The only human resource strategy you really need is the tangible expression of values and the implementation of values... unless you get the human resource values right you can forget all the rest.'

The Finance Director commented that: 'There's a lot of interaction, prior to and during the top board discussion, which tends to be concerned with culturally-based issues and the way we manage people'.

And the Director of Operations indicated that the organization developed its HR strategy: 'Through evolution; it's an aggregation of things that have come together, not necessarily in the right order'.

The approach to developing HR strategy was described by the Head of HR as follows:

> In our original HR strategy we tried to encompass the emerging values and principles that we felt should determine how we should conduct our business in terms of people. HR strategies come from the ideas we share together and the problems and issues that managers are working on... It's very much a team effort, working with line colleagues in whatever they do... I use e-mail to flash ideas round to groups of managers and thus build up draft policy papers. E-mail is a very powerful device for getting ideas back rapidly.

Comments

In all the organizations referred to above:

- there is a well-defined corporate or business strategy, although the extent to which it is formalized varies;
- HR strategy is seen as part of the business strategy;
- HR strategy or policy issues appeared to be of interest to all members of the board and, contrary to popular opinion, this included the finance director.

Philosophy on managing people

The philosophy on managing people is a broad strategic issue associated with management style, and it is one that may never be articulated and so often remains on a 'taken for granted' basis, like other manifestations of corporate culture. The philosophy may lead to a 'hard HRM' or a 'soft HRM' approach or a combination of the two as described in Chapter 1. But to adapt a common if somewhat inadequate definition of corporate culture, strategic HRM is about 'the way things should be done around here in the future'. Questions can be asked about the traditional or underlying philosophy, the extent to which it is still relevant and the directions in which it might usefully change.

The philosophy of the Managing Director of Megastores on managing people was expressed as follows:

> There is immense strength and talent in any body of people numbering 50,000 and we are negligent if we don't tap that resource as far as we possibly can... The contribution of our managers to added value is immense because they are people managers... They are not managing systems, they are not managing machinery and they are not managing shops – you can't manage a shop, you manage people within a shop.
>
> I have always advocated the employment of the highest calibre of people we can find, and I think we've got that... We are in the vanguard of retailing. Our net profit to sales ratio is about the highest in the high street and in profit terms we are growing at a faster rate than the market. The biggest challenge will be to maintain that competitive advantage and to do that we need to maintain and continue to attract very high calibre people.

Corporate issues

Vision and mission

In the broadest terms strategic HRM is concerned with the people implications of top management's vision of the future of the organization and the mission it is there to fulfil. HR strategies, like those of all the other functions, are there to support the realization of the vision and mission of the organization and the achievement of its goals.

The HR Director at Mercia Systems made the following comment about vision and strategy: 'The first thing is that the organization has to know where it is going. That is why it needs a vision. It has to know why it exists and who its customers are. This leads to the development of strategies which in turn lead to action plans. The plans follow three lanes: systems, processes and people.'

Two of the other functional directors at Mercia Systems commented on the significance of vision and a sense of purpose or mission:

I would put it in a single word – which is vision. If you can create a vision and communicate it to people you can release a colossal current of energy... Communication and vision means education and training and I am one of the operational guys who believe that whatever you are currently spending on education and training you start by doubling it.

What contributes most to success is a clear sense of purpose and definition of where you are trying to get to. Unless you have a top team with a clear and unified understanding of purpose and direction it can be difficult to cascade it throughout the organization.

The Managing Director of Welland Water commented that: 'We look at our vision for the company and we say: "how do we maximize the contribution that our people can make to achieving that vision?"'

Organization

HR strategy may address such issues as structure, teamworking, performance or quality and customer care.

Structure

The Managing Director of ABC Distribution said: 'I do not see any difference between the HR strategy and the business strategy on organization because we evolve our organization to reflect where the business is going'.

As the Managing Director of Megastores said: 'You cannot fully maximize business opportunities unless you have the proper management structure to create them'.

Teamworking

At Mercia Systems the background to the work on teambuilding was the demolition of traditional hierarchies over the last two to three years. In manufacturing and engineering there are never more than three layers between team members and the Director. In 80 per cent of the engineering teams there are now only two layers – the Team Manager and the Engineering Manager. It is believed that these changes have had far-reaching effects on flexibility and performance and have contributed significantly to the achievement of better coordination in manufacturing and engineering.

Performance

A performance strategy will be based on an analysis of the critical success factors and the performance levels reached in relation to them. Steps can then be agreed as to what needs to be done to improve performance through training, development, reorganization, the development of performance management processes, some form of business process re-engineering, or simply 'taking cost out of the business'.

This is how a cost reduction strategy works in one of the key divisions of ABC Distribution as described by the Managing Director:

We know that over the next three years we have to take more than £10 million-worth of cost out of the business. So our HR Director sits down with the business head of the division and they identify the areas we need to focus on. It could be productivity enhancement, it could be changing work practices, it could be making sure that we have no anomalies round the depots in terms of payment, it could even be taking tea breaks out. A three-year strategy is agreed, targets are set and then they get on with it.

The approach at Loamshire Council was described by the Director of HR as follows: 'We have a general strategy of performance measurement and management from which grew our performance appraisal system, which has worked extremely well... We spent a lot of time ensuring that people understood that this was a development process and it was about not just their competence, but also the ability of the organization to achieve what it wants to achieve.'

The strategy for improving performance at Megastores involves the use of a performance management system, which was introduced, as the Director of HR explained: 'Because we didn't have any mechanism through which we could run the business through the people'. He went on to say that: 'Line management own it totally. It's not a HR system, it's a line management system for running the business.'

The Director of HR for Megastores also made the following comments on performance strategies:

We set out to understand the differences between successful and less successful performance within the organization and we call those our competency frameworks... By developing these frameworks we have educated the whole of our line management throughout the organization into how to think about their people in a much wider sense. Our key HR strategy question is: 'How do we actually get the people to deliver what the business requires?'

The process of performance improvement could mean, as Mercia Systems' Marketing Director put it: 'Going through a lot of effort to ensure that we have the correct level of performance in what we do and underpinning this with financial and commercial stability'.

Mercia Systems successfully used a functional analysis process, which, as described by the HR Director, was carried out as shown in Figure 6.1.

At Welland Water, the Head of HR thought that: 'Performance improvement lies not so much in creating the hard issues at the bottom line but in creating an environment within which people will accept change and cooperate in different methods of working. And I believe our partnership approach does create such an environment, one in which we can manage change successfully and which encourages people to accept new responsibilities and acquire new skills.'

The majority of the organizations covered by the research had installed performance management processes in which the emphasis was on performance improvement and development and not reward. The scheme in Mercia

FIGURE 6.1

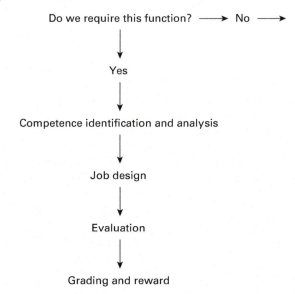

Focus:
- whole work roles
- outcome approach
- top down method

Do we require this function? ⟶ No ⟶

↓

Yes

↓

Competence identification and analysis

↓

Job design

↓

Evaluation

↓

Grading and reward

Systems emphasized the new priorities of involvement, teamwork and self-development as well as more standard measures.

Quality and customer care

Quality, which in essence means customer satisfaction, is generally recognized today as the key to the achievement of competitive advantage. Innovation and cost reduction are still important but they are to no avail if, ultimately, customers reject the product because it does not meet their expectations. Quality is achieved through people and, in accordance with a basic HRM principle, investment in people is a prerequisite for achieving high quality standards.

A strategy for total quality is a true HRM strategy in the sense that it is owned and delivered by management. It should therefore be built into their business strategy as it is, for example, by Mercia Systems.

The Chief Executive of Loamshire Council said that: 'We have a performance appraisal system and one area that we are particularly keen should be dealt with as part of that process is the contribution of the individual to our customer care standards'.

At Mercia Systems, the HR Director stated that in pursuit of their goal of world-class performance, HR strategy must help to ensure that they are a best-practice company. An important aspect of this strategy 'is to educate everyone to build quality into every job, aiming to convey to people that if you get it right first time they will be saving a lot of unnecessary work'.

Achieving integration

The integration of HR and business strategies is seen by some commentators as a main distinguishing feature of strategic HRM. Doubts have been cast by a number of commentators such as Storey (1992) on the extent to which such integration does take place, often on the grounds that integration is not an issue when there are no corporate strategies. This was not the case in any of the organizations referred to earlier. In all but two of them the HR strategies, in Walker's (1992) terms, were fully integrated, while in the other cases the strategies were 'aligned'.

As the Managing Director of ABC Distribution pointed out: 'Our HR strategy has to respond to our business strategy... The challenge for HR is to look at all the areas that they encompass and make sure they are integrated into the main plan.' But he admitted that: 'One of the problems this company used to have up to a few years ago was that HR strategy was seen as something completely separate from the corporate strategy. What we have tried to do in the past few years is to make them one and the same thing.'

The Director of HR for ABC Distribution recognized that: 'The development of HR strategies should be shared more widely with the business controllers. If we don't do that we run the risk of not developing the consistent themes we need to have.' But the Director of Finance was positive that: 'In terms of performance improvement the business and HR strategies are very closely linked. Productivity is a major area and the HR implications of pursuing these policies is critical.'

These, incidentally, were not the only positive contributions from finance directors. It was found that, without exception, the finance directors interviewed were all fully aware of the significance of the HR perspective for their organizations, although they were obviously concerned with financial performance and budgets.

In Loamshire Council, the approach to integration as described by the Director of HR was simply to get the top team together and ask them: 'What are the real strategies that will help the organization and its functioning?' And the Director of Planning for the authority commented on the important integrating role of the Director of HR as follows:

> In the old days, the HR manager was not a member of the management team, and I got used to a culture where HR advice was not really part of strategic direction. And any debate there may have been at the corporate level came out in the wash. It was not led by someone like our Director of HR. She is now on a par with the rest of us in terms of status and contribution and she brings the whole of the human resource angle into the debate.

Also, in reply to the question: 'How well are corporate and HR strategies integrated?' the Director of Technical Services for the authority said: 'The short answer is that they are inextricably linked... you cannot do anything without having worked through the human resource implications and it's all about better performance by teams and individuals.'

The approach of Megastores was described by the Director of Stores as follows:

> The starting point is the operating plan emerging from and contributing to the business plan. There is only a certain level of change we can cope with and what we have is a funnel of brilliant ideas and strategies, but they all end up in the stores. So we only commit to a plan we can deliver and we identify the levels of change that we can manage and calculate how much time the stores have to implement it. That is fed into the planning process so that it becomes realistic. The human resource strategy is integral to the process, it's not linked.

At Mercia Systems, integration was not an issue. As explained by the Marketing Director: 'We do not think of ourselves as having a human resource strategy per se. We just see it as one aspect of the overall business strategy. From what I have observed going on in the business I find it quite difficult to separate a strand of activity which I would call HR strategy because it is so integral to everything which is going on... HR strategy is effectively a part of the overall vision.'

He gave the example of the Technical Director who is developing technical route maps, and the HR function which is working with technical management to produce forecasts as a basis for finding and developing the right people with the right skills. His own role is to explain the nature of the competences required in the business groups, including business management, programme management and sales and marketing: 'Only by understanding these can we equip ourselves for the future'.

The Director of Finance for Welland Water pointed out that: 'The HR side is a fundamental part of the business planning process, and it's not something you just bolt on somewhere along the way. There's a lot of interaction, prior to and during the top board discussion, which tends to be concerned with culturally-based issues and the way we manage people.'

On the basis of these comments, integration is most likely to be achieved when:

- there are well-articulated corporate or business strategies operating in the context of a clear mission;
- there is a powerful driving force in the shape of commitment to certain values and overall strategies for change;
- the chief executive or managing director recognizes the contribution that people make to increasing added value and achieving competitive advantage and ensures that people issues are fully taken into account at the time corporate or business strategies are being prepared;

- the other members of the top team generally share the views of their chief executive on the added value that can be created by considering HR and corporate/business issues simultaneously;
- the HR director is capable of making a full contribution to the formulation of corporate/business strategies as well as those relating to people;
- the views of the HR director are listened to, respected and acted upon;
- unions are involved in developing change strategies on a partnership basis;
- HR strategies relate to the critical success factors of the organization and the impact high quality and committed people can make on the delivery of the results the organization is expected to achieve.

KEY LEARNING POINTS

The most characteristic features of strategic HRM in action in the case study organizations mentioned above were:

- a clear and purposeful corporate or business strategy exists;
- the HR strategies in most cases are fully integrated and owned by the whole of the top management team;
- the HR strategies are very much concerned with developing the organization and the people in it;
- most if not all of the organizations could be described as 'unitarist' in their approach (ie they believe in the commonality of the interests of management and employees), and they are all striving to develop a 'commitment-orientated' culture;
- but in many cases they have still taken pains to involve the trade unions.

References

Storey, J (1992) *New Developments in the Management of Human Resources*, Blackwell, Oxford
Tyson, S and Witcher, M (1994) Human resource strategy emerging from the recession, *HR Management, August*, pp 20–23
Walker, J W (1992) *Human Resource Strategy*, McGraw-Hill, New York

07 **Strategic international HRM**

KEY CONCEPTS AND TERMS

Convergence
Divergence
Globalization
Strategic international human resource management (SIHRM)

LEARNING OUTCOMES

On completing this chapter you should be able to define the key concepts above. You should also know about:

- the meaning of strategic international HRM;
- issues in international HRM;
- approaches to strategic international HRM.

Introduction

It was stated by Chris Brewster et al (2005: 949) that: 'A critical challenge for organizations from both the public and private sectors in the twenty-first century is the need to operate across national boundaries'. As Dave Ulrich (1998: 126) pointed out, faced with globalization, organizations must 'increase their ability to learn and collaborate and to manage diversity, complexity, and ambiguity'. The following observations on the international scene were made by Raymond Schuler and his colleagues (1999).

To deal with these issues, a coherent approach is required that involves deliberating on the implications of international operations for the management of people, and then developing strategies that point in the right direction to what needs to be done and how it should be done. This is the process of strategic international human resource management, which will be defined and explained in this chapter.

Strategic international human resource management defined

Strategic international human resource management (SIHRM) is the process of planning how best to develop and implement policies and practices for managing people across international boundaries by multinational companies. As defined by Schuler et al (1999: 321) it consists of: 'Human resource management issues, functions and policies and practices that result from the strategic activities of multinational enterprises and the impact on the international concerns and goals of those enterprises'.

The aims of SIHRM are to ensure that HR strategies, policies and practices are developed and implemented that will help the enterprise to operate profitably in a number of different countries and ensure that each unit can operate effectively within its context – its culture and the legal, political and economic factors that affect it. In doing this, the organization has to bear in mind the point made by Pucik (2007: 203) that 'The global firm must manage the contradictions of global integration, local responsiveness and worldwide coordination'.

International SHRM strategic issues

The fundamental strategic HRM issue for multinational companies is how to cope with 'complex cultural, geographical and constitutional pressures' (Sparrow and Braun, 2007: 187). They have to 'enhance the ability of specific functions to perform globally' (ibid: 188). The specific issues that affect international as distinct from domestic HRM are the impact of globalization, the influence of environmental and cultural differences, the extent to which operations should be centralized or decentralized, and the extent to which HRM policy and practice should vary in different countries (convergence or divergence). The last two issues are of particular concern when framing international HR strategies.

Globalization

Globalization is the process of international economic integration in world-wide markets. It involves the development of single international markets for goods or services accompanied by an accelerated growth in world trade. Any company that has economic interests or activities extending across a number of international boundaries is a global company. This involves a number of issues not present when the activities of the firm are confined to one country. As Ulrich (1998: 126) put it: 'Globalization requires organizations to move people, ideas, products and information around the world to meet local needs'.

SOURCE REVIEW   The distinction between international and global HRM – Brewster et al (2005: 996)

Traditionally, international HR has been about managing an international workforce – the higher-level organizational people working as expatriates, frequent commuters, cross-cultural team members and specialists involved in international knowledge transfer. Global HRM is not simply about these staff. It concerns managing all HRM activities, wherever they are, through the application of global rule sets.

Bartlett and Ghoshal (1991) argued that the main issue for multinational companies was the need to manage the challenges of global efficiency and multinational flexibility. They had to manage the risks and exploit the opportunities that arise from the diversity and volatility of the global environment.

Research conducted over a number of years by Brewster and Sparrow (2007: 48) has shown that the nature of international human resource management is changing fast. They noted that among some of the larger international organizations, '... these changes have created a completely different approach to international human resource management, one we have dubbed "globalized HRM". Whereas international human resource management has tended to operate in the same way as local HRM but on a wider scale, globalized HRM exploits the new technologies available in order to manage all the company's staff around the world in the same way that it has traditionally managed staff in the home country.'

Environmental differences

Environmental differences between countries have to be taken into account in managing globally. As described by Gerhart and Fang (2005: 971), these include 'differences in the centrality of markets, institutions, regulation, collective bargaining and labour-force characteristics'. For example, in Western Europe collective bargaining coverage is much higher than in countries like the United States, Canada and Japan. Works councils are mandated by law in Western European countries like Germany, but not in Japan or the United States. In China, Eastern Europe and Mexico, labour costs are significantly lower than in Western Europe, Japan and the United States.

Cultural differences

Cultural differences must also be taken into account. Hiltrop (1995) noted the following HR areas that may be affected by national culture:

- decisions on what makes an effective manager;
- giving face-to-face feedback;
- readiness to accept international assignments;
- pay systems and different concepts of social justice;
- approaches to organizational structuring and strategic dynamics.

The significance of cultural differences was the influential message delivered by Hofstede (1980, 1991). He claimed that 'organizations are culture-bound' (1980: 372). Using worldwide data on IBM employees he identified four national cultural dimensions: uncertainty avoidance, masculinity/femininity, power distance and individualism/collectivism. One of the conclusions Hofstede reached was that the cultural values within a nation are substantially more similar than the values of individuals from different nations. This has been taken up by subsequent commentators such as Adler (2002), who claimed that Hofstede's study explained 50 per cent of the difference between countries in employees' attitudes and behaviours. But this view has been challenged by Gerhart and Fang (2005). They subjected Hofstede's findings to further analysis and established that at the level of the individual as distinct from the country, only 2 per cent to 4 per cent of the difference was explained by national differences and that therefore: 'Hofstede's study should not be interpreted as showing that national culture explains 50 per cent of behaviours' (ibid: 977). They also established from Hofstede's data that culture varies more between organizations than countries. In their view, cross-country cultural differences, while real, have been overestimated and may well pale in importance when compared with other unique country characteristics when it comes to explaining the effectiveness of HR practices. But they accepted that national culture differences can be critical and that insensitivity to national culture differences can and does result in business failure (as well as failures and career consequences for individual managers).

On the basis of research conducted in 30 multinational companies, Stiles (2007: 37) commented that 'while national cultural differences were not insignificant, they were less important than we imagined; organizational culture actually had more influence on HR practice'. The conclusion from the research was that: 'To think there is one best way to manage human resources is simplistic and wrong, but the variation and contextualization of HR, at least for the companies we studied, owes little to national culture' (ibid: 41).

Centralization or decentralization

As Pucik (2007: 201) declared: 'Many firms competing globally are being pointed in contradictory strategic directions. In order to survive and prosper in the new global competition, companies must embrace closer regional and global integration to cut cost and improve efficiency, while at the same time, meet demands for local responsiveness to increase local acceptance, flexibility and speed.' On the basis of his research, Pucik (2007: 201) identified three strategic approaches to this issue:

1 A mega-national strategy, which means that the whole company operates in a centralized fashion. Worldwide facilities are centralized in the parent company, products are standardized, and overseas operations are used as delivery pipelines to serve international markets. There is tight central control of strategic decisions, resources and information. As a result, the competitive strength of the mega-national firm is its global integration resulting in cost efficiencies. However, the firm's ability to respond to variations in local conditions is limited and the international operation can become bureaucratic and inflexible.

2 A multi-domestic strategy, which emphasizes local differences by decentralizing operations to their subsidiaries and local business units in order to be close to customers, to create a heightened sense of local accountability and to encourage more local innovation and entrepreneurship. But this can lead to an inability to compete on global terms with fully integrated competitors, slowness in responding to change and failure to benefit from pooled resources,

including knowledge and management expertise. Decentralized companies meeting these problems tend to veer towards centralization until bureaucracy, lack of responsiveness and the inability to retain good people locally leads the pendulum to swing again towards centralization.

3 Dual centralized/decentralized strategy, which aims to benefit from both approaches. Firms adopting a dual strategy recognize that decentralization (local autonomy) and centralization (global integration) are not contradictory, but form a duality. They attempt to maximize the benefits from both approaches in order to achieve high integration while remaining locally responsive. This can mean following the old adage of 'think globally and act locally' and can get the best out of both worlds. But it is a hard strategy to implement. It requires managers with what Pucik calls a 'global mindset', who can behave and act in a way that recognizes the global nature of the firm and who can focus both on worldwide strategies and the need to encourage the development of local initiatives and allow a reasonable degree of local autonomy within a global framework.

Convergence and divergence

According to Brewster et al (2002) the effectiveness of global HRM depends on the ability to judge the extent to which an organization should implement similar practices across the world or adapt them to suit local conditions. This is a strategic decision that is an aspect of the choice between centralization or decentralization referred to above. The dilemma facing all multinational corporations is that of achieving a balance between international consistency and local autonomy. They have to decide on the extent to which their HR policies should either 'converge' worldwide to be basically the same in each location, or 'diverge' to be differentiated in response to local requirements.

SOURCE REVIEW   Convergence and divergence issues – Perkins and Shortland (2006: 33)

Strategic choices surrounding employment relationships may be influenced primarily by 'home country' values and practices. But those managing operations in one or a range of host country environments face the challenge of transplanting 'ethnocentric' principles, justifying the consequential policies and practices in their interactions with local managers, other employees and external representatives.

Brewster (2004) believes that convergence may be increasing as a result of the power of the markets, the importance of cost, quality and productivity pressures, the emergence of transaction cost economies, the development of like-minded international cadres, and benchmarking 'best practice'. Stiles (2007) noted that common practices across borders may be appropriate: 'Organizations seek what works and for HR in multinational companies, the range of options is limited to a few common practices that are believed to secure high performance'. Brewster et al (2005) think that it is quite possible for some parts of a HR system to converge while other parts may diverge. But there is a choice. The factors that affect the choice include the extent to which the unit is operating mainly at a local level, the strength of local norms, and the degree to which financial, managerial, technical and people resources flow from the parent company to the subsidiary. A further factor is that some international companies are much more prone to the exercise of central control than others, whatever the local circumstances.

Sparrow and Braun (2007: 170) identified three approaches to global HR strategy:

1   The wholesale transfer of HRM policies and practices successful in the parent company to affiliates.

2   The creation of HR systems with a maximum of adaptation to local context and conditions.

3   The transfer of best practice from wherever it may be found among affiliates in the organization.

Approaches to strategic international HRM

Bartlett and Ghoshal (1991) set out the following fundamental assumptions governing the approach to strategic international HRM:

SOURCE REVIEW   Fundamental assumptions in SIHRM – Bartlett and Ghoshal (1991: 59)

Balancing the needs of control and autonomy and maintaining the appropriate balance are critical to the success of the multinational enterprise in being globally competitive, sensitive to the local environment, flexible and capable of creating an organization in which learning and the transfer of knowledge are feasible.

Strategic management is always about making choices and this is particularly the case in international strategic management. The fundamental strategic choices are on the degree of centralization/decentralization and convergence/divergence to be adopted. There is choice on how to follow the advice of Sparrow and Braun (2007: 173) that 'It is the utilization of organizational capabilities worldwide that provides multinational companies with competitive advantage'. Multinational companies have to make strategic choices on how to find and develop talented managers with a global mindset and how to make the maximum use of expertise by transferring learning across units in order to 'enhance an organization's capability to gain and use its knowledge resources' Sparrow and Braun (2007: 178).

The research conducted by Brewster et al (2005: 949) identified three processes that constitute global HRM: (1) management and employer branding; (2) global leadership through international assignments; and (3) managing an international workforce and evaluation of HR contribution. They found that organizations such as Rolls Royce had set up centres of excellence operating on a global basis. They observed that global HR professionals are acting as the guardians of culture, operating global values and systems.

It was established by the Global HR Research Alliance study (Stiles, 2007) that global HR policies and practices were widespread in the areas of maintaining global performance standards, the use of common evaluation processes, common approaches to rewards, the development of senior managers, the application of competency frameworks and the use of common performance management criteria.

Generally the research has indicated that while global HR policies in such areas as talent management, performance management and reward may be developed, communicated and supported by centres of excellence, often through global networking, a fair degree of freedom has frequently been allowed to local management to adopt their own practices in accordance with the local context, as long as in principle these are consistent with global policies.

KEY LEARNING POINTS

Strategic international human resource management (SIHRM) defined

SIHRM is the process of planning how best to develop and implement policies and practices for managing people across international boundaries by multinational companies.

The aims of SIHRM

To ensure that HR strategies, policies and practices are developed and implemented that will help the enterprise to operate profitably in a number of different countries and ensure that each unit can operate effectively within its context.

SIHRM issues

The fundamental strategic HRM issue for multinational companies is how to cope with 'complex cultural, geographical and constitutional pressures' (Sparrow and Braun, 2007: 187).

The specific issues that affect international as distinct from domestic HRM are the impact of globalization, the influence of environmental and cultural differences, the extent to which operations should be centralized or decentralized, and the extent to which HRM policy and practice should vary in different countries (convergence or divergence). The last two issues are of particular concern when framing international HR strategies.

Approaches to strategic HRM

Strategic management is always about making choices and this is particularly the case in international strategic management. The fundamental strategic choices are on the degree of centralization/decentralization and convergence/divergence to be adopted. Multinational companies also have to make strategic choices on how to find and develop talented managers with a global mindset and how to make the maximum use of expertise by transferring learning across units.

While global HR policies in such areas as talent management, performance management and reward may be developed, communicated and supported by centres of excellence, often through global networking, a fair degree of freedom has frequently been allowed to local management to adopt their own practices in accordance with the local context, as long as in principle these are consistent with global policies.

References

Adler, N J (2002) *International Dimensions of Organizational Behaviour*, South-Western, Cincinatti, OH

Bartlett, C A and Ghoshal, S (1991) *Managing Across Borders: The transnational solution*, London Business School, London

Brewster, C (2004) European perspectives of human resource management, *Human Resource Management Review*, **14** (4), pp 365–82

Brewster, C and Sparrow, P (2007) Advances in technology inspire a fresh approach to international HRM, *People Management*, 8 February, p 48

Brewster, C, Harris, H and Sparrow, P (2002) *Globalizing HR*, CIPD, London

Brewster, C, Sparrow, P and Harris, H (2005) Towards a new model of globalizing HRM, *The International Journal of Human Resource Management*, **16** (6), pp 949–70

Gerhart, B and Fang, M (2005) National culture and human resource management: assumptions and evidence, *The International Journal of Human Resource Management*, **16** (6), pp 971–86

Hiltrop, J M (1995) The changing psychological contract: the human resource challenge of the 1990s, *European Management Journal*, **13** (3), pp 286–94

Hofstede, G (1980) *Cultural Consequences: International differences in work-related values*, Sage, Beverley Hills, CA

Hofstede, G (1991) *Culture and Organization: Software of the mind*, Sage, London

Perkins, S J and Shortland, S M (2006) *Strategic International Human Resource Management*, Kogan Page, London

Pucik, V (2007) Reframing global mindset: from thinking to acting, in *Strategic Human Resource Management*, (eds) R S Schuler and S E Jackson, pp 200–13, Blackwell, Malden, MA

Schuler, R S, Dowling, P J and De Cieri, H (1999) Framework of strategic international HRM, in *Strategic Human Resource Management*, (eds) R S Schuler and S E Jackson, pp 319–55, Blackwell, Oxford

Sparrow, P R and Braun, W (2007) Human resource strategy in international context, *Strategic Human Resource Management*, (eds) R S Schuler and S E Jackson, pp 162–99, Blackwell, Malden, MA

Stiles, P (2007) A world of difference? *People Management*, 15 November, pp 36–41

Ulrich, D (1998) A new mandate for human resources, *Harvard Business Review*, January/February, pp 124–34

PART THREE
HR strategies

The framework of HR strategy

LEARNING OUTCOMES

On completing this chapter you should be able to define the key concepts above. You should also understand:

- what HR strategies are and their purpose;
- the main types of HR strategies;
- how to evaluate the effectiveness of a HR strategy;
- how to develop strategy;
- how to implement strategy.

Introduction

HR strategies provide a framework within which is set out what the organization is proposing to do about people management generally or in particular areas of HRM. Tyson and Witcher (1994: 21) defined HR strategies as '... the intentions and plans for using human resources to achieve business objectives'. HR strategies set out aspirations that have to be expressed as intentions, which then in turn have to be converted into actions. The strategies may be defined formally as part of a strategic human resource management process, which leads to the development of overall or specific HR strategies as considered in this chapter for implementation by HR and, vitally, line managers.

However, it should be remembered that HR strategies, like any other aspects of business strategy, can come into existence through an emergent, evolutionary and possibly unarticulated process influenced by the business strategy as it develops and changes in the internal and external environment. Pettigrew and Whipp (1991: 30) emphasized that strategy '... far from being a straightforward, rational phenomenon, is in fact interpreted by managers according to their own frame of reference, their particular motivations and information'. But there are still strong arguments for a systematic approach to identifying strategic directions that can provide a framework for decision-making and action, as examined in this chapter.

What are HR strategies?

HR strategies set out what the organization intends to do about its human resource management policies and practices and how they should be integrated with the business strategy and each other. They were described by Dyer and Reeves (1995: 656) as 'internally consistent bundles of human resource practices', and in the words of Boxall (1996: 61) they provide 'a framework of critical ends and means'. Richardson and Thompson (1999: 3) suggested that: 'A strategy, whether it is an HR strategy or any other kind of management strategy, must have two key elements: there must be strategic objectives (ie things the strategy is supposed to achieve), and there must be a plan of action (ie the means by which it is proposed that the objectives will be met)'. Purcell (2001: 72) made the point that: 'Strategy in HR, like in other areas, is about continuity and change, about appropriateness in the circumstances, but anticipating when the circumstances change. It is about taking strategic decisions.'

What is the purpose of HR strategies?

The purpose of HR strategies is to articulate what an organization intends to do about its human resource management policies and practices now and in the longer term in order to ensure that they contribute to the achievement of business objectives. However, it is necessary to bear in mind the dictum of Fombrun et al (1984) that business and managers should perform well in the present to succeed in the future. HR strategies may set out intentions and provide a sense of purpose and direction, but they are not just long-term plans.

Perhaps the main argument for articulating HR strategies is that unless you know where you are going, you will not know how to get there or know when you have arrived.

The nature of HR strategies

Because all organizations are different, all HR strategies are different. There is no such thing as a standard strategy, and research into HR strategy conducted by Armstrong and Long (1994) and Armstrong and Baron (2002) revealed many variations.

HR strategies may not be deliberate. It was pointed out by Mintzberg (1987: 67) that: 'An organization can have a pattern (a realized strategy) without knowing it, let alone making it explicit'. He produced the principle of 'emergent strategy', stating that: 'A realized strategy can emerge in response to an evolving situation' (ibid: 68). As Mintzberg et al (1988) suggested, strategies can simply exist in the 'collective minds' of the people on whom they make an impact. The fact that they have not been articulated may not matter as long as people in the organization share the same perspective through their intentions or their actions.

Mintzberg's concept of 'emergent strategy' rings true, but Grant (1998) has argued that the Mintzberg approach, which downplays the role of systematic analysis and emphasizes the role of intuition and vision, fails to provide a clear basis for reasoned choices. However, Mintzberg (1987: 69) accepted that 'purely emergent strategy making precludes control'. He took the realistic position that there is no such thing as a purely deliberate strategy or a purely emergent one, and that 'deliberate and emergent strategy form the end points of a continuum along which the strategies which are crafted in the real world may be found' (ibid: 69). Thompson and Strickland (1996: 20) noted that 'a company's actual strategy is partly planned and partly reactive to changing circumstances'.

Types of HR strategies

Deliberate HR strategies provide guidelines for planning and implementation. Three types can be identified: (1) broad statements of intent under various headings; (2) overall HR strategies concerned with high performance working, high commitment management or high involvement management; and (3) specific strategies relating to the different aspects of human resource management such as talent management, learning and development and reward.

Broad statements of intent

HR strategy may simply consist of a broad statement of intent that provides the framework for more specific strategic plans in individual HR areas. Mintzberg (1987) referred to this approach as 'umbrella strategy' in which senior management sets out broad guidelines, leaving the specifics to people lower down in the organization.

The CIPD-sponsored research conducted by Armstrong and Baron (2002) found that there was a surprising convergence on the objectives of the strategies in the organizations they studied – to modify values, behaviours and attitudes. However, the paths taken to get there were quite different.

Research into the formulation of HR strategy in a number of US companies by Wright et al (2004: 43) established that 'the core components of HR strategies seem to be building a performance culture, developing leadership capability, attracting and retaining the best talent, and providing state of the art HR systems, processes, and services'. The following are UK examples of overall HR strategic statements of intent.

Aegon

The human resources integrated approach aims to ensure that from whatever angle staff now look at the elements of pay management, performance, career development and reward, they are consistent and linked.

NG Bailey

As described by Marsh and Sweeney (2010: 97), what was referred to as an 'integrated framework model' at NG Bailey (a construction company) had as its first element: 'Climate, which requires interventions in three main areas: on behaviour; on culture; and on knowledge, skills and competence'.

B&Q

- Enhance employee commitment and minimize the loss of B&Q's best people.
- Position B&Q as one of the best employers in the UK.

Egg

'The major factor influencing HR strategy was the need to attract, maintain and retain the right people to deliver it. The aim was to introduce a system that complemented the business, that reflected the way we wanted to treat our customers – treating our people the same. What we would do for our customers we would also do for our people. We wanted to make an impact on the culture – the way people do business' (HR Director).

GlaxoSmithKline

We want GSK to be a place where the best people do their best work.

An insurance company

'Without the people in this business we don't have anything to deliver. We are driven to getting the people issues right in order to deliver the strategy. To a great extent it's the people that create and implement the strategy on behalf of the organization. We put people very much at the front of our strategic thought process. If we have the right people, the right training, the right qualifications and the right sort of culture then we can deliver our strategy. We cannot do it otherwise' (Chief Executive).

Lands' End

Based on the principle that staff who are enjoying themselves, who are being supported and developed, and who feel fulfilled and respected at work, will provide the best service to customers.

A local authority

As expressed by the chief executive of this borough council, their HR strategy is about 'having a very strong focus on the overall effectiveness of the organization, its direction and how it's performing; here is commitment to, and belief in, and respect for individuals, and I think that these are very important factors'.

A public utility

'The only HR strategy you really need is the tangible expression of values and the implementation of values... unless you get the human resource values right you can forget all the rest' (Managing Director).

A manufacturing company

'The HR strategy is to stimulate changes on a broad front aimed ultimately at achieving competitive advantage through the efforts of our people. In an industry of fast followers, those who learn quickest will be the winners' (HR Director).

A retail stores group

'The biggest challenge will be to maintain (our) competitive advantage and to do that we need to maintain and continue to attract very high calibre people. The key differentiator on anything any company does is fundamentally the people, and I think that people tend to forget that they are the most important asset. Money is easy to get hold of, good people are not. All we do in terms of training and manpower planning is directly linked to business improvement' (Managing Director).

Overall HR approaches

The second category of HR strategy consists of the deliberate introduction of overall approaches to human resource management, such as high performance management, high involvement management and high commitment management, which are described below. There is some overlap between these approaches, especially the latter two.

High performance management

High performance management aims to make an impact on the performance of the organization through its people in such areas as productivity, quality, levels of customer service, growth, profits and, ultimately, the delivery of increased shareholder value. The objective is to achieve this by rigorous recruitment and selection procedures, extensive and relevant training and management development activities, incentive pay systems and performance management processes. As a bundle, these practices are often called high performance work systems (HPWS). This term is more frequently used than either high involvement management or high commitment management. High performance work system strategies are considered in more detail in Chapter 10.

High involvement management

High involvement management practices were described by Wood (2010) as follows:

SOURCE REVIEW   High involvement management defined
– Wood (2010: 410)

High involvement management includes: first, practices such as teamworking, flexible job descriptions, and idea capturing schemes, which are means of ensuring greater flexibility, proactivity and collaboration; and second, practices that give workers the opportunities for the acquisition of skills and knowledge that are needed to ensure they have the capacities to work in an involved way. They include intensive training geared towards teamworking, functional flexibility and information sharing, particularly about the economics and market of the business.

The practices included in a high involvement system have sometimes expanded beyond this original concept and included high performance practices. For example, as defined by Benson et al (2006: 519): 'High-involvement work practices are a specific set of human resource practices that focus on employee decision-making, power, access to information, training and incentives'. As noted above, high performance practices usually include relevant training and incentive pay systems. Sung and Ashton (2005) include high involvement practices as one of the three broad areas of a high performance work system (the other two being human resource practices and reward and commitment practices).

The way in which high involvement made an impact was explained by Guest (1997). He suggested that the commitment and flexibility provided by highly involving action led to behaviour changes among employees. Because they show high levels of motivation, commitment and organizational citizenship, they adopt better-performing behaviours, leading to lower absenteeism and turnover rates, increased productivity and higher levels of quality.

High commitment management

One of the defining characteristics of the concept of HRM is its emphasis on mutuality – enhancing mutual commitment (Walton, 1985). High commitment management has been described by Wood (1996: 41) as: 'A form of management which is aimed at eliciting a commitment so that behaviour is primarily self-regulated rather than controlled by sanctions and pressures external to the individual, and relations within the organization are based on high levels of trust'.

The approaches to achieving high commitment as described by Beer et al (1984) and Walton (1985) are:

● the development of career ladders and emphasis on trainability and commitment as highly valued characteristics of employees at all levels in the organization;

● a high level of functional flexibility with the abandonment of potentially rigid job descriptions;

● the reduction of hierarchies and the ending of status differentials;

● a heavy reliance on team structure for disseminating information (team briefing), structuring work (teamworking) and problem solving (quality circles).

Wood and Albanese (1995) added to this list:

● job design as something management consciously does in order to provide jobs that have a considerable level of intrinsic satisfaction;

● a policy of no compulsory lay-offs or redundancies and permanent employment guarantees with the possible use of temporary workers to cushion fluctuations in the demand for labour;

● new forms of assessment and payment systems and, more specifically, merit pay and profit sharing;

● a high involvement of employees in the management of quality.

Specific HR strategies

Specific HR strategies set out what the organization intends to do in areas such as:

- Human capital management – obtaining, analysing and reporting on data that informs the direction of value-adding people management strategic, investment and operational decisions.
- Corporate social responsibility – a commitment to managing the business ethically in order to make a positive impact on society and the environment.
- Organization design and development – designing and modifying organization structures and planning and implementation of programmes designed to enhance the effectiveness with which an organization functions and responds to change.
- Engagement – the development and implementation of policies designed to increase the level of employees' engagement with their work and the organization.
- Knowledge management – creating, acquiring, capturing, sharing and using knowledge to enhance learning and performance.
- Resourcing – attracting and retaining high quality people.
- Talent management – how the organization ensures that it has the talented people it needs to achieve success.
- Learning and development – providing an environment in which employees are encouraged to learn and develop.
- Reward – defining what the organization wants to do in the longer term to develop and implement reward policies, practices and processes that will further the achievement of its business goals and meet the needs of its stakeholders.
- Employee relations – defining the intentions of the organization about what needs to be done and what needs to be changed in the ways in which the organization manages its relationships with employees and their trade unions.

These strategies may be developed individually, or preferably the HR strategy includes specific and articulated plans to create 'bundles' of HR practices and develop a coherent HR system.

The following are some examples of specific HR strategies.

The Children's Society

- Implement the rewards strategy of the Society to support the corporate plan and secure the recruitment, retention and motivation of staff to deliver its business objectives.

- Manage the development of the human resources information system to secure productivity improvements in administrative processes.
- Introduce improved performance management processes for managers and staff of the Society.
- Implement training and development which supports the business objectives of the Society and improves the quality of work with children and young people.

Diageo

There are three broad strands to the Organization and People Strategy:

1 Reward and recognition: use recognition and reward programmes to stimulate outstanding team and individual performance contributions.

2 Talent management: drive the attraction, retention and professional growth of a deep pool of diverse, talented employees.

3 Organizational effectiveness: ensure that the business adapts its organization to maximize employee contribution and deliver performance goals.

It provides direction to the company's talent, operational effectiveness and performance and reward agendas. The company's underlying thinking is that the people strategy is not for the human resource function to own but is the responsibility of the whole organization, hence the title 'Organization and People Strategy'.

A government agency

The key components of the HR strategy are:

- Investing in people – improving the level of intellectual capital.
- Performance management – integrating the values contained in the HR strategy into performance management processes and ensuring that reviews concentrate on how well people are performing those values.
- Job design – a key component concerned with how jobs are designed and how they relate to the whole business.
- The reward system – developing reward strategies, taking into account that this is a very hard-driven business.

Higher education institutions (The Higher Education Funding Council)

1 Address recruitment and retention difficulties in a targeted and cost-effective manner.

2 Meet specific staff development and training objectives that not only equip staff to meet their current needs but also prepare them for

future changes, such as using new technologies for learning and teaching. This would include management development.

3 Develop equal opportunity targets with programmes to implement good practice throughout an institution. This would include ensuring equal pay for work of equal value, using institution-wide systems of job evaluation. This could involve institutions working collectively – regionally or nationally.

4 Carry out regular reviews of staffing needs, reflecting changes in market demands and technology. The reviews would consider overall numbers and the balance of different categories of staff.

5 Conduct annual performance reviews of all staff, based on open and objective criteria, with reward connected to the performance of individuals including, where appropriate, their contribution to teams.

6 Take action to tackle poor performance.

A local authority

The focus is on the organization of excellence. The strategy is broken down into eight sections: employee relations, recruitment and retention, training, performance management, pay and benefits, health and safety, absence management and equal opportunities.

Evaluating HR strategy

HR strategies should be evaluated by comparing achievements against goals. This is not possible where strategies are emergent rather than deliberate. In this case they can only be judged by reference to the degree to which the organization is successful in achieving its objectives through people, insofar as this judgement is possible. As Boxall and Purcell (2003: 28) observed, '... strategy is best discerned in behaviour'.

Deliberate strategies, as long as they incorporate strategic goals and strategic plans, can be evaluated according to the extent to which, ideally, they:

- 'indicate something of genuine significance for the future of the firm' (Boxall and Purcell, 2003: 30);
- satisfy the needs of the business and its employees;
- are founded on detailed analysis and study, not just wishful thinking;
- can be turned into actionable programmes that anticipate implementation requirements and problems;
- are coherent and integrated, being composed of components that fit with and support each other.

In the real world these prescriptions may be difficult to realize, but at least they provide a number of aiming points.

Ultimately, even deliberate strategies incorporating detailed strategic plans can sometimes only be assessed by the extent to which they meet the sort of broad criteria produced by the chief executive of a housing trust interviewed by the author:

> A good strategy is one which actually makes people feel valued. It makes them knowledgeable about the organization and makes them feel clear about where they sit as a group, or team, or individual. It must show them how what they do either together or individually fits into that strategy. Importantly, it should indicate how people are going to be rewarded for their contribution and how they might be developed and grow in the organization.

Developing HR strategies

When considering approaches to the formulation of HR strategy it is necessary to underline the interactive (not unilinear) relationship between business strategy and HRM, as have Hendry and Pettigrew (1990). They emphasized the limits of excessively rationalistic models of strategic and HR planning. The process by which strategies come to be realized is not only through formal HR policies or written directions: strategy realization can also come from actions by managers and others. Since actions provoke reactions (acceptance, confrontation, negotiation etc), these reactions are also part of the strategy process. It is desirable to treat HR strategy as a perspective rather than a rigorous procedure for mapping the future. This does not preclude the preparation of strategic plans that programme a defined strategy in which specific innovations have been proposed, but it does emphasize the fact that those strategic plans cannot be treated as inviolable; strategic plans need to evolve as circumstances change. Mintzberg (1987: 66) made it clear that strategic management is a learning process: 'Formulation and implementation merge into a fluid process of learning through which creative strategies evolve'.

Many different routes may be followed when formulating HR strategies – there is no one right way. On the basis of their research in 30 well-known companies, Tyson and Witcher (1994: 22) noted that: 'The process of formulating HR strategy was often as important as the content of the strategy ultimately agreed. It was argued that by working through strategic issues and highlighting points of tension, new ideas emerged and a consensus over goals was found.'

They also commented that: 'The different approaches to strategy formation reflect different ways to manage change and different ways to bring the people part of the business into line with business goals' (ibid: 24). In developing HR strategies, process may be as important as content.

Propositions on formulating HR strategy

Boxall (1993) drew up the following propositions about the formulation of HR strategy:

- the strategy formation process is complex, and excessively rationalistic models that advocate formalistic linkages between strategic planning and HR planning are not particularly helpful to our understanding of it;
- business strategy may be an important influence on HR strategy but it is only one of several factors;
- implicit (if not explicit) in the mix of factors that influence the shape of HR strategies is a set of historical compromises and trade-offs from stakeholders.

It is also necessary to stress that coherent and integrated HR strategies are only likely to be developed if the top team understands and acts upon the strategic imperatives associated with the employment, development and engagement of people. This will be achieved more effectively if there is a HR director who is playing an active and respected role as a member of the top management team.

A further vital consideration is that the effective implementation of HR strategies depends on engaging the stakeholders – line managers, staff and their representatives – by involving them in the design process. This is particularly important in the case of line managers, who will be directly concerned with implementing the strategy.

Finally, there is too often a wide gap between the rhetoric of strategic HRM and the reality of its impact, as Gratton et al (1999) stress. Good intentions can too easily be subverted by the harsh realities of organizational life. For example, strategic objectives such as increasing commitment by providing more security and offering training to increase employability may have to be abandoned or at least modified because of the short-term demands made on the business due to financial pressures.

Schools of strategy development

Purcell (2001: 74–75) has identified three main schools of strategy development: the design school, the process school and the configuration school.

The design school is deliberate and is 'based on the assumption of economic rationality'. It uses quantitative rather than qualitative tools of analysis and focuses on market opportunities and threats. What happens inside the company is 'mere administration or operations'.

The process school adopts a variety of approaches and is concerned with how strategies are made and what influences strategy formulation. 'It is much more a study of what actually happens with explanations coming from experience rather than deductive theory' (Purcell, 2001). As Purcell suggests, the implication of the design concept is that 'everything is possible', while that of the process school is that 'little can be done except swim with the tide of events'. The rationalist approach adopted by Purcell's design school broadly corresponds with the classical approach to strategy, and Porter (1985), with his concepts of competitive advantage and the value chain, is a typical representative of it. Purcell's process school is the post-modern version of strategy, of which Mintzberg is the most notable exponent.

The configuration school draws attention to the beliefs that: first, strategies vary according to the life-cycle of the organization; second, that they will be contingent to the sector of the organization; and third, that they will be about change and transformation. The focus is on implementation strategies, which is where Purcell thinks HR can play a major role.

Approaches to HR strategy formulation

Ideally, the formulation of HR strategy is conceived as a process that is closely aligned to the formulation of business strategies. HR strategy can influence as well as be influenced by business strategy. Sparrow et al (2010: 69–70) go further: 'Strategy ceases to exist in the ideal situation; there is business strategy, and this will be associated with an HR process. The two become synonymous with HR nested within the business strategy. You only have a separate HR strategy when HR is not playing at the highest level.'

The process of defining HR strategy involves the initial step of answering the following questions posed by Becker et al (2001: 41):

- Which strategic goals/objectives/outcomes are critical rather than just nice to have?
- What are the performance drivers for each goal?
- How would we measure progress towards these goals?
- What are the barriers to the achievement of each goal?
- How would employees need to behave to ensure that the company achieves these goals?
- Is the HR function providing the company with the employee competencies and behaviours necessary to achieve these objectives?
- If not, what needs to change?

Research conducted by Wright et al (2004) identified two approaches that can be adopted by HR in strategy formulation: the 'inside-out' approach and the 'outside-in' approach. The inside-out approach begins with the status quo HR function (in terms of skills, processes, technologies etc) and then attempts (with varying degrees of success) to identify linkages to the business (usually through focusing on 'people issues'), making minor adjustments to HR activities along the way. The 'outside-in' starts with the customer, competitor and other issues the business faces. The HR strategy then derives directly from these challenges to 'create real solutions and add real value' (ibid: 37). Wright et al made the point that 'the most advanced linkage was the "integrative" linkage in which the senior HR executive was part of the top management team, and was able to sit at the table and contribute during development of the business strategy' (ibid: 37). Their recommendations on adopting an outside-in approach are set out below.

SOURCE REVIEW   Adopting an outside-in approach to the formulation of HR strategy – Wright et al (2004: 45–46)

- Develop a formal process for involving line executives in the development of HR strategy.

- Have formal mechanisms for tracking developments in the external environment as part of the process.

- Begin with the assumption that everything the current HR function is doing is either wrong or does not exist.

- Identify the key business and people metrics that will determine or indicate the success of the business, then constantly track and communicate those metrics to the entire internal HR community.

- Based on the business issues and metrics, develop the HR strategy that will maximally drive performance on those metrics.

- Remember that the HR strategy is a process, not a document, intervention, or event. Any strategy is a pattern in a stream of decisions, and as business and people issues change or obstacles appear, the pattern (strategy) will also have to change.

In reality, however, HR strategies will often flow from business strategies, which will be dominated by product/market and financial considerations. But there is still room for HR to make a useful, even essential, contribution at the stage when business strategies are conceived, for example, by focusing on resource issues. This contribution may be more significant if strategy formulation is an emergent or evolutionary process – HR strategic issues will then be dealt with as they arise during the course of formulating and implementing the corporate strategy.

Strategic options and choices

The process of developing HR strategies involves generating strategic HRM options and then making appropriate strategic choices. It has been noted by

Cappelli (1999: 8) that: 'The choice of practices that an employer pursues is heavily contingent on a number of factors at the organizational level, including their own business and production strategies, support of HR policies, and cooperative labour relations'. The process of developing HR strategies involves the adoption of a contingent approach in generating strategic HRM options and then making appropriate strategic choices. There is seldom if ever one right way forward.

Choices should relate to but also anticipate the critical needs of the business and the people in it. They should be founded on detailed analysis and study, not just wishful thinking, and should incorporate the experienced and collective judgement of top management about the organizational requirements while also taking into account the needs of line managers and employees generally. The emerging strategies should anticipate the problems of implementation that may arise if line managers are not committed to the strategy and/or lack the skills and time to play their part, and the strategies should be capable of being turned into actionable programmes. Consideration needs to be given to the impact of the five forces on HR policy choice identified by Baron and Kreps (1999):

1 the external environment (social, political, legal and economic);
2 the workforce;
3 the organization's culture;
4 the organization's strategy;
5 the technology of production and organization of work.

A methodology for formulating HR strategies

Wright et al (2004: 40) pointed out that the basic approach to the development of a people strategy resembles that of any strategic decision process:

1 Scan the firm's external environment.
2 Identify the strategic business issues that need to be addressed.
3 Pinpoint people issues critical to the success of the business.
4 Develop a strategy to address the relevant issues, including connecting relevant metrics to the strategy.
5 Communicate the strategy.

Considerations to be taken into account

The main considerations to be taken into account in formulating HR strategies are achieving vertical and horizontal fit.

Achieving vertical fit – integrating business and HR strategies

Wright and Snell (1998) suggested that seeking fit required knowledge of the skills and behaviours necessary to implement the strategy, knowledge of the HRM practices needed to elicit those skills and behaviours, and the ability to quickly implement the desired system of HRM practices.

When considering how to integrate business and HR strategies, it should be remembered that business and HR issues influence each other and in turn influence corporate and business unit strategies. It is also necessary to note that in establishing these links, account must be taken of the fact that strategies for change have also to be integrated with changes in the external and internal environments. Fit may exist at a point in time but circumstances will change and then fit no longer exists. An excessive pursuit of 'fit' with the status quo will inhibit the flexibility of approach that is essential in turbulent conditions. This is the 'temporal' factor in achieving fit identified by Gratton et al (1999). An additional factor that will make the achievement of good vertical fit difficult is that the business strategy may not be clearly defined – it could be in an emergent or evolutionary state. This would mean that there could be nothing with which to fit the HR strategy.

Achieving horizontal fit (bundling)

Horizontal fit or integration is achieved when the various HR strategies cohere and are mutually supporting. This can be attained by the process of 'bundling' as described in Chapter 3. Bundling is carried out by first identifying appropriate HR practices, and then assessing how the items in the bundle can be linked together so that they become mutually reinforcing and therefore coherent. This may mean identifying integrating processes and finally drawing up programmes for the development of these practices, paying particular attention to the links between them.

The use of high performance, high involvement or high commitment systems as described earlier in this chapter is an integrating process. The essence of these systems is that they each consist of a set of complementary work practices that are developed and maintained as a whole.

Setting out the strategy

There is no standard model of how a HR strategy should be set out; it all depends on the circumstances of the organization. But the following are the typical areas that may be covered in a written strategy.

1 Basis:
   - business needs in terms of the key elements of the business strategy;
   - environmental factors and analysis (SWOT/PESTLE);
   - cultural factors, ie possible helps or hindrances to implementation.

2 Content – details of the proposed HR strategy.

3 Rationale – the business case for the strategy against the background of business needs and environmental/cultural factors.

4 Implementation plan:
- action programme;
- responsibility for each stage;
- resources required;
- proposed arrangements for communication, consultation, involvement and training;
- project management arrangements.

5 Costs and benefits analysis – an assessment of the resource implications of the plan (costs, people and facilities) and the benefits that will accrue for the organization as a whole, for line managers and for individual employees (so far as possible these benefits should be quantified in terms of return on investment or value added).

Implementing HR strategies

Strategies cannot be left as generalized aspirations or abstractions. If, in Rosabeth Moss Kanter's (1984: 301) phrase, they are to be action vehicles, they must be translated into HR policies that provide guidelines on decision-making and HR practices which enable the strategy to work. These can be the basis for implementation programmes with clearly stated objectives and deliverables. It is necessary to avoid saying, in effect: 'We need to get from here to there but we don't care how'. But getting strategies into action is not easy. The problem is that intent does not always lead to action. Too often strategists act like Mr Pecksmith, who was compared by Dickens (Penguin Classics, 2004: 23) to 'a direction-post which is always telling the way to a place and never goes there'.

The term 'strategic HRM' has been devalued in some quarters; sometimes to mean no more than a few generalized ideas about HR policies, at other times to describe a short-term plan, for example, to increase the retention rate of graduates. It must be emphasized that HR strategies are not just aspirations that the HR department happens to feel are important. Aspirations have to be expressed as intentions and these have to be converted into actions. The problem with strategic HRM as noted by Gratton et al (1999: 202) is that too often there is a gap between what the strategy states will be achieved and what actually happens to it. In their words: 'One principal strand that has run through this entire book is the disjunction between rhetoric and reality in the area of human resource management, between HRM theory and HRM practice, between what the HR function says it is doing and how that practice is perceived by employees, and between what senior management believes to be the role of the HR function, and the role it actually plays.'

The factors identified by Gratton et al (1999) that contributed to creating this gap included:

● the tendency of employees in diverse organizations to accept only initiatives they perceive to be relevant to their own areas;

● the tendency of long-serving employees to cling to the status quo;

● complex or ambiguous initiatives may not be understood by employees or will be perceived differently by them, especially in large, diverse organizations;

● it is more difficult to gain acceptance of non-routine initiatives;

● employees will be hostile to initiatives if they are believed to be in conflict with the organization's identity, eg downsizing in a culture of 'job-for-life';

● the initiative is seen as a threat;

● inconsistencies between corporate strategies and values;

● the extent to which senior management is trusted;

● the perceived fairness of the initiative;

● the extent to which existing processes could help to embed the initiative;

● a bureaucratic culture that leads to inertia.

Barriers to the implementation of HR strategies

Each of the factors listed by Gratton et al (1999) can create barriers to the successful implementation of HR strategies. To overcome them it is necessary to: (1) conduct a rigorous preliminary analysis of needs and requirements; (2) formulate the strategy; (3) enlist support for the strategy; (4) assess barriers; (5) prepare action plans; (6) project-manage implementation; and (7) follow up and evaluate progress so that remedial action can be taken as necessary.

Other major barriers include failure to understand the strategic needs of the business (which may be difficult), inadequate assessment of the environmental and cultural factors, including internal politics, which affect the content of the strategies, the development of ill-conceived, unmanageable and irrelevant initiatives, possibly because they are current fads or because there has been a poorly-digested analysis of 'best practice' that does not fit the organization's requirements and, importantly, failure to involve stakeholders in the formulation of strategy. These problems are compounded when insufficient attention is paid to practical implementation problems, particularly where line managers are concerned and there is a need for supporting systems.

The role of line managers in implementing strategy

HR strategies have to be converted into policies and practices and these have to be implemented by line managers. As Purcell et al (2003) stress, it is front-line managers who 'bring policies to life'. They point out that: 'Implementing and enacting policies is the task of line managers. The way they exercise leadership in the sense of communicating, solving problems, listening to suggestions, asking people's opinions, coaching and guiding, and controlling lateness, absence and quality make the vital difference' (ibid: 72).

Jonathon Trevor (2010) established through his research into the implementation of reward strategy that too often line managers compromised, even sabotaged, the implementation of HR strategies because they were not convinced that they were necessary or lacked the skills or motivation to put them into practice. It could be said that HR may propose but line managers dispose – line managers can bring HR policies to life but they can also put them to death.

There are three ways of dealing with this problem. First, involve line managers in the development of HR strategy – bear in mind that things done with line managers are much more likely to work than things done to line managers. Second, ensure that the HR policies they are expected to put into practice are manageable with the resources available. Third, provide them with the training and on-the-spot guidance they need.

Supporting processes

HR initiatives may not work unless supporting processes are available. One of the main reasons why performance-related pay has failed is because an effective performance management system is not available.

KEY LEARNING POINTS

HR strategies defined

- HR strategies provide a framework within which is set out what the organization is proposing to do about people management generally or in particular areas of HRM.
- HR strategies set out what the organization intends to do about its human resource management policies and practices and how they should be integrated with the business strategy and with each other.

Purpose of HR strategies

The purpose of HR strategies is to articulate what an organization intends to do about its human resource management policies and practices now and in the longer-term in order to ensure that they contribute to the achievement of business objectives.

Types of HR strategies

- Because all organizations are different, all HR strategies are different.
- HR strategies can be deliberate, or they can emerge in response to evolving situations, or they may be partly deliberate and partly emergent.
- HR strategy may simply consist of a broad statement of intent that provides the framework for more specific strategic plans in individual HR areas, or it may include the deliberate introduction of overall approaches to human resource management such as high performance management, or it may include plans for specific areas of HRM such as talent management and reward.

Evaluating HR strategies

Where strategies are emergent rather than deliberate their effectiveness cannot be assessed by a formal process of evaluating their achievements against their goals. They can only be judged by reference to the degree to which the organization is successful in achieving its objectives through people. Deliberate strategies can be evaluated according to the extent to which they meet specified objectives.

Developing HR strategies

- The three main schools of strategy development: the design school, the process school and the configuration school.
- The main considerations to be taken into account in formulating HR strategies are achieving vertical and horizontal fit.

Implementing HR strategies

Strategies may be expressed as abstractions and if that is the case they must be translated into programmes with clearly stated objectives and deliverables. To implement strategies it is necessary to: (1) conduct a rigorous preliminary analysis of needs and requirements; (2) formulate the strategy; (3) enlist support for the strategy; (4) assess barriers; (5) prepare action plans; (6) project-manage implementation; and (7) follow up and evaluate progress so that remedial action can be taken as necessary.

References

Armstrong, M and Baron, A (2002) *Strategic HRM: The route to improved business performance*, CIPD, London

Armstrong, M and Long, P (1994) *The Reality of Strategic HRM*, Institute of Personnel and Development, London

Baron, J and Kreps, D (1999) Consistent human resource practices, *California Management Review*, **41** (3), pp 29–53

Becker, B E, Huselid, M A and Ulrich, D (2001) *The HR Score Card: Linking people, strategy, and performance*, Harvard Business School Press, Boston, MA

Beer, M et al (1984) *Managing Human Assets*, The Free Press, New York

Benson, G S, Young, S M and Lawler, E E (2006) High involvement work practices and analysts' forecasts of corporate performance, *Human Resource Management*, **45** (4), pp 519–27

Boxall, P F (1993) The significance of human resource management: a reconsideration of the evidence, *The International Journal of Human Resource Management*, **4** (3), pp 645–65

Boxall, P F (1996) The strategic HRM debate and the resource-based view of the firm, *Human Resource Management Journal*, **6** (3), pp 59–75

Boxall, P F and Purcell, J (2003) *Strategy and Human Resource Management*, Palgrave Macmillan, Basingstoke

Cappelli, P (1999) *Employment Practices and Business Strategy*, Oxford University Press, New York

Dickens, C (1843) *Martin Chuzzlewit*, Chapman & Hall, London (Penguin Classics 2004)

Dyer, L and Reeves, T (1995) Human resource strategies and firm performance: what do we know and where do we need to go? *The International Journal of Human Resource Management*, **6** (3), pp 656–70

Fombrun, C J, Tichy, N M and Devanna, M A (1984) *Strategic Human Resource Management*, Wiley, New York

Grant, R M (1998) *Contemporary Strategic Analysis*, Blackwell, Malden, MA

Gratton, L A et al (1999) *Strategic Human Resource Management*, Oxford University Press, Oxford

Guest, D E (1997) Human resource management and performance; a review of the research agenda, *The International Journal of Human Resource Management*, **8** (3), 263–76

Hendry, C and Pettigrew, A (1990) Human resource management: an agenda for the 1990s, *International Journal of Human Resource Management*, **1** (1), 17–44

Kanter, R M (1984) *The Change Masters*, Allen & Unwin, London

Marsh, C and Sweeney, H (2010) NG Bailey: constructing business model change, in *Leading HR*, (eds) P Sparrow, A Hesketh, M Hird, and C Cooper, pp 90–102, Palgrave Macmillan, Basingstoke

Mintzberg, H (1987) Crafting strategy, *Harvard Business Review*, July/August, pp 66–74

Mintzberg, H, Quinn, J B and James, R M (1988) *The Strategy Process: Concepts, contexts and cases*, Prentice-Hall, New York

Pettigrew, A and Whipp, R (1991) *Managing Change for Competitive Success*, Blackwell, Oxford

Porter, M E (1985) *Competitive Advantage: Creating and sustaining superior performance*, The Free Press, New York

Purcell, J (2001) The meaning of strategy in human resource management, in *Human Resource Management: A critical text*, 2nd edn, (ed) J Storey, pp 59–77, Thompson Learning, London

Purcell, J et al (2003) *Understanding the People and Performance Link: Unlocking the black box*, CIPD, London

Richardson, R and Thompson, M (1999) *The Impact of People Management Practices on Business Performance: A literature review*, Institute of Personnel and Development, London

Sparrow, P et al (2010) Using business model change to tie HR into strategy: reversing the arrow, in *Leading HR*, (eds) P Sparrow, A Hesketh, M Hird and C Cooper, pp 68–89, Palgrave Macmillan, Basingstoke

Sung, J and Ashton, D (2005) *High Performance Work Practices: Linking strategy and skills to performance outcomes*, DTI in association with CIPD, available online at http://www.cipd.co.uk/subjects/corpstrtgy/

Thompson, A A and Strickland, A J (1996) *Strategic Management: Concepts and cases*, 9th edn, Irwin, Georgetown, Ontario

Trevor, J (2010) Can pay be strategic? A critical exploration of the pay practices of leading firms, presentation at The Reward Management Update, e-reward, 3 November (unpublished)

Tyson, S and Witcher, M (1994) Human resource strategy emerging from the recession, *Personnel Management*, August, pp 20–23

Walton, R E (1985) Towards a strategy of eliciting employee commitment based on principles of mutuality, in *HRM Trends and Challenges*, (eds) R E Walton and P R Lawrence, Harvard Business School Press, Boston, MA

Wood, S (1996) High commitment management and organization in the UK, *International Journal of Human Resource Management*, 7 (1), pp 41–58

Wood, S (2010) High involvement and performance, in *The Oxford Handbook of Participation in Organizations*, (eds) A Wilkinson, P J Gollan, M Marchington and D Lewins, pp 407–26, Oxford University Press, Oxford

Wood, S and Albanese, M (1995) Can we speak of a high commitment management on the shop floor? *Journal of Management Studies*, 32 (2), pp 215–47

Wright, P M and Snell, S A (1998) Towards a unifying framework for exploring fit and flexibility in strategic human resource management, *Academy of Management Review*, 23 (4), pp 756–72

Wright, P M, Snell, S A and Jacobsen, H H (2004) Current approaches to HR strategies: inside-out versus outside-in, *Human Resource Planning*, 27 (4), pp 36–46

Business model innovation

KEY CONCEPTS AND TERMS

Business model

Business model innovation

Change management

Knowledge management

Organization development

Talent management

Workforce planning

LEARNING OUTCOMES

On completing this chapter you should be able to define the key concepts above. You should also understand:

- how the concept of business models developed;
- the rationale for business models;
- the rationale for business model innovation;
- the relationship between business model innovation and strategy;
- the process of analysing and designing business models;
- the role of HR in business model innovation.

Introduction

Business model innovation is an approach to the development of a business. Johnson (2010: 7) stated that a business model 'defines the way the company delivers value to a set of customers at a profit'. He explained that business model innovation involves 'the creation or reinvention of a business' and that 'it results in an entirely different type of company that competes not only on the value proposition of its offerings, but aligns its profit formula, resources, and processes to enhance that value proposition, capture new market segments, and alienate competitors' (Johnson, 2010: 20). A survey by IBM (Pohle and Chapman, 2006: 34) found that 'competitive pressures have pushed business model innovation much higher than expected on CEOs' priority lists. Business leaders are seeking and finding new ways to adapt their business models to remain competitive in their current industry – or to seek growth by entering new industries'.

Business models provide a picture of an organization that explains how it works. Business model innovation is concerned with how the organization should change its business model to improve its performance. Such changes impact on people. They involve employees in planning and implementing them. They are therefore the concern of the HR function as well as operational management. HR has a major role in ensuring that innovation or change is carried out effectively through people. HR needs to be involved in planning the change and implementing it by developing and facilitating the introduction of appropriate HR strategies. As Sparrow et al (2010: 9) indicated: 'Describing business models helps to articulate the key components of effective strategic performance, thereby providing an opportunity to link HR more closely to the challenges faced during strategy execution'. They also remarked that: 'A central task for HR directors is to identify how they, as a leader, and how their function's own delivery model structure, and the people processes it manages, add value during periods of business model change' (ibid: 14–15).

Strategic HRM is about the integration of HR and business plans. This means being involved in business model innovation when it takes place as part of those plans. The aim of this chapter is to explain how this can happen by defining the concept of a business model and the part it plays in strategic management, examining the process of business model innovation, describing how business models can be analysed as part of strategic HRM, and examining the role of HR in business model innovation.

Business models defined

Business models, as defined by Joan Magretta (2002: 87), '... are at heart stories – stories that explain how enterprises work... They answer the fundamental questions every manager needs to ask: How do we make money in this business? What is the underlying economic logic that explains how we can deliver value to customers at an appropriate cost?' She explained that a business model 'focuses attention on how all the elements in a system fit into a working whole' (ibid: 90).

It was suggested by Chesbrough (2010: 355) that: 'A business model articulates the value proposition... and defines the structure of the value chain'. According to Teece (2010: 173): 'In essence, a business model is a conceptual rather than a financial model of a business'. A major contribution to understanding business models was made by Johnson et al (2008: 52), who stated that: 'A business model, from our point of view, consists of four inter-locking elements that, taken together, create and deliver value'. These four elements are:

1 The customer value proposition: how the business will create value for its customers. This is the most important element.

2 The profit formula: the blueprint that defines how the company creates value for itself while providing value to the customer. It consists of the revenue model, cost structure, margin model (the contribution needed from each transaction to achieve desired profits) and resource velocity (how fast the business needs to turn over inventory and assets and how well resources should be utilized).

3 Key resources: assets such as people, technology, products, facilities, equipment, channels and brand required to deliver the value proposition to the targeted customer.

4 Key processes: recurrent tasks such as training, development, manufacturing, budgeting, planning and sales that allow firms to deliver value in a way they can successfully repeat and increase in scale. Key processes also include a company's rules, metrics and norms.

Development of the concept

The notion of business models was in a sense created by Peter Drucker (1955: 41–46) who said that companies should be able to answer four questions: 'What is our business?', 'Who is the customer?', 'What is value to the customer?' and 'What will our business be?' The concept of business models as it developed owes something to the competitive positioning approach to strategy adopted by Porter (1980), ie analysing the external environment (competitors, customers and markets) and then considering its internal implications. As Schweizer (2005: 42) pointed out, it was later influenced by the resource-based view, which suggests that the value embedded in a business model 'increases as the bundle of resources and capabilities it comprises become more and more difficult to imitate, less transferable and more complementary'. The term business model gained currency and to a degree lost its reputation when it was used by the dot com companies in the 1990s boom and bust era. But over the last decade it has become increasingly prominent as a means of describing a business.

Rationale for business models

Business models provide a picture of what the firm is doing or intends to do. Magretta (2002: 92) argued that: 'Because a business model tells a good story, it can be used to get everyone aligned around the kind of value the company wants to create. Stories are easy to grasp and easy to remember.' As Casedusus-Masanel and Ricart (2010: 196) suggested, the notion of business models became popular as a means of defining 'the logic of the firm – the way it operates and creates value for its stakeholders'.

Business model innovation defined

Business model innovation is the process of developing new business models or changing existing ones in order to deliver better value to customers, achieve competitive advantage and increase profitability. Mark Johnson (2010) defined the concept in more detail as follows.

SOURCE REVIEW   Business model innovation defined
– Johnson (2010: 20)

Business model innovation (BMI) refers to the creation or reinvention of a business. Though innovation is more often seen in the form of a new product or service offering, a business model innovation results in an entirely different type of company that competes not only on the value proposition of its offerings, but aligns its profit formula, resources, and processes to enhance that value proposition, capture new market segments, and alienate competitors.

He also observed that: 'Business model innovation thrives in cultures of inquiry, environments in which new value propositions and ideas for new business models are met with interest and encouragement' (ibid: 177).

Rationale for business model innovation

'Business model innovation can empower organizations to transform existing markets, create new ones or recast whole industries' (Johnson, 2010: 20). As Casedusus-Masanel and Ricart (2010: 195) put it, companies believe in the need to innovate business models 'in order to compete differently'.

Sparrow et al (2010: 6) argued that 'Organizations are using business models to articulate what they consider must be the dominant performance logic inherent in their strategy'.

An analysis of an IBM survey of 765 corporate leaders by Pohle and Chapman (2006) came to the following conclusions.

SOURCE REVIEW   Views of CEOs on business model innovation – Pohle and Chapman (2006: 35)

Because businesses are so often defined in terms of the products and services they take to market, their leaders have traditionally focused innovative energy there. But with technological advances and globalization presenting so many new opportunities – and threats – CEOs are looking to business model innovation to create sustainable competitive advantage and differentiation for them in their marketplaces. In fact, according to CEOs, business model innovation is now on par with innovation in operations and nearly as important as innovation around products and services.

They also found that:

> Cost reduction and strategic flexibility were considered top benefits from business model innovation – reported by over half of all business model innovators. Business model innovation allows companies to specialize and move more quickly to seize growth opportunities as they emerge. Overall, CEOs' rankings suggest that business model innovation is helping their organizations become more nimble and responsive, while, at the same time, lowering costs (ibid: 38).

Chesbrough (2010: 356) confirmed that: 'A company has at least as much value to gain from developing an innovative new business model as from developing an innovative new technology'. *The Economist* (2007: 7) also noted that: 'Business model innovation is far more radical than conventional product or process innovation. Globalisation and the spread of IT allow the creation of unexpected and disruptive business models.'

Business model innovation and strategy

What is the relationship between business models and strategy? The following categorical answer to this question was produced by Joan Magretta (2002).

SOURCE REVIEW Business models and strategy – Magretta (2002: 91)

A business model isn't the same thing as a strategy, even though many people use the terms interchangeably today. Business models describe as a system how the pieces of a business fit together. But they don't factor in one critical dimension of performance: competition. Sooner or later – and it is usually sooner – every enterprise runs into competitors. Dealing with that reality is strategy's job. A competitive strategy explains how you will do better than your rivals. And doing better, by definition, means being different.

However, business model innovation is clearly linked to strategy, so what's the link? Sparrow et al (2010: 5) argued that 'whilst strategy concerns the long-term creation of value and the process of making strategic choices, analysis of the business model facilitates clearer analysis, testing and validation of these choices'. They also pointed out that business models 'can be used to weave together and demonstrate the importance of a range of components to the execution of a strategy' (ibid: 8).

Teece (2010: 179) explained that: 'A business model is more generic than a business strategy. Coupling strategy analysis with business model analysis is necessary in order to protect whatever competitive advantage results from the design and implementation of new business models.' Casedusus-Masanel and Ricart (2010: 196) proposed a closer link when they suggested that strategy 'refers to the choice of business model through which the firm will compete in the market place'.

Business model analysis and design

Business model analysis is a necessary part of business model innovation. It is concerned with two key issues: (1) how the organization creates value; and (2) how the organization establishes unique resources, assets or positions that will achieve competitive advantage. It may involve an analysis of how value is generated at each stage of the value chain (a value chain identifies those activities in a firm that are strategically relevant and underlie its key capabilities).

An overall approach to business model analysis advocated by Johnson et al (2008: 52) consists of three steps: 'The first is to realize that success starts by not thinking about business models at all. It starts with thinking about the opportunity to satisfy a real customer who needs a job done. The second step is to construct a blueprint laying out how your company will fulfil that need at a profit... The third is to compare that model to your existing model to see how much you'd have to change it to capture the opportunity'.

They recommend that the analysis should focus on the four elements of the business model:

1 The customer value proposition: This means finding out what customers value or do not value about the present offering, assessing what they might want in the future and, importantly, because this is where the innovation comes in, identifying new products or services or improvements to existing products or services that customers will value.

2 The profit formula: Gaining a better understanding about how well the present profit formula functions under each of its four headings (revenue model, cost structure, margin model and resource velocity) and establishing areas for improvement.

3 Key resources: Examining each of the key resources (people, money, brand, equipment etc) to determine the extent to which they are adequate for the task in hand and will enable the organization to develop and compete in the future.

4 Key processes: Reviewing each of the key managerial and operational processes to assess their effectiveness now and for the future.

The design follows the analysis but as Chesbrough (2010: 362) put it: 'Designing a new business model requires creativity, insight and a good deal of competition and supplier information and intelligence'. And Teece (2010: 181) was certain that: 'Business model innovation is vitally important and yet very difficult to achieve'. The design may be difficult but implementation is harder. Sparrow et al (2010: 15) asserted that: 'In order for organizations to make their models work, they have to understand the potentially deep implications they have for people management'. The HR function has an important role to play in ensuring that businesses gain this understanding and act on it.

The role of HR in business model innovation

On the basis of extensive research into how HR departments dealt with business model innovation, their role was spelt out by Paul Sparrow and his colleagues (2010) as follows:

SOURCE REVIEW   The role of HR in business model innovation
– Sparrow et al (2010: 14–15)

A central task for HR directors is to identify how they as a leader, and how their function's own delivery model, structure, and the people processes it manages, add value during periods of business model change. In order for organizations to make their models work, they have to understand the potentially deep implications they have for people management. People management experts have to make sure that those engineering the new business models are working on assumptions that can reasonably be executed.

To contribute to business model innovation HR directors need to:

- understand the implications of the existing and potential business model in terms of the organization structure and the new or enhanced capabilities the people involved will require;

- contribute to the redesign of the organization to meet the requirements of the business model change programme;

- plan organization development activities that systematically improve organizational capability in terms of process – how things get done;

- mastermind change management programmes that provide for the acceptance and smooth implementation of change;

- conduct workforce planning exercises that identify more specifically the numbers of people required with specified skills and knowledge;

- formulate and implement talent management strategies that provide for the development, deployment, recruitment and retention of talented people – those individuals who can make a difference to organizational performance through their immediate contribution and in the longer term;

- develop performance management and contingent reward systems – what Sparrow et al (2010: 16) call 'performance-driven processes';

- plan and manage learning programmes to ensure that people have the skills required to implement the new or changed business model;

- establish knowledge management procedures for storing and sharing the wisdom, understanding and expertise accumulated in the organization about its processes, techniques and operations.

In addition, as Schuler and Jackson (2007: 31) point out, '... because an innovation strategy requires risk taking and tolerance of inevitable failures, HRM in firms pursuing this strategy should be used to give employees a sense of security and encourage a long-term commitment'.

KEY LEARNING POINTS

Business models defined

- A business model 'defines the way the company delivers value to a set of customers at a profit' (Johnson, 2010: 7).
- Business models provide a picture of an organization that explains how it works.
- Business models consist of a customer value proposition, the profit formula, key resources and key processes.

Business model innovation defined

- Business model innovation (BMI) is a strategic approach to business management and development.
- It is concerned with how the organization should change its business model to improve its performance.
- Business model innovation is clearly linked to strategy.

Business model innovation analysis and design

- Business models should be analysed in terms of the customer value proposition, the profit formula, key resources and key processes.
- 'Designing a new business model requires creativity, insight and a good deal of competition and supplier information and intelligence' (Chesbrough, 2010: 362).
- 'In order for organizations to make their models work, they have to understand the potentially deep implications they have for people management' (Sparrow et al, 2010: 15).

The role of HR

HR has a major role in ensuring that innovation or change is carried out effectively through people. HR needs to be involved in planning the change and implementing it by developing and facilitating the introduction of appropriate HR strategies.

To contribute to business model innovation, HR directors need to understand the implications of the existing and potential business model in terms of the organization structure and the new or enhanced capabilities the people involved will require. They are then concerned with the development of strategies and processes to ensure that the organization has the skills and expertise required.

References

Casedusus-Masanel, R and Ricart, J E (2010) From strategy to business models and on to tactics, *Long Range Planning*, **43** (2–3), pp 195–215

Chesbrough, H W (2010) Business model innovation: opportunities and barriers, *Long Range Planning*, **43** (2–3), pp 354–62

Drucker, P (1955) *The Practice of Management*, Heinemann, London

The Economist (2007) Something new under the sun: a special report on innovation, *The Economist*, 11 October, **385** (8550), pp 7–8

Johnson, M (2010) *Seizing the White Space*, Harvard Business Press, Boston, MA

Johnson, M, Christensen, C and Kagermann, H (2008) Reinventing your business model, *Harvard Business Review*, December, pp 52–59

Magretta, J (2002) Why business models matter, *Harvard Business Review*, May, 86–93

Pohle, G and Chapman, M (2006) IBM's global CEO report 2006: business model innovation matters, *Strategy and Leadership*, **34** (5), pp 34–40

Porter, M E (1980) *Competitive Strategy: Techniques for analyzing industries and competitors*, The Free Press, New York

Schuler, R S and Jackson, S E (2007) Understanding human resource management in the context of organizations and their environments, in *Strategic Human Resource Management*, (eds) R S Schuler and S E Jackson, pp 23–48, Blackwell, Oxford

Schweizer, L (2005) Concept and evolution of business models, *Journal of General Management*, **31** (2), pp 37–56

Sparrow, P et al (2010) Introduction: performance-led HR, in *Leading HR*, (eds) P Sparrow, A Hesketh, M Hird and C Cooper, Palgrave Macmillan, Basingstoke

Teece, D (2010) Business models, business strategy and innovation, *Long Range Planning*, **43** (2–3), pp 172–94

High performance strategy

Introduction

A high performance strategy sets out the aspirations and intentions of the organization on how it can achieve competitive advantage by improving performance through people, and spells out how those aspirations and intentions will be attained. The aim is to support the achievement of the organization's strategic objectives by means of high performance work systems (HPWS) as described in this chapter. Becker et al (2001: 13) stated that: 'In an HPWS, each element of the HR system is designed to maximize the overall quality of the human capital throughout the organization'. They also claimed that: 'An HPWS is a strategy implementation system embedded with the firm's larger strategy implementation system' (ibid: 18).

High performance work systems are also known as high performance work practices (Sung and Ashton, 2005). Thompson and Heron (2005: 1029–30) refer to them as high performance work organizations, which 'invest in the skills and abilities of employees, design work in ways that enable employee collaboration in problem-solving, and provide incentives to motivate workers to use their discretionary effort'.

There is much common ground between the practices included in high performance, high commitment and high involvement work systems as described in Chapter 8. Sung and Ashton (2005: 8) noted that:

> In some cases high performance work practices are called 'high commitment practices' (Walton, 1985) or 'high involvement management' (Lawler, 1986). More recently they have been termed 'high performance organizations' (Lawler et al, 1998, Ashton and Sung, 2002) or 'high involvement' work practices (Wood et al, 2001). Whilst these studies are referring to the same general phenomena the use of different 'labels' has undoubtedly added to the confusion.

High performance work system defined

High performance work systems provide the means for creating a performance culture. They embody ways of thinking about performance in organizations and how it can be improved. They are concerned with developing and implementing bundles of complementary practices, which as an integrated whole will make a much more powerful impact on performance than if they were dealt with as separate entities. Becker et al (2001: 19) pointed out that: 'In an HPWS a firm's HR policies and practices show a strong alignment with the firm's competitive strategy and operational goals'.

As defined by Appelbaum et al (2000), high performance work systems are comprised of practices that can facilitate employee involvement, skill enhancement and motivation. Research conducted by Armitage and Keble-Allen (2007) indicated that people management basics formed the foundation of high performance working. They identified three themes underpinning the HPWS concept:

1 An open and creative culture that is people-centred and inclusive, where decision-taking is communicated and shared through the organization.

2 Investment in people through education and training, loyalty, inclusiveness and flexible working.

3 Measurable performance outcomes such as benchmarking and setting targets, as well as innovation through processes and best practice.

Sung and Ashton (2005) defined what they call high performance work practices as a set of 35 complementary work practices covering three broad areas: high employee involvement work practices; human resource practices; and reward and commitment practices. They refer to them as 'bundles' of practices.

Characteristics of a high performance work system

A high performance work system is described by Becker and Huselid (1998) as: 'An internally consistent and coherent HRM system that is focused on solving operational problems and implementing the firm's competitive strategy'. They suggest that such a system 'is the key to the acquisition, motivation and development of the underlying intellectual assets that can be a source of sustained competitive advantage'. This is because it:

- links the firm's selection and promotion decisions to validated competency models;
- develops strategies that provide timely and effective support for the skills demanded by the firm's strategy implementation;
- enacts compensation and performance management policies that attract, retain and motivate high performance employees.

As described by Appelbaum et al (2000), a HPWS is 'generally associated with workshop practices that raise the levels of trust within workplaces and increase workers' intrinsic reward from work, and thereby enhance organizational commitment'.

Nadler and Gerstein (1992) have characterized a HPWS as a way of thinking about organizations. It can play an important role in strategic human resource management by helping to achieve a 'fit' between information, technology, people and work.

Components of a HPWS

The intentions contained in a high performance strategy will include the development and application of HR practices, which it is believed will result in high performance. Typically, these will include performance management, reward management (eg performance pay and recognition schemes), talent management, and learning and development programmes. These are, of course, standard HR practices. The difference provided by a high performance system is that these practices are bundled together so that they support one another and make a greater impact on performance as an integrated whole. Ashton and Sung (2002) noted that HPWS practices may be more effective when they are grouped together in 'bundles'. For example, the isolated use of quality circles is not as effective as when the practice is supported by wider employee involvement/empowerment practices.

A number of lists of HPWS practices have been produced as set out in Table 10.1. These lists have certain items in common, such as some form of incentive rewards and performance appraisal or feedback, but there is considerable variation. Gephart (1995) notes that research has not clearly identified any single set of high performance practices.

Such lists reflect a 'best practice' or 'universalistic' viewpoint and Sung and Ashton (2005: 8) comment that: 'It would be wrong to seek one magic list. After all, it is quite possible to replace one practice with another practice, or with combinations of other practices that deliver the same results'. However, it may be reasonable to assume that, in essence, some practices are desirable, although the form they take in a particular organization must take account of the context of that organization. For example, some form of performance management system may be worth having, which might include such features as the joint agreement of performance goals, feedback and reviews. But how these features are applied will vary according to the organization's circumstances.

Impact of high performance work systems

A considerable amount of studies (as summarized below) have been conducted that demonstrate that the impact of high performance work systems is positive. A more negative study is also summarized.

US Department of Labor (1993)

In a survey of 700 organizations, the US Department of Labor found that firms that used innovative human resource practices showed a significantly higher level of shareholder and gross return on capital.

King (1995)

Jeffrey King cites a survey of Fortune 1000 companies in the US, revealing that 60 per cent of those using at least one practice increasing the responsibility of employees in the business process reported that the result was an increase in productivity, while 70 per cent reported an improvement in quality.

He examined the impact of the use of certain practices in detail. A study of 155 manufacturing firms showed that those that had introduced a formal training programme experienced a 19 per cent larger rise in productivity over three years than firms that did not introduce a training programme. Research in the use of gainsharing in 112 manufacturing firms revealed that

TABLE 10.1

US Department of Labor (1993)	Appelbaum et al (2000)	Sung and Ashton (2005)	Thompson and Heron (2005)
• Careful and extensive systems for recruitment, selection and training.	• Work is organized to permit front-line workers to participate in decisions that alter organizational routines.	• High involvement work practices – eg self-directed teams, quality circles, and sharing/ access to company information.	• Information sharing.
• Formal systems for sharing information with employees.			• Sophisticated recruitment.
			• Formal induction programme.
• Clear job design.	• Workers require more skills to do their jobs successfully, and many of these skills are firm-specific.		• Five or more days of off-the-job training in the last year.
• High-level participation processes.		• Human resource practices – eg sophisticated recruitment processes, performance appraisals, work redesign and mentoring.	• Semi or totally autonomous work teams; continuous improvement teams; problem-solving groups.
• Monitoring of attitudes.	• Workers experience greater autonomy over their job tasks and methods of work.		
• Performance appraisals.			• Interpersonal skill development.
• Properly functioning grievance procedures.	• Incentive pay motivates workers to expend extra effort on developing skills.		• Performance feedback.
• Promotion and compensation schemes that provide for the recognition and reward of high-performing employees.	• Employment security provides front-line workers with a long-term stake in the company and a reason to invest in its future.	• Reward and commitment practices – eg various financial rewards, family-friendly policies, job rotation and flexi hours.	• Involvement – works council, suggestion scheme, opinion survey.
			• Team-based rewards, employee share ownership scheme, profit-sharing scheme.

defect and downtime rates fell 23 per cent in the first year after the approach was introduced. His review of 29 studies on the effects of workplace participation on productivity indicated that 14 had a positive effect on productivity, only two had negative effects, and the rest were inconclusive.

However, he noted that such work practices may have only a limited effect unless they are elements of a coherent work system. Further research examined changes over time in 222 firms and found that these and other practices are associated with even greater productivity when implemented together in systems.

He concluded that the evidence suggests that it is the use of comprehensive systems of work practices in firms that is most closely associated with stronger firm performance. Yet he noted that 'the nature of the relationship between high performance work practices and productivity is not clear'.

Varma et al (1999)

A survey of 39 organizations was conducted to examine the antecedents, design and effectiveness of high performance initiatives. Results indicated that HPWS are primarily initiated by strong firms that are seeking to become stronger. First and foremost, firms reported that in general their HPWS:

- had a significant impact on financial performance;
- created a positive culture change in the organization (eg cooperation and innovation);
- created higher degrees of job satisfaction among employees;
- positively influenced the way in which work was designed;
- led to marked improvement in communication processes within the organization.

In particular, the use of team-based and non-financial rewards was closely related to improved performance, as was rewarding people for improving their competencies.

Ramsay et al (2000)

The aim of this research was to explore linkages from HPWS practices to employee outcomes and via these to organizational performance. They refer to the existence of a 'black box', meaning that while the introduction of a HPWS may be associated with improved performance, no researchers have yet established how this happens.

Their research was based on data from the UK 1998 Workplace Employee Relations Survey. They commented that 'the widely held view that positive performance outcomes from HPWS flow via positive employee outcomes has been shown to be highly questionable', a finding that ran counter to most if not all other studies. They admit that their analysis was 'perhaps too simplistic to capture the complex reality of the implementation and operation of HPWS', but they note, realistically, that 'there are major limitations to the strategic management of labour which severely constrain the potential for innovative approaches to be implemented successfully'.

Appelbaum et al (2000)

A multifaceted research design was used by the authors in their study of the impact of HPWS. This included management interviews, the collection of plant performance, and data surveys of workers on their experiences with workshop practices. Nearly 4,400 employees were surveyed and 44 manufacturing facilities were visited.

The findings of the research in industry were that:

- in the steel industry HPWS produced string positive effects on performance, for example, substantial increases in uptime;
- in the apparel industry the introduction of a 'module system' (ie group piecework rates linked to quality as well as quantity rather than individual piecework, plus multiskilling) dramatically speeded up throughput times, meeting consumer demands for fast delivery;
- in the medical electronics and imaging industry those using a HPWS ranked highly on eight diverse indicators of financial performance and production efficiency and quality.

The impact of HPWS on individual workers was to enhance:

- trust by sharing control and encouraging participation;
- intrinsic rewards because workers are challenged to be creative and use their skills and knowledge – discretion and autonomy are the task level decisions most likely to enhance intrinsic rewards;
- organizational commitment through opportunity to participate, and incentives that make people feel that organizational relationships are beneficial for them;
- job satisfaction because of participation, perception of fairness in pay and adequate resources to do jobs (inadequate resources is a cause of dissatisfaction, as is working in an unsafe or unclean environment).

Taken as a whole, the results suggested that the core characteristics of HPWS – having autonomy over task-level decision making, membership of self-directing production and off-line teams, and communication with people outside the work group – generally enhance workers' levels of organizational commitment and satisfaction.

Sung and Ashton (2005)

This survey of high performance work practices (HPWP) was conducted in 294 UK companies. It included 10 case studies. Its aim was to study the relationship between the adoption of such practices and a range of organizational outcomes. A list of 35 HPWP practices was drawn up under the three headings of high involvement practices, human resource practices, and reward and commitment practices.

The survey provided evidence that the level of HPWP adoption as measured by the number of practices in use is linked to organizational performance. Those adopting more of the practices as 'bundles' had greater employee involvement and were more effective in delivering adequate training provision, managing staff and providing career opportunities.

Ericksen (2007)

Research was conducted in 196 small businesses to test the hypothesis that HPWS create a human resource advantage by aligning key employee attributes and the strategic goals of the firm and by adapting their workforce attributes in response to new strategic circumstances. Dynamic workforce alignment exists when firms have 'the right types of people, in the right places, doing the right things right', and when adjustments are readily made to their workforces as the situation changes.

The research showed that there was a strong positive relationship between workforce alignment and sales growth when adaptation was high.

Developing a high performance strategy

A high performance strategy has to be aligned to the context of the organization and to its business strategy. Every organization will therefore develop a different strategy, as is illustrated by the case study examples set out in Table 10.2.

Approach to development

A high performance strategy is focused on what needs to be done to reach the organization's goals. The aim is to create and maintain a high performance culture. The approach to development is therefore based on an understanding of what those goals are and how people can contribute to their achievement, and on assessing what type of performance culture is required as a basis for developing a high performance work system.

The characteristics of a performance culture are that:

- a clear line of sight exists between the strategic aims of the organization and those of its departments and its staff at all levels;
- people know what's expected of them – they understand their goals and accountabilities;

TABLE 10.2

Organization	High performance working ingredients
Halo Foods	• A strategy that maintains competitiveness by increasing added value through the efforts and enhanced capability of all staff. • The integration of technical advance with people development. • Continuing reliance on teamworking and effective leadership, with innovation and self- and team-management skills.
Land Registry	• Organizational changes to streamline processes, raise skill levels and release talents. • Managers who could see that the problems were as much cultural as organizational. • Recruitment of people whose attitudes and aptitudes match the needs of high performance work practices.
Meritor Heavy Vehicle Braking Systems	• Skill enhancement, particularly of management and self-management skills using competence frameworks. • Teamworking skills and experience used on improvement projects. • Linking learning, involvement and performance management.
Orangebox	• A strategy that relies on constant reinvention of operational capability. • Engagement and development of existing talent and initiative in productivity improvement. • Increasing use of cross-departmental projects to tackle wider opportunities.
Perkinelmer	• A vision and values worked through by managers and supervisors. • Engagement of everyone in the organization and establishment of a continuous improvement culture. • Learning as a basis for change.
United Welsh Housing Association	• Linking of better employment relations with better performance. • Using staff experience to improve customer service. • Focusing management development on the cascading of a partnership culture.

SOURCE: Stevens (2005)

- people feel that their job is worth doing, and there is a strong fit between the job and their capabilities;
- people are empowered to maximize their contribution;
- management defines what it requires in the shape of performance improvements, sets goals for success, and monitors performance to ensure that the goals are achieved;
- there is strong leadership from the top that engenders a shared belief in the importance of continuing improvement;
- there is a focus on promoting positive attitudes that result in an engaged, committed and motivated workforce;
- performance management processes are aligned to business goals to ensure that people are engaged in achieving agreed objectives and standards;
- capacities of people are developed through learning at all levels to support performance improvement, and people are provided with opportunities to make full use of their skills and abilities;
- a pool of talent ensures a continuous supply of high performers in key roles;
- people are valued and rewarded according to their contribution;
- people are involved in developing high performance practices;
- there is a climate of trust and teamwork, aimed at delivering a distinctive service to the customer.

The development programme requires strong leadership from the top. Stakeholders – line managers, team leaders, employees and their representatives – should be involved as much as possible through surveys, focus groups and workshops.

Developing a high performance work system

The steps required are described below. The more line managers and other employees can be involved at every stage, the better.

1 Analyse the business strategy:
   - Where is the business going?
   - What are the strengths and weaknesses of the business?
   - What threats and opportunities does the business face?
   - What are the implications of the above on the type of people required by the business, now and in the future?
   - To what extent do we – can we – obtain competitive advantage through people?

2 Define the desired performance culture of the business and the objectives of the exercise. Use the list of characteristics above as a starting point and produce a list that is aligned to the culture and context of the business and a statement of the objectives of developing a HPWS.

3 Analyse the existing arrangements – start from the headings defined at stage 2 and analyse against each heading:
- what is happening now in the form of practices, attitudes and behaviours (what do you want people to do differently?);
- what should be happening;
- what people feel about it (the more involvement in this analysis there is by all stakeholders, the better).

4 Identify the gaps between what is and what should be – clarify specific practices where there is considerable room for improvement.

5 Draw up a list of practices that need to be introduced or improved – at this stage only a broad definition should be produced of what ideally needs to be done.

6 Establish complementarities – identify the practices that can be linked together in 'bundles' in order to complement and support one another.

7 Assess practicality – the ideal list of practices, or preferably bundles of practices, should be subjected to a reality check:
- Is it worth doing? What's the business case in terms of added value? What contribution will it make to supporting the achievement of the organization's strategic goals?
- Can it be done?
- Who does it?
- Have we the resources to do it?
- How do we manage the change?

8 Prioritize – in the light of the assessment of practicalities, decide on the priorities that should be given to introducing new or improved practices. A realistic approach is essential. There will be limits on how much can be done at once or at any future time. Priorities should be established by assessing:
- the added value the practice will create;
- the availability of the resources required;
- anticipated problems in introducing the practice, including resistance to change by stakeholders (too much should not be made of this, change can be managed, but there is much to be said for achieving some quick wins);
- the extent to which they can form bundles of mutually supporting practices.

9 Define project objectives – develop the broad statement of objectives produced at stage 2 and define what is to be achieved, why and how.

10 Get buy in – this should start at the top with the chief executive and members of the senior management team, but so far as possible it should extend to all the other stakeholders (best to involve them at earlier stages and communicate intentions in full).

11 Plan the implementation – this is where things become difficult. Deciding what needs to be done is fairly easy; getting it done is the hard part. The implementation plan needs to cover:

- who takes the lead – this must come from the top of the organization; nothing will work without it;
- who manages the project and who else is involved;
- the timetable for development and introduction;
- the resources (people and money required);
- how the change programme will be managed, including communication and further consultation;
- the success criteria for the project.

12 Implement – too often, 80 per cent of the time spent on introducing a HPWS is spent on planning and only 20 per cent on implementation. It should be the other way round. Whoever is responsible for implementation must have very considerable project and change management skills.

KEY LEARNING POINTS

High performance strategy

A high performance strategy sets out the intentions of the organization on how it can achieve competitive advantage by improving performance through people. This can involve the introduction of high performance work systems.

High performance work systems defined

High performance work systems are comprised of practices that can facilitate employee involvement, skill enhancement and motivation. They provide the means for creating a performance culture and embody ways of thinking about performance in organizations and how it can be improved. They are concerned with developing and implementing bundles of complementary practices that as an integrated whole will make a much more powerful impact on performance than if they were dealt with as separate entities.

The practices may be more effective when they are grouped together in 'bundles'. A considerable number of studies have been conducted that demonstrate that the impact of high performance work systems is positive.

Developing a high performance strategy

A high performance strategy has to be aligned to the context of the organization and to its business strategy. Every organization will therefore develop a different strategy. A high performance strategy is focused on what needs to be done to reach the organization's goals. The aim is to create and maintain a high performance culture.

The approach to development is therefore based on an understanding of what those goals are and how people can contribute to their achievement, and on assessing what type of performance culture is required as a basis for developing a high performance work system.

References

Appelbaum, E et al (2000) *Manufacturing Advantage: Why high performance work systems pay off*, ILR Press, Ithaca, NY

Armitage, A and Keble-Allen, D (2007) Why people management basics form the foundation of high-performance working, *People Management*, 18 October, p 48

Ashton, D and Sung, J (2002) *Supporting Workplace Learning for High Performance*, ILO, Geneva

Becker, B E and Huselid, M A (1998) High performance work systems and firm performance: a synthesis of research and managerial implications, *Research on Personnel and Human Resource Management*, **16**, pp 53–101

Becker, B E, Huselid, M A and Ulrich, D (2001) *The HR Score Card: Linking people, strategy, and performance*, Harvard Business School Press, Boston, MA

Ericksen, J (2007) High performance work systems: dynamic workforce alignment and firm performance, *Academy of Management Proceedings*, pp 1–6

Gephart, M A (1995) The road to high performance: steps to create a high-performance workplace, *Training and Development*, June, p 29

King, J (1995) High performance work systems and firm performance, *Monthly Labour Review*, May, pp 29–36

Lawler, E E (1986) *High Involvement Management*, Jossey-Bass, San Francisco

Lawler, E E, Mohrman, S and Ledford, G (1998) *Strategies for High Performance Organizations: Employee involvement, TQM, and re-engineering programs in Fortune 1000*, Jossey-Bass, San Francisco

Nadler, D A and Gerstein, M S (1992) Designing high-performance work systems: organizing people, technology, work and information, *Organizational Architecture*, Summer, pp 195–208

Ramsay, H, Scholarios, D and Harley, B (2000) Employees and high-performance work systems: testing inside the black box, *British Journal of Industrial Relations*, **38** (4), pp 501–31

Stevens, J (2005) *High Performance Wales: Real experiences, real success*, Wales Management Council, Cardiff

Sung, J and Ashton, D (2005) *High Performance Work Practices: Linking strategy and skills to performance outcomes*, DTI in association with CIPD, available online at http://www.cipd.co.uk/subjects/corpstrtgy/

Thompson, M and Heron, P (2005) Management capability and high performance work organization, *International Journal of Human Resource Management*, **16** (6), pp 1029–48

US Department of Labor (1993) *High Performance Work Practices and Work Performance*, US Government Printing Office, Washington DC

Varma, A et al (1999) High performance work systems: exciting discovery or passing fad? *Human Resource Planning*, **22** (1), pp 26–37

Walton, R E (1985) From control to commitment in the workplace, *Harvard Business Review*, March/April, pp 77–84

Wood, S, de Menezes, L M and Lasaosa, A (2001) High involvement management and performance, paper delivered at the Centre for Labour Market Studies, University of Leicester, May

Human capital management strategy

KEY CONCEPTS AND TERMS

Evidence-based human resource management
Human capital
Human capital management

LEARNING OUTCOMES

On completing this chapter you should be able to define the key concepts above. You should also understand:

- the meaning and significance of human capital management (HCM);
- the aims of HCM;
- the role of HCM strategy;
- the link between HRM and business strategy;
- developing an HCM strategy.

Introduction

Human capital management (HCM) is concerned with obtaining, analysing and reporting on data that informs the direction of value-adding people management strategy. A HCM strategy is therefore closely associated with strategic HRM. In the words of Manocha (2005: 29) it can also provide 'evidence of a robust people strategy mapped to the business strategy'.

The defining characteristic of HCM is the use of metrics to guide an approach to managing people that regards them as assets. It emphasizes that competitive advantage is achieved by strategic investments in those assets through employee engagement and retention, talent management, and learning and development programmes. HCM is a bridge between HR and business strategy. It provides the basis for 'evidence-based human resource management', ie the process of ensuring that decisions and proposals on the development and application of HR strategies and practices are backed up with hard data derived from research, benchmarking and the analysis and evaluation of the organizational context and management activities.

The Accounting for People Task Force Report (2003: 3) stated that HCM involves 'the systematic analysis, measurement and evaluation of how people policies and practices create value'. HCM was defined as 'an approach to people management that treats it as a high level strategic issue rather than an operational matter "to be left to the HR people"' (ibid: 7). The Task Force expressed the view that HCM had been underexploited as a way of gaining competitive edge.

Scarborough and Elias (2002: 3) defined human capital as 'something that employees bring to the organization but is also developed through training and experience within the organization'. Nalbantian et al (2004: 75) described human capital as 'The accumulated stock of skills, experience and knowledge that resides in an organization's workforce and drives productive labour' and suggested that human capital management involves 'putting into place the metrics to measure the value of these attributes and using that knowledge to effectively manage the organization'.

HCM is sometimes defined more broadly without the emphasis on measurement and this approach makes it almost indistinguishable from strategic HRM. Chatzkel (2004: 139) pointed out that 'Human capital management is an integrated effort to manage and develop human capabilities to achieve significantly higher levels of performance'. And Kearns (2004: 14) asserted that 'everything done in the name of HRM is done in the name of value'. He described HCM as 'The total development of human potential expressed as organizational value'. He believes that 'HCM is about creating value through people' and that it is 'a people development philosophy, but the only development that means anything is that which is translated into value' (ibid: 205).

Aims of human capital management

The four fundamental objectives of HCM are:

1 to determine the impact of people on the business and their contribution to value;

2 to demonstrate that HR practices produce value for money in terms, for example, of return on investment;

3 to provide guidance on future HR and business strategies;

4 to provide data that will inform strategies and practices designed to improve the effectiveness of people management in the organization.

As Manocha (2005: 28) stated: 'Essentially, it [HCM] is a discipline that enables organizations to identify how their people contribute to and drive business performance'.

The role of human capital management strategy

Human capital strategy was defined by Nalbantian et al (2004: 79) as '... a blueprint for securing, managing and motivating the workforce needed to support the organization's strategic goals. To be effective, the management practices that influence the workforce should be consistent with one another and mutually reinforcing'.

The whole area of human capital management presents both an opportunity and a challenge. An opportunity to recognize people as an asset that contributes directly to organizational performance, and a challenge to develop the skills necessary to identify, analyse and communicate that contribution and ensure it is recognized in business decision making. By developing strategies to generate better and more accurate information on human capital, and communicating this information both internally and externally, organizations will not only improve their business decision making but will also enable stakeholders to make more accurate assessments about the long-term future performance of the organization. There is evidence of a growing demand, from the investment community in particular, for better information to explain intangible value. Many organizations are beginning to understand that, in an increasingly knowledge-intensive environment, the key to good management lies in understanding the levers that can be manipulated to change employee behaviour and develop commitment and engagement. This in turn encourages individuals to deliver discretionary behaviour or willingly share their knowledge and skills to achieve organizational goals.

A human capital management strategy that includes the systematic collection and analysis of human capital data can help managers to begin to understand factors that will have a direct impact on the people they manage. It can also help executives to understand and identify areas in which there are issues regarding the effective management of staff and to design management development programmes to address these.

The link between HCM and business strategy

It is often asserted that HCM and business strategy are closely linked and that a HCM approach provides guidance on both HR and business strategy. For example:

- 'By linking good HR practice and strategic management to human capital measurement firms are able to make a number of better informed decisions that will help to ensure long-term business success' (Scarborough and Elias, 2002: 17).

- 'If HR people can demonstrate they can articulate the worth and contribution of the organization's people by linking the human capital strategy to the overall business strategy, they will not only prove invaluable but play a part in improving management practices' (Manocha, 2005: 28).

- The HCM proposition 'emphasizes the connections and value flows between strategy, statistical analysis and the key stakeholders – employees, customers and investors' (Donkin, 2005: 3).

The issue is to determine what this link is and how to make it work. A bland statement that HCM informs HR strategy, which in turn informs business strategy, tells us nothing about what is involved in practice. If we are not careful we are saying no more than that all business strategic plans for innovation, growth and price/cost leadership depend on people for their implementation. This is not a particularly profound or revealing statement and is in the same category as the discredited cliché 'Our people are our greatest asset'. We must try to be more specific, otherwise we are only doing things – more training, succession planning, performance management, performance-related pay and so on – in the hope rather than the expectation that they will improve business results.

One way of being more specific is to use HCM assessments of the impact of HR practices on performance to justify these practices and improve the likelihood that they will work. The future of HCM as a strategic management process largely depends on getting this done.

A second way of specifying the link is to explore in more detail the people implications of business strategy and, conversely, the business implications of HR strategy. This can be done by analysing the elements of the business strategy and the business drivers and deciding on the HR-supporting activities and HCM data required, as illustrated in Table 11.1.

A third (and potentially the most productive) way of linking HR and business strategy is to relate business results to HR practices to determine how they can best contribute to improving performance.

TABLE 11.1

	Content	HR-supporting activities	Supporting data required
Business strategy	• Growth – revenue/profit • Maximize shareholder value • Growth through acquisitions/mergers • Growth in production/servicing facilities • Product development • Market development • Price/cost leadership	• Human resource planning • Talent management • Skills development • Targeted recruitment • Retention policies • Leadership development	• Workforce composition • Attrition rates • Skills audit • Outcome of recruitment campaigns • Learning and development activity levels • Outcome of leadership surveys

TABLE 11.1 *Continued*

Content	HR-supporting activities	Supporting data required
Business drivers	• Innovation • Maximize added value • Productivity • Customer service • Quality • Satisfy stakeholders – investors, shareholders, employees, elected representatives	• Talent management • Skills development • Total reward management • Performance management • Develop high performance working • Enhance motivation, engagement and commitment • Leadership development	• Balanced scorecard data • Added value ratios (eg added value per employee, added value per £ of employment cost) • Productivity ratios (eg sales revenue per employee, units produced or serviced per employee) • Outcomes of general employee opinion survey and other surveys covering engagement and commitment, leadership, reward management and performance management • Analysis of competence level assessments • Analysis of performance management assessments • Analysis of customer surveys • Analysis of outcomes of total quality programmes • Return on investment from training activities • Internal promotion rate • Succession planning coverage

Developing a human capital management strategy

The programme for introducing human capital management is illustrated in Figure 11.1.

FIGURE 11.1   Developing an HCM strategy

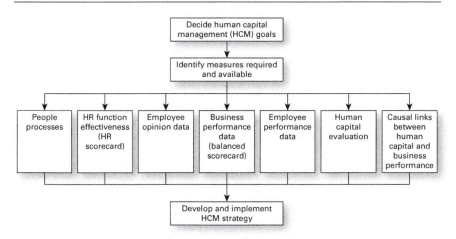

The development programme starts with a definition of the aims of the HCM strategy, for example, to:

- obtain, analyse and report on data that inform the direction of HR strategies and processes;
- inform the development of business strategy;
- use measurements to prove that superior HRM strategies and processes deliver superior results;
- reinforce the belief that HRM strategies and processes create value through people;
- determine the impact of people on business results;
- assess the value of the organization's human capital;
- improve the effectiveness of HR;
- provide data on the performance of the organization's human capital for the Operating and Financial Report;
- demonstrate that HR processes provide value for money.

The programme continues with the identification of possible measures and how they can be used, as set out in Table 11.2.

TABLE 11.2

Possible measures	Possible use – analysis leading to action
Workforce composition – gender, race, age, full-time, part-time	• Analyse the extent of diversity • Assess the implications of a preponderance of employees in different age groups, eg extent of losses through retirement • Assess the extent to which the organization is relying on part-time staff
Length of service distribution	• Indicate level of success in retaining employees • Indicate preponderance of long or short-serving employees • Enable analyses of performance of more experienced employees to be assessed
Skills analysis/assessment – graduates, professionally/ technically qualified, skilled workers	• Assess skill levels against requirements • Indicate where steps have to be taken to deal with shortfalls
Attrition – employee turnover rates for different categories of management and employees	• Indicate areas where steps have to be taken to increase retention rates • Provide a basis for assessing levels of commitment
Attrition – cost of	• Support business case for taking steps to reduce attrition
Absenteeism/sickness rates	• Identify problems and need for more effective attendance management policies
Average number of vacancies as a percentage of total workforce	• Identify potential shortfall problem areas
Total payroll costs (pay and benefits)	• Provide data for productivity analysis

TABLE 11.2 *Continued*

Possible measures	Possible use – analysis leading to action
Compa-ratio – actual rates of pay as a percentage of policy rates	• Enable control to be exercised over management of pay structure
Percentage of employees in different categories of contingent pay or payment-by-result schemes	• Demonstrate the extent to which the organization believes that pay should be related to contribution
Total pay review increases for different categories of employees as a percentage of pay	• Compare actual with budgeted payroll increase costs • Benchmark pay increases
Average bonuses or contingent pay awards as a % of base pay for different categories of managers and employees	• Analyse cost of contingent pay • Compare actual and budgeted increases • Benchmark increases
Outcome of equal pay reviews	• Reveal pay gap between male and female employees
Personal development plans completed as a % of employees	• Indicate level of learning and development activity
Training hours per employee	• Indicate actual amount of training activity (note that this does not reveal the quality of training achieved or its impact)
Percentage of managers taking part in formal management development programmes	• Indicate level of learning and development activity
Internal promotion rate (% of promotions filled from within)	• Indicate extent to which talent management programmes are successful

TABLE 11.2 *Continued*

Possible measures	Possible use – analysis leading to action
Succession planning coverage (% of managerial jobs for which successors have been identified)	• Indicate extent to which talent management programmes are successful
Percentage of employees taking part in formal performance reviews	• Indicate level of performance management activity
Distribution of performance ratings by category of staff and department	• Indicate inconsistencies, questionable distributions and trends in assessments
Accident severity and frequency rates	• Assess health and safety programmes
Cost savings/revenue increases resulting from employee suggestion schemes	• Measure the value created by employees
Measures of impact of HR practices	• Evaluation of effectiveness

The analysis of possible measures leads to the development of a strategy for introducing and using them. It is often best to start with information that is readily available and extend the range of data as experience is gained. And it is important to remember that it is the quality of the information that counts, not the quantity.

KEY LEARNING POINTS

Human capital management defined

Human capital management (HCM) is concerned with obtaining, analysing and reporting on data that informs the direction of value-adding people management. HCM involves the systematic analysis, measurement and evaluation of how people policies and practices create value.

Objectives of human capital management

The four fundamental objectives of HCM are:

1 to determine the impact of people on the business and their contribution to value;

2 to demonstrate that HR practices produce value for money in terms, for example, of return on investment;

3 to provide guidance on future HR and business strategies;

4 to provide data that will inform strategies and practices designed to improve the effectiveness of people management in the organization.

By developing strategies to generate better and more accurate information on human capital, and communicating this information both internally and externally, organizations will not only improve their business decision making but also enable stakeholders to make more accurate assessments about the long-term future performance of the organization.

Human capital management strategy

A human capital management strategy that includes the systematic collection and analysis of human capital data can help managers to begin to understand factors that will have a direct impact on the people they manage. HCM assessments of the impact of HR practices on performance can be used to justify these practices and improve the likelihood that they will work.

Developing a human capital management strategy

The development programme starts with a definition of the aims of the HCM strategy, for example, to:

- obtain, analyse and report on data that inform the direction of HR strategies and processes;
- inform the development of business strategy;
- use measurements to prove that superior HRM strategies and processes deliver superior results;
- reinforce the belief that HRM strategies and processes create value through people;
- determine the impact of people on business results;
- assess the value of the organization's human capital;
- improve the effectiveness of HR;
- provide data on the performance of the organization's human capital for the Operating and Financial Report;
- demonstrate that HR processes provide value for money.

The programme continues with the identification of possible measures and how they can be used. The analysis of possible measures leads to the development of a strategy for introducing and using them. It is often best to start with information that is readily available and extend the range of data as experience is gained.

References

Accounting for People Task Force (2003) *Accounting for People*, DTI, London
Chatzkel, J L (2004) Human capital: the rules of engagement are changing, *Lifelong Learning in Europe*, 9 (3), pp 139–45
Donkin, R (2005) *Human Capital Management: A management report*, Croner, London
Kearns, P (2004) *Human Capital Management*, Personnel Today, London
Manocha, R (2005) Grand totals, *People Management*, 7 April, pp 27–31
Nalbantian, R et al (2004) *Play to Your Strengths: Managing your internal labour markets for lasting competitive advantage*, McGraw-Hill, New York
Scarborough, H and Elias, J (2002) *Evaluating Human Capital*, CIPD, London

Corporate social responsibility strategy

Introduction

Corporate social responsibility (CSR) strategy is concerned with planning how to ensure that the organization conducts its business in an ethical way, taking account of the social, environmental and economic impact of its operations and going beyond compliance. As Windsor (2006: 99) commented: 'Ethical managers engage in impartial moral reflection beyond the law'.

Wood (1991: 695) reflected that: 'The basic idea of corporate social responsibility is that business and society are interwoven rather than distinct entities; therefore, society has certain expectations for appropriate business behaviour and outcomes'. CSR, as explained in this chapter, is largely a strategic matter that impinges strongly on the behaviour of organizations as it affects their stakeholders. Strategic HRM has an important contribution to make.

Corporate social responsibility defined

As defined by McWilliams et al (2006: 1), CSR refers to the actions taken by businesses 'that further some social good beyond the interests of the firm and that which is required by law'. CSR has also been described by Husted and Salazar (2006) as being concerned with 'the impact of business behaviour on society'. Porter and Kramer (2006: 83) argued that to advance CSR: '... we must root it in a broad understanding of the interrelationship between a corporation and society while at the same time anchoring it in the strategies and activities of specific companies'. They see CSR as a process of integrating business and society.

The rationale for CSR

The philosophy of CSR is largely based on stakeholder theory, which was originated by Freeman (1984). This proposes that managers should tailor their policies to satisfy a number of constituents, not just shareholders. Stakeholding is based on the idea that a company is responsible not just to its shareholders but to a plurality of groups. The inclusion of such groups assumes that they all have an interest in the operation of the company. Investors, employees, suppliers and customers come into this category.

The rationale for CSR as defined by Hillman and Keim (2001) is based on two propositions: first, there is a moral imperative for businesses to 'do the right thing' without regard to how such decisions affect firm performance (the social issues argument); and second, firms can achieve competitive advantage (achieving and sustaining better results than business rivals thus placing the firm in a competitive position) by tying CSR activities to primary stakeholders (the stakeholders argument). Their research in 500 firms implied that investing in stakeholder management may be complementary to shareholder value creation and could indeed provide a basis for competitive advantage, as important resources and capabilities are created that differentiate a firm from its competitors (the resource-based view). The arguments identified by Porter and Kramer (2006) that support CSR are:

1 The moral appeal – the argument that companies have a duty to be good citizens.

2 Sustainability – an emphasis on environmental and community stewardship. As expressed by the World Business Council for Sustainable Social Development (2006: 1), this involves 'meeting the needs of the present without compromising the ability of future generations to meet their own needs'.

3 Licence to operate – every company needs tacit or explicit permission from government, communities and other stakeholders to do business.

4 Reputation – CSR initiatives can be justified because they improve a company's image, strengthen its brand, enliven morale and even raise the value of its stock.

Much research has been conducted on the relationship between CSR and firm performance. Russo and Fouts (1997) found that there was a positive relationship with environmental performance and Waddock and Graves (1997) established that CSR results in an improvement in firm performance. But McWilliams and Siegel (2000) discovered only a neutral relationship between CSR and profitability.

The opposing view was expressed forcibly by Theodore Levitt, marketing expert. In a *Harvard Business Review* article, 'The dangers of social responsibility' (Levitt, 1958: 44), he emphasized that: 'The essence of free market enterprise is to go after profit in any way that is consistent with its own survival as an economic system'. Milton Friedman (1970), the Chicago monetarist, expressed the same sentiment. His view was that the social responsibility of business is to maximize profits within the bounds of the law. He argued that the mere existence of CSR was an agency problem within the firm in that it was a misuse of the resources entrusted to managers by owners, which could be better used on value-added internal projects or returned to the shareholders.

But it can be argued, as do Moran and Ghoshal (1996), that what is good for society does not necessarily have to be bad for the firm, and what is good for the firm does not necessarily have to come at a cost to society. This notion may support a slightly cynical view that there is room for enlightened self-interest that involves doing well by doing good.

Strategic CSR defined

CSR can be an integral element of a firm's business and corporate-level differentiation strategies. Therefore, it should be considered as a form of strategic investment. Even when it is not directly tied to a product feature or production process, CSR can be viewed as a form of reputation building or maintenance. Baron (2001) pointed out that CSR is what a firm does when its business and marketing strategy is concerned with the public good. And Husted and Salazar (2006: 83) commented that: 'There are additional benefits that the firm extracts from a given level of social output... precisely because the firm has designed a strategy so as to appropriate such benefits'.

Strategic CSR is about deciding initially whether or not the firm should be involved in social issues and then creating a corporate social agenda – deciding what social issues to focus on and to what extent. Porter and Kramer (2006: 85) believe that: 'It is through strategic CSR that the company will make the greatest social impact and reap the greatest business benefits'. They also stress that: 'Strategy is always about making choices, and success in corporate social responsibility is no different. It is about choosing which social issues to focus on... organizations that make the right choices and build focused, proactive and integrated social initiatives in concert with their core strategies will increasingly distance themselves from the pack' (ibid: 91). McWilliams and Siegel (2000) suggest that CSR activities should be included in strategy formulation and that the level of resources devoted to CSR should be determined through cost/benefit analysis.

CSR strategy needs to be integrated with the business strategy but it is also closely associated with HR strategy. This is because it is concerned with ethical behaviour both outside and within the firm – with society generally and with the internal community. In the latter case this means creating a working environment where personal and employment rights are upheld and HR policies and practices provide for the fair and ethical treatment of employees.

CSR activities

CSR activities as listed by McWilliams et al (2006) include incorporating social characteristics or features into products and manufacturing processes, adopting progressive human resource management practices, achieving higher levels of environmental performance through recycling and pollution abatement, and advancing the goals of community organizations.

Business in the Community (2007) surveyed the CSR activities of 120 leading British companies and summarized them under four headings:

1 Community – skills and education, employability and social exclusion were frequently identified as key risks and opportunities. Other major activities were support for local community initiatives and being a responsible and safe neighbour.

2 Environment – most companies reported climate change and resource-use as key issues for their business. Eighty-five

per cent of them managed their impacts through an environmental management system.

3 Marketplace – the issues most frequently mentioned by companies were research and development, procurement and supply chain, responsible selling, responsible marketing, and product safety. There was a rising focus on fair treatment of customers, providing appropriate product information and labelling, and on the impacts of products on customer health.

4 Workplace – this was the strongest management performing area as most companies have established employment management frameworks that can cater for workplace issues as they emerge. Companies recognized the crucial role of employees in achieving responsible business practices. Increasing emphasis was placed on internal communications and training to raise awareness and understanding of why it is relevant to employees and valuable for the business. More attention was being paid to health and well-being issues as well as the traditional safety agenda. More work was being done on diversity, both to ensure the business attracts a diverse workforce and to communicate the business case for diversity internally.

Business in the Community (2007) also reported a growing emphasis on responsible business as a source of competitive advantage as firms move beyond minimizing risk to creating opportunities.

Role of HR

The CIPD (2003: 5) stated that: 'The way a company treats its employees will contribute directly to the picture of a company that is willing to accept its wider responsibilities'. The CIPD (2009: 2) also expressed the view that: 'HR has a key role in making CSR work. CSR without HR runs the risk of being dismissed as PR or shallow "window-dressing". And CSR is an opportunity for HR to demonstrate a strategic focus and act as a business partner.'

The arguments for HR people taking the CSR agenda seriously were summarized by the CIPD (2003, 2009) as follows:

- Companies are increasingly required to take account of the impact of their activities on society.
- The credibility of CSR is dependent on delivery, not on rhetoric, and HR is responsible for many of the key systems and processes (eg recruitment, training and communications) on which effective delivery depends.
- HR people have relevant knowledge and skills in relation to CSR, eg organizational learning and culture change.
- Managing trust and risk raises fundamental issues about how people are managed.

- CSR offers the HR community opportunities to demonstrate its strategic focus.
- The way a company treats its employees, including its practices on diversity, employee representation and development, will contribute to the picture of a company that is willing to accept its wider responsibilities.
- HR already works at communicating and implementing ideas, policies, and cultural and behavioural change across organizations. Its role in influencing attitudes and links with line managers and the top team mean it is ideally placed to do the same with CSR.

Developing a CSR strategy

The basis for developing a CSR strategy is provided by the *Competency Framework* of the CSR Academy (2006), which is made up of six characteristics:

1 Understanding society – understanding how the business operates in the broader context and knowing the social and environmental impacts that the business has on society.

2 Building capacity – building the capacity of others to help manage the business effectively. For example, suppliers understand the business's approach to the environment and employees can apply social and environmental concerns in their day-to-day roles.

3 Questioning business as usual – individuals continually questioning the business in relation to a more sustainable future and being open to improving the quality of life and the environment.

4 Stakeholder relations – understanding who the key stakeholders are and the risks and opportunities they present. Working with them through consultation and taking their views into account.

5 Strategic view – ensuring that social and environmental views are included in the business strategy, such that they are integral to the way the business operates.

6 Harnessing diversity – respecting the fact that people are different, which is reflected in fair and transparent business practices.

To develop and implement a CSR strategy based on these principles it is necessary to:

- understand the business and social environment in which the firm operates;
- understand the business and HR strategies and how the CSR strategy should be aligned to them;

- know who the stakeholders are (including top management) and find out their views and expectations on CSR;
- identify the areas in which CSR activities might take place by reference to their relevance in the business context of the organization and an evaluation of their significance to stakeholders;
- prioritize as necessary on the basis of an assessment of the relevance and significance of CSR to the organization and its stakeholders and the practicalities of introducing the activity or practice;
- draw up the strategy and make the case for it to top management and the stakeholders;
- obtain approval for the CSR strategy from top management and key stakeholders;
- communicate information on the whys and wherefores of the strategy comprehensively and regularly;
- provide training to employees on the skills they need to use in implementing the CSR strategy;
- measure and evaluate the effectiveness of CSR.

KEY LEARNING POINTS

Corporate social responsibility (CSR) strategy defined

CSR strategy is concerned with planning how to ensure that the organization conducts its business in an ethical way, taking account of the social, environmental and economic impact of how it operates and going beyond compliance.

Rationale for CSR

The philosophy of CSR is largely based on stakeholder theory, which was originated by Freeman (1984). This states that managers should tailor their policies to satisfy a number of constituents, not just shareholders.

The rationale for CSR as defined by Hillman and Keim (2001) is based on two propositions. First, there is a moral imperative for businesses to 'do the right thing' without regard to how such decisions affect firm performance (the social issues argument), and second, firms can achieve competitive advantage by tying CSR activities to primary stakeholders (the stakeholders argument).

Strategic CSR

CSR can be an integral element of a firm's business and corporate-level differentiation strategies. Therefore, it should be considered as a form of strategic investment. McWilliams and Siegel (2000) suggest that CSR activities be included in strategy formulation and that the level of resources devoted to CSR be determined through cost/benefit analysis.

CSR activities

CSR activities as listed by McWilliams et al (2006) include incorporating social characteristics or features into products and manufacturing processes, adopting progressive human resource management practices, achieving higher levels of environmental performance through recycling and pollution abatement, and advancing the goals of community organizations.

The role of HR

'The way a company treats its employees will contribute directly to the picture of a company that is willing to accept its wider responsibilities' (CIPD, 2003). 'HR has a key role in making CSR work' (CIPD, 2009: 2).

Developing CSR strategy

To develop and implement a CSR strategy it is necessary to:

- understand the business and social environment in which the firm operates;
- understand the business and HR strategies and how the CSR strategy should be aligned to them;
- know who the stakeholders are (including top management) and find out their views and expectations on CSR;
- identify the areas in which CSR activities might take place by reference to their relevance in the business context of the organization and an evaluation of their significance to stakeholders;
- prioritize as necessary on the basis of an assessment of the relevance and significance of CSR to the organization and its stakeholders and the practicalities of introducing the activity or practice;
- draw up the strategy and make the case for it to top management and the stakeholders;
- obtain approval for the CSR strategy from top management and key stakeholders;
- communicate information on the whys and wherefores of the strategy comprehensively and regularly;
- provide training to employees on the skills they need to use in implementing the CSR strategy;
- measure and evaluate the effectiveness of CSR.

References

Baron, D (2001) Private policies, corporate policies and integrated strategy, *Journal of Economics and Management Strategy*, **10** (1), pp 7–45

Business in the Community (2007) *Benchmarking Responsible Business Practice*, available online at bits.org.uk

Chartered Institute of Personnel and Development (2003) *Corporate Social Responsibility and HR's Role*, CIPD, London

Chartered Institute of Personnel and Development (2009) *Corporate Social Responsibility*, CIPD, London

CSR Academy (2006) *The CSR Competency Framework*, Stationery Office, Norwich

Freeman, R E (1984) *Strategic Management: A stakeholder perspective*, Prentice Hall, Englewood Cliffs, New Jersey

Friedman, M (1970) The social responsibility of business is to increase its profits, *New York Times Magazine*, September, p 13

Hillman, A and Keim, G (2001) Shareholder value, stakeholder management and social issues: what's the bottom line? *Strategic Management Journal*, **22** (2), pp 125–39

Husted, B W and Salazar, J (2006) Taking Friedman seriously: maximizing profits and social performance, *Journal of Management Studies*, **43** (1), pp 75–91

Levitt, T (1958) The dangers of social responsibility, *Harvard Business Review*, September/October, pp 41–50

McWilliams, A and Siegel, D (2000) Corporate social responsibility: a theory of the firm perspective, *Academy of Management Review*, **26** (1), pp 117–27

McWilliams, A, Siegel, D S and Wright, P M (2006) Corporate social responsibility: strategic implications, *Journal of Management Studies*, **43** (1), pp 1–12

Moran, P and Ghoshal, S (1996) Value creation by firms, *Best Paper Proceedings*, Academy of Management Annual Meeting, Cincinnati, Ohio

Porter, M E and Kramer, M R (2006) Strategy and society: the link between competitive advantage and corporate social responsibility, *Harvard Business Review*, December, pp 78–92

Russo, M V and Fouts, P A (1997) A resource-based perspective on corporate environmental performance and profitability, *Academy of Management Review*, **40** (3), pp 534–59

Waddock, S A and Graves, S B (1997) The corporate social performance – financial performance link, *Strategic Management Journal*, **18** (4), pp 303–19

Windsor, D (2006) Corporate social responsibility: three key approaches, *Journal of Management Studies*, **43** (1), pp 93–114

Wood, D J (1991) Corporate social performance revisited, *Academy of Management Review*, **16** (4), 691–718

World Business Council for Sustainable Social Development (2006) *From Challenge to Opportunity: The role of business in tomorrow's society*, WBCSSD, Geneva

13 Organization development strategy

KEY CONCEPTS AND TERMS

Action research
Behavioural science
Change management
Force-field analysis
Group dynamics
Interventions

Organizational/corporate culture
Organizational transformation
Organization capability
Organization development
Process consultation
Survey feedback

LEARNING OUTCOMES

On completing this chapter you should be able to define the key concepts above. You should also understand:

- how organization development got to where it is;
- how organization development is applied as a strategic process.

Introduction

Organization development in its traditional form as 'OD' was defined by Rowlandson (1984: 90) as 'an intervention strategy that uses group processes to focus on the whole culture of an organization in order to bring about planned change'. More recently, the CIPD (2010: 1) defined it broadly as a 'planned and systematic approach to enabling sustained organization performance through the involvement of its people'. In its original form as

'OD' it was based on behavioural science concepts, ie the field of enquiry dedicated to the study of human behaviour through sophisticated and rigorous methods. However, during the 1980s and 1990s a number of other approaches were introduced, and further changes occurred in the following decade, although the behavioural sciences still play an important part in OD 'interventions' (in OD jargon, interventions are planned activities designed to improve organizational effectiveness or manage change). It was these changes that led to the broader definition produced by the CIPD.

OD used to be the province of specialized consultants, with HR playing a supporting role if it played any role at all. But *HR Magazine* (2007) spelt out the close relationship between HR and organization development as follows:

SOURCE REVIEW HR and organization development
– *HR Magazine* (2007: 1)

To remain competitive in today's global marketplace, organizations must change. One of the most effective tools to promote successful change is organization development (OD). As HR increasingly focuses on building organizational learning, skills and workforce productivity, the effective use of OD to help achieve company business goals and strategies is becoming a broad HR competency as well as a key strategic HR tool. While there are variations regarding the definition of OD, the basic purpose of organization development is to increase an organization's effectiveness through planned interventions related to the organization's processes (often company-wide), resulting in improvements in productivity, return on investment and employee satisfaction.

The CIPD (2010: 3) stated that: 'We place considerable importance on OD, seeing it as one of the ten professional areas within the HR profession map which emphasizes its importance as a HR skill'. The CIPD also commented that:

> OD is not a new discipline and has always had a focus on people but has only relatively recently become considered as a mainstream discipline of HR. Supporters of OD argue that its strength is its ability to understand the whole organization and as such it may be inhibiting to root it too firmly in the HR function. However, given the increasing need for the HR profession to act as a business partner, OD and its methods have a part to play in developing HR's strategic role and its involvement in organizational change, organizational culture and employee engagement (ibid: 3).

The strategic nature of organization development as an integral part of HRM arises because it can play a significant role in the implementation of business strategy. For example, business model innovation as a strategy could result in the need for new organization structures and processes. This would involve organization development and change management activities. The aim of this chapter is to explain the strategic purpose of organization development in the light of an analysis of the history of the concept and how it can be applied as part of a strategic HRM approach.

The story of organization development

There are three chapters in the story of organization development: the original version of the 1960s and 1970s, the extensions and modifications to the original approach in the 1980s and 1990s, and the new look at organization development of the 2000s.

The first chapter – the original version

Organization development emerged as the 'OD' movement in the 1960s. It was based on the strong humanistic values of its early founders, who wanted to improve the conditions of people's lives in organizations by applying behavioural science knowledge. Its origins can be traced to the writings of behavioural scientists such as Lewin (1947, 1951) on group dynamics (the improvement of group processes through various forms of training, eg teambuilding, interactive skills training or T-groups) and change management. Other behavioural scientists included Maslow (1954), who produced his needs theory of motivation, Herzberg (Herzberg et al, 1957), who wrote about the motivation to work, and Argyris (1957), who emphasized the need to plan for integration and involvement. McGregor (1960) produced his 'Theory Y', which advocated the recognition of the needs of both the organization and the individual on the basis that given the chance, people will not only accept but seek responsibility. Likert (1961) added his theory of supportive relationships.

The two founders of the organization development movement were Beckhard (1969), who probably coined the term, and Bennis (1969) who, according to Buchanan and Huczynski (2007: 575) described OD as a 'truth, trust, love and collaboration approach'. Ruona and Gibson (2004: 53) explained that: '... early OD interventions can be categorized as primarily focusing on individuals and interpersonal relations. OD was established as a social philosophy that emphasized a long-term orientation, the applied behavioural sciences, external and process-oriented consultation, change managed from the top, a strong emphasis on action research and a focus on creating change in collaboration with managers.'

The assumptions and values of OD

The assumptions and values of OD as originally conceived were that:

- Most individuals are driven by the need for personal growth and development as long as their environment is both supportive and challenging.

- The work team, especially at the informal level, has great significance for feelings of satisfaction and the dynamics of such teams have a powerful effect on the behaviour of their members.

- OD programmes aim to improve the quality of working life of all members of the organization.

- Organizations can be more effective if they learn to diagnose their own strengths and weaknesses.

- Managers often do not know what is wrong and need special help in diagnosing problems, although the outside 'process consultant' ensures that decision making remains in the hands of the client.

The OD toolkit

OD during this time was practised predominantly by external consultants working with senior managers. Personnel specialists were not involved to any great extent. OD programmes consisted then of 'interventions' such as those listed below. These often feature in current programmes.

- Process consultation – helping clients to generate and analyse information that they can understand and, following a thorough diagnosis, act upon. The information will relate to organizational processes such as intergroup relations, interpersonal relations and communications.

- Change management – often using the techniques advocated by Lewin (1951), which consisted of processes of managing change by unfreezing, changing and freezing, and force-field analysis (analysing and dealing with the driving forces that affect transition to a future state).

- Action research – collecting data from people about process issues and feeding it back in order to identify problems and their likely causes. This can then be used as a basis for an action plan to deal with the problem.

- Survey feedback – a variety of action research in which data is systematically collected about the system through attitude surveys and workshops, leading to action plans.

- Personal interventions – developing interpersonal skills through such processes as T-groups, transactional analysis, behaviour modelling and, a later method, neuro-linguistic programming (NLP).

The second chapter – criticisms of the original version of OD and new approaches

The OD movement as originally conceived and practised was characterized by what Buchanan and Huczynski (2007: 559) called 'quasi-religious values', with some of the features of a religious movement. This, they claim, is one reason why it has survived as a concept in spite of the criticisms that began to be levelled at it in the 1980s. Weidner (2004: 39) wrote that: 'OD was something that practitioners felt and lived as much as they *believed*' (original emphasis).

One of the earliest critics was McLean (1981: 13), who asserted that:

> It is becoming increasingly apparent that there exists a considerable discrepancy between OD as practiced and the prescriptive stances taken by many OD writers... The theory of change and change management which is the foundation of most OD programmes is based on over-simplistic generalizations which offer little specific guidance to practitioners faced with the confusing complexity of a real change situation.

Armstrong (1984: 113) commented that: 'Organization development has lost a degree of credibility in recent years because the messianic zeal displayed by some practitioners has been at variance with the circumstances and real needs of the organization'. Burke (1995: 8) stated that 'in the mid-1970s, OD was still associated with T-groups, participative management and consensus, Theory Y, and self-actualization – the soft, human, touchy-feely kinds of activities'.

An even more powerful critic was Karen Legge (1995: 212) who commented that the OD rhetoric fitted the era of 'flower power' and that: 'OD was seen on the one hand as a form of devious manipulation, and on the other as "wishy-washy" and ineffectual'. She noted 'the relative lack of success of OD initiatives in effecting major and lasting cultural change, with the aim of generating commitment to new values in the relatively small number of organizations in which it was tried' (ibid: 213) and produced the following devastating critique.

SOURCE REVIEW   A critique of organization development –
Legge (1995: 213)

In order to cope with an increasingly complex and changing environment, many of the initiatives were, in retrospect, surprisingly inward looking, involving schemes of management development, work system design, attempts at participation, almost as a good in their own right, without close attention as to how they were to deliver against market-driven organizational success criteria. The long-term nature of OD activities, together with difficulties in clearly establishing to sceptics their contribution to organizational success criteria (and within a UK culture of financial short-termism) rendered the initiatives at best marginal... and at worst to be treated with a cynical contempt.

The main criticisms of OD as noted by Marsh et al (2010: 143) were that it was: 'Orientated to process and tools rather than results... where techniques are considered to be ends in themselves rather than a means to deliver organizational performance'. However, during the 1980s and 1990s, attention was drawn to the concept of organizational or corporate culture – the pattern of values, norms, beliefs, attitudes and assumptions that may not have been articulated but that shape the ways in which people in organizations behave and get things done. This led to culture management, which aimed to achieve cultural change as a means of enhancing organizational capability. Culture change or management programmes start with an analysis of the existing culture, which may involve the use of a diagnostic such as the Organizational Culture Inventory devised by Cooke and Lafferty (1989). The desired culture is then defined – one that enables the organization to function effectively and achieve its strategic objectives. As a result, a 'culture gap' is identified that needs to be filled. This analysis of culture identifies behavioural expectations so that HR processes can be used to develop and reinforce them. This sounds easier than it really is. Culture is a complex notion that is often hard to define, and it is usually strongly embedded and therefore difficult to change. Culture management became a process in its own right but OD consultants also jumped on the bandwagon.

Other movements in this period that could be described as organization development activities (but again can exist as distinct entities) included total quality management (TQM) and quality circles. TQM aims to ensure that all activities within an organization happen in the way they have been planned in order to meet the defined needs of customers. Its approach is holistic – quality management is not a separate function to be treated in isolation, but is an integral part of all operations. Quality circles are groups of volunteers engaged in related work who meet regularly to discuss and propose ways of improving working methods under a trained leader.

Another approach more closely related to OD that emerged at this time was organizational transformation. This was defined by Cummins and Worley (2005: 752) as: 'A process of radically altering the organization's strategic direction, including fundamental changes in structures, processes and behaviours'.

Other holistic approaches to improving organizational capability that emerged in this period, which were not part of what was conventionally known as OD, included high performance working, high commitment management and high involvement management. This was also the time when performance management systems came to the fore. The further development of these systems in the 2000s led to a radically changed view on what constituted organization development.

The third chapter – changing the focus

The most significant change in the 2000s was the shift to a strategic perspective. As noted by Cummins and Worley (2005: 12), 'Change agents have proposed a variety of large-scale or strategic-change models; each of these models recognizes that strategic change involves multiple levels of the organization and a change in its culture, is driven from the top by powerful executives, and has important effects on performance'. They also commented that the practice of organization development therefore went far beyond its humanistic origins.

There was also an increasing emphasis on associating organization design and organization development. Marsh et al (2010) proposed that organization design and organization development need to be merged into one HR capability, with organization design taking precedence. They considered that this should all be brought in-house as a necessary part of the business model innovation process. But as they commented: 'We do not believe that the field of organization development has passed its sell-by date. Far from it. It just needs to be repositioned as a HR capability' (ibid: 143). However, Weidner (2004: 37) made the following more pessimistic comment in the *Organization Development Journal* about OD: 'Unfortunately, after sixty years – despite the best efforts and intentions of many talented people – OD finds itself increasingly at the margins of business, academe, and practice. The field continues to affirm its values, yet has no identifiable voice.' OD 'interventions' still have a role to play in improving performance, but as part of an integrated business and HR strategy planned and implemented by HR in conjunction with senior management, with or without outside help.

Organization development strategy

Organization development strategy is based on the aspiration to improve organizational capability, which is broadly the capacity of an organization to function effectively in order to achieve desired results. It has been defined more specifically by Ulrich and Lake (1990: 40) as 'the ability to manage people for competitive advantage'. It is concerned with mapping out intentions on how the organization should be structured to meet new demands, on system-wide change in fields such as reward and performance management, on how change should be managed, on what needs to be done to improve organizational processes involving people such as teamwork, communications and participation, and on how the organization can acquire, retain, develop and engage the talent it needs. These intentions will be converted into actions on structure design, systems development and, possibly, OD-type interventions.

The process of integrated strategic change as conceived by Worley et al (1996) can be used to formulate and implement organization development strategies. The steps required are:

1 Strategic analysis – a review of the organization's strategic orientation (its strategic intentions within its competitive environment) and a diagnosis of the organization's readiness for change.

2 Develop strategic capability – the ability to implement the strategic plan quickly and effectively.

3 Integrate individuals and groups throughout the organization into the processes of analysis, planning and implementation to maintain the firm's strategic focus, direct attention and resources to the organization's key competencies, improve coordination and integration within the organization, and create higher levels of shared ownership and commitment.

4 Create the strategy, gain commitment and support for it and plan its implementation.

5 Implement the strategic change plan, drawing on knowledge of motivation, group dynamics and change processes, dealing with issues such as alignment, adaptability, teamwork and organizational and individual learning.

6 Allocate resources, provide feedback and solve problems as they arise.

KEY LEARNING POINTS

Organization development defined

Organization development in its traditional form as 'OD' was defined by Rowlandson (1984: 90) as 'an intervention strategy that uses group processes to focus on the whole culture of an organization in order to bring about planned change'. The CIPD (2010: 1) defined organization development as a 'planned and systematic approach to enabling sustained organization performance through the involvement of its people'.

Strategic nature of organization development

The strategic nature of organization development as an integral part of HRM arises because it can play a significant role in the implementation of business strategy.

Assumptions and values of OD

The assumptions and values of OD as originally conceived were that:

● Most individuals are driven by the need for personal growth and development as long as their environment is both supportive and challenging.

- The work team, especially at the informal level, has great significance for feelings of satisfaction, and the dynamics of such teams have a powerful effect on the behaviour of their members.
- OD programmes aim to improve the quality of working life of all members of the organization.
- Organizations can be more effective if they learn to diagnose their own strengths and weaknesses.
- Managers often do not know what is wrong and need special help in diagnosing problems, although the outside 'process consultant' ensures that decision making remains in the hands of the client.

OD interventions

OD interventions include process consultation, change management, action research and survey feedback.

Criticisms of OD

The main criticisms of OD as noted by Marsh et al (2010: 143) were that it was: 'Orientated to process and tools rather than results... where techniques are considered to be ends in themselves rather than a means to deliver organizational performance'.

Organization development strategy

Organization development strategy is based on the aspiration to improve organizational capability, which is broadly the capacity of an organization to function effectively in order to achieve desired results.

References

Argyris, C (1957) *Personality and Organization*, Harper & Row, New York

Armstrong, M (1984) *A Handbook of Personnel Management Practice*, 2nd edn, Kogan Page, London

Beckhard, R (1969) *Organization Development: Strategy and models*, Addison-Wesley, Reading, MA

Bennis, W G (1969) *Organization Development: Its nature, origin and prospects*, Addison-Wesley, Reading, MA

Buchanan, D and Huczynski, A (2007) *Organizational Behaviour*, FT Prentice-Hall, Harlow

Burke, W W (1995) Organization development: then, now and tomorrow, *Organization Development Journal*, **13** (4), pp 7–17

Chartered Institute of Personnel and Development (2010) *Organization Development Fact Sheet*, CIPD, London

Cooke, R and Lafferty, J (1989) *Organizational Culture Inventory*, Human Synergistic, Plymouth, MI

Cummins, T G and Worley, C G (2005) *Organization Development and Change*, South Western, Mason, Ohio

Herzberg, F, Mausner, B and Snyderman, B (1957) *The Motivation to Work*, Wiley, New York

HR Magazine (2007) Organization development: a strategic HR tool, *HR Magazine*, **52** (9), pp 1–10

Legge, K (1995) *Human Resource Management: Rhetorics and realities*, Macmillan, London

Lewin, K (1947) Frontiers in group dynamics, *Human Relations*, **1** (1), pp 5–42

Lewin, K (1951) *Field Theory in Social Science*, Harper & Row, New York

Likert, R (1961) *New Patterns of Management*, Harper & Row, New York

Marsh, C, Sparrow, P and Hird, M (2010) Improving organization design: the new priority for HR directors, in *Leading HR*, (eds) P Sparrow, A Hesketh, M Hird and C Cooper, pp 136–61, Palgrave Macmillan, Basingstoke

Maslow, A (1954) *Motivation and Personality*, Harper & Row, New York

McGregor, D (1960) *The Human Side of Enterprise*, McGraw-Hill, New York

McLean, A (1981) Organization development: a case of the emperor's new clothes? *Personnel Review*, **10** (1), pp 3–14

Rowlandson, P (1984) The oddity of OD, *Management Today*, November, pp 91–93

Ruona, W E A and Gibson, S K (2004) The making of twenty-first century HR: the convergence of HRM, HRD and OD, *Human Resource Management*, **43** (1), pp 49–66

Ulrich, D and Lake, D (1990) *Organizational Capability: Competing from the inside out*, Wiley, New York

Weidner, C K (2004) A brand in dire straits: organization development at sixty, *Organization Development Journal*, **22** (2), pp 37–47

Worley, C, Hitchin, D and Ross, W (1996) *Integrated Strategic Change: How organization development builds competitive advantage*, Addison-Wesley, Reading, MA

Engagement strategy

Introduction

Engagement happens when people are committed to their work and the organization and are motivated to achieve high levels of performance. Engaged people at work are positive, interested in, and even excited about their jobs and are prepared to put discretionary effort into their work beyond the minimum to get it done. As Macey et al (2009: 6) put it, in an engaged workforce 'employees will think and act proactively: engaged employees anticipate opportunities to take action – and actually do take action – in ways that are aligned with organizational goals'.

Engagement defined

The concept of engagement was defined by Gallup (2009) as: 'The individual's involvement and satisfaction with, as well as enthusiasm for, work'. Balain and Sparrow (2009) noted that a number of other well-known applied research and consultancy organizations have defined engagement on similar lines, often emphasizing the importance of discretionary effort as the key outcome or distinguishing feature of an engaged employee. MacLeod and Clarke (2009: 9) defined engagement generally as 'a workplace approach designed to ensure that employees are committed to their organization's goals and values, motivated to contribute to organizational success, and are able at the same time to enhance their own sense of well-being'. Reilly and Brown (2008) commented that the terms job satisfaction, motivation and commitment are generally being replaced now in business by engagement, because it appears to have more descriptive force and face validity.

A comprehensive analysis of the concept of engagement was made by Balain and Sparrow (2009: 17). They concluded that: 'To understand what really causes engagement, and what it causes in turn, we need to embed the idea in a well-founded theory. The one that is considered most appropriate is social exchange theory, which sees feelings of loyalty, commitment, and discretionary effort as all being forms of social reciprocation by employees to a good employer. This work separates out job engagement from organizational engagement'. Following Saks (2006) they summarized the main causes, types and consequences of employee engagement at the individual level as shown in Table 14.1.

How important is engagement?

A considerable amount of research has indicated that higher levels of engagement produce a range of organizational benefits, for example:

- higher productivity/performance – engaged employees perform 20 per cent better than the average (Conference Board, 2006);
- lower staff turnover – engaged employees are 87 per cent less likely to leave (Corporate Leadership Council, 2004);
- better attendance – engaged employees have lower sick leave (CIPD 2007);
- improved safety (Vance, 2006).

TABLE 14.1

Antecedents of engagement	Types of employee engagement	Consequences
• Enriched and challenging jobs (job characteristics) • Quality of the employee-organization relationship (perceived organizational support) • Quality of the employee-supervisor relationship (perceived supervisor support) • Rewards and recognition • Fairness in the processes that allocate resources or resolve disputes (procedural justice) • What is considered just or right in the allocation of goods in a society (distributive justice)	• Job engagement • Organizational engagement	• Job satisfaction • Organizational commitment • Level of intention to quit • Organizational citizenship behaviour

Gallup (2006a) examined 23,910 business units and compared top quartile and bottom quartile financial performance with engagement scores. They found that:

- Those with engagement scores in the bottom quartile averaged 31–51 per cent more employee turnover, 51 per cent more inventory shrinkage, and 62 per cent more accidents.
- Those with engagement scores in the top quartile averaged 12 per cent higher customer advocacy, 18 per cent higher productivity, and 12 per cent higher profitability.

A study by Gallup (2006b) of earnings per share (EPS) growth of 89 organizations found that the EPS growth rate of organizations with engagement scores in the top quartile was 2.6 times that of organizations with below-average engagement scores.

Engagement and discretionary behaviour

There is a close link between high levels of engagement and positive discretionary behaviour. As described by Purcell et al (2003), discretionary behaviour refers to the choices that people at work often have on the way they do the job and the amount of effort, care, innovation and productive behaviour they display. It can be positive when people 'go the extra mile' to achieve high levels of performance. It can be negative when they exercise their discretion to slack at their work. Discretionary behaviour is hard for the employer to define, monitor and control. But positive discretionary behaviour is more likely to happen when people are engaged with their work.

The propositions made by Purcell et al (2003) on discretionary behaviour as a result of their longitudinal research were that:

- Performance-related practices only work if they positively induce discretionary behaviour.

- Discretionary behaviour is more likely to occur when enough individuals have commitment to their organization and/or when they feel motivated and/or when they gain high levels of job satisfaction.

- Commitment, motivation and job satisfaction, either together or separately, will be greater when people positively experience the application of HR policies concerned with creating an able workforce, motivating valued behaviours and providing opportunities to participate.

- This positive experience will be greater if the wide range of HR policies necessary to develop ability, motivation and opportunity are both in place and mutually reinforcing.

- The way HR and reward policies and practices are implemented by front-line managers, and the way top-level espoused values and organizational cultures are enacted by them, will enhance or weaken the effect of HR policies in triggering discretionary behaviour by influencing attitudes.

- The experience of success seen in performance outcomes helps reinforce positive attitudes.

What are the factors that influence employee engagement?

Research cited by IDS (2007) identified two key elements that have to be present if genuine engagement is to exist. The first is the rational aspect, which relates to an employee's understanding of their role, where it fits in the wider organization, and how it aligns with business objectives. The second is the emotional aspect, which has to do with how the person feels about the organization, whether their work gives them a sense of personal accomplishment, and how they relate to their manager. These two overall aspects can be analysed into a number of factors that influence levels of job and organizational engagement as set out below.

The work itself

The work itself can create job satisfaction leading to intrinsic motivation (the self-generated factors affecting people's behaviour, which may arise from the work itself) and increased engagement. The factors involved are interesting and challenging work, responsibility (feeling that the work is important and having control over one's own resources), autonomy (freedom to act), scope to use and develop skills and abilities, the availability of the resources required to carry out the work, and opportunities for advancement.

The work environment

An enabling, supportive and inspirational work environment creates experiences that impact on engagement by influencing how people regard their roles and carry them out. An enabling environment will create the conditions that encourage high performance and effective discretionary behaviour. These include work processes, equipment and facilities, and the physical conditions in which people work. A supportive environment will be one in which proper attention is paid to achieving a satisfactory work–life balance, emotional demands are not excessive, care is taken to provide healthy and safe working conditions, job security is a major consideration, and personal growth needs are taken into consideration. An inspirational environment will be one where there is what Purcell et al (2003: 13) refer to as 'the big idea', which is '... a clear sense of mission underpinned by values, and a culture expressing what the firm is and its relationship with its customers and employees'. The organization has a clear vision and a set of integrated values that are 'embedded, collective, measured and managed'.

The environment is affected by the organization's climate, which consists of the continuing perceptions members of the organization have about its culture and how it affects them. As Purcell (2001) suggests, the way HR practices are experienced by employees is affected by organizational values and operational strategies, such as staffing policies or hours of work, as well as the way they are implemented. He also emphasizes that work climate – the impression made by the organization on people – and the experience of actually doing the job – pace, demand and stress – all influence the way employees experience the work environment. This has an important effect on how they react to HR and reward practices and how these influence organizational outcomes. Employees react in a number of different ways to practices in their organization and this affects the extent to which they want to learn more, are committed and feel satisfied with their jobs. This, in turn, influences engagement – how well they do their jobs and whether they are prepared to contribute discretionary effort.

The quality of leadership and management

The degree to which jobs encourage engagement and positive discretionary behaviour very much depends upon the ways in which job holders are led and managed. Managers and team leaders often have considerable discretion when it comes to how jobs are designed, how they allocate work, and how much they delegate and provide autonomy. They can spell out the significance of the work people do. They can give people the opportunity to achieve and develop, and provide feedback that recognizes their contribution.

Opportunities for personal growth

Most people want to get on. The opportunity to grow and develop is a motivating factor that directly impacts on engagement when it is an intrinsic element of the work.

Opportunities to contribute

Engagement is enhanced if employees have a voice that is listened to. This enables them to feed their ideas and views upwards and feel that they are making a contribution.

Commitment to the organization

The three characteristics of commitment identified by Mowday et al (1982) are:

1 A strong desire to remain a member of the organization.
2 A strong belief in, and acceptance of, the values and goals of the organization.
3 A readiness to exert considerable effort on behalf of the organization.

Kochan and Dyer (1993) indicated that the factors affecting the level of commitment in what they call mutual commitment firms are as follows:

1 Strategic level: supportive business strategies, top management value commitment and effective voice for HR in strategy making and governance.
2 Functional (human resource policy) level: staffing based on employment stabilization, investment in training and development

and contingent compensation that reinforces cooperation, participation and contribution.

3 Workplace level: selection based on high standards, broad task design and teamwork, employee involvement in problem solving and a climate of cooperation and trust.

Purcell et al (2003) identified the following key policy and practice factors influencing levels of commitment:

● received training last year;
● satisfied with career opportunities;
● satisfied with the performance appraisal system;
● thinks managers are good in people management (leadership);
● finds their work challenging;
● thinks their firm helps them achieve a work–life balance;
● satisfied with communication and company performance.

On the basis of his research in flexible production manufacturing plants in the United States, MacDuffie (1995: 201) noted that discretionary effort (one of the first times this phrase was used) on problem solving will only be contributed if workers 'believe that their individual interests are aligned with those of the company, and that the company will make a reciprocal investment in their well-being'.

Following research, it was concluded by Boswell (2006: 1506) that to get employees to contribute effectively: 'The most fruitful efforts are likely to come in the form of directly linking employee behaviours to firm success through performance feedback, goal setting and employee involvement initiatives.'

Strategies for enhancing engagement

When developing engagement strategies the first step is to establish what is happening now and in the light of that determine what should happen in each of the areas described above. This means measuring levels of engagement regularly in order to identify successes and failures and analyse any gaps between what is wanted and what is actually going on. This can be done through published surveys such as those operated by Gallup, which enable benchmarking to take place with the levels of engagement achieved in other organizations. An example of a survey is provided in the SHRM toolkit in Part 4 of this book. Alternatively, organizations can develop their own surveys to suit their circumstances. Engagement strategies can be developed under the headings of the factors affecting engagement set out above.

The work itself

Intrinsic motivation through the work itself, and therefore engagement, depends largely on the way in which work or jobs are designed. Hackman and Oldham (1974) identified the following characteristics of jobs that are motivating:

1 variety;
2 autonomy;
3 required interaction;
4 optional interaction;
5 knowledge and skill required;
6 responsibility.

The work environment

A strategy for increasing engagement through the work environment will be generally concerned with developing a culture that encourages positive attitudes to work, promoting interest and excitement in the jobs people do and reducing stress. Lands' End believes that staff who are enjoying themselves, who are being supported and developed, and who feel fulfilled and respected at work will provide the best service to customers. The thinking behind why the company wants to inspire staff is straightforward – employees' willingness to do that little bit extra arises from their sense of pride in what the organization stands for, ie quality, service and value. It makes the difference between a good experience for customers and a poor one.

The strategy also needs to consider particular aspects of the work environment, especially communications, involvement, work–life balance and working conditions. It can include policies that are concerned with building effective relationships with people in their roles, treating individual employees fairly, recognizing their value, giving them a voice and providing opportunities for growth.

Leadership

The leadership strategy should concentrate on what line managers have to do as leaders in order to play their vital and immediate part in increasing levels of engagement. This will include the implementation of learning programmes that help them to understand how they are expected to act and the skills they need to use. The programmes can include formal training (especially for potential managers or those in their first leadership role) but more impact will be made by 'blending' various learning methods such as e-learning, coaching and mentoring.

It should also be recognized that a performance management process can provide line managers with a useful framework in which they can deploy their skills in improving performance though increased engagement. This applies particularly to the performance management activities of role definition, performance improvement planning, joint involvement in monitoring performance, and feedback. The strategy should therefore include the steps required to make performance management more effective by increasing the commitment of managers to it and developing the skills they require.

Opportunities for personal growth

A strategy for providing development and growth opportunities should be based on the creation of a learning culture. This is one that promotes learning because it is recognized by top management, line managers and employees generally as an essential organizational process to which they are committed and in which they engage continuously. Reynolds (2004: 21) describes a learning culture as a 'growth medium' that will 'encourage employees to commit to a range of positive discretionary behaviours, including learning' and that has the following characteristics: empowerment not supervision; self-managed learning not instruction; and long-term capacity building not short-term fixes. It will encourage discretionary learning, which Sloman (2003) believes takes place when individuals actively seek to acquire the knowledge and skills that promote the organization's objectives.

Specifically, the strategy should define the steps required to ensure that people have the opportunity and are given the encouragement to learn and grow in their roles. This includes the use of policies that focus on role flexibility – giving people the chance to develop their roles by making better and extended use of their talents. This means going beyond talent management for the favoured few and developing the abilities of the core people on whom the organization depends. The philosophy should be that everyone has the ability to succeed, and the aim should be to 'achieve extraordinary results with ordinary people'. It includes using performance management primarily as a developmental process with an emphasis on personal development planning.

The strategy should also cover career development opportunities and how individuals can be given the guidance, support and encouragement they need if they are to fulfil their potential and achieve a successful career with the organization, in tune with their talents and aspirations. Finally, the strategy should include the actions required to provide men and women of promise with a sequence of learning activities and experiences that will equip them for whatever level of responsibility they have the ability to reach.

Opportunities to contribute

Providing people with the opportunity to contribute is not just a matter of setting up formal consultative processes, although they can be important. It is also about creating a work environment that gives people a voice by encouraging them to have their say, and emphasizes as a core value of the organization that management at all levels must be prepared to listen and respond to any contributions their people make.

Organizational engagement and commitment strategy

An organizational engagement and commitment strategy will be concerned with both strategic goals and values. The components of the strategy may include initiatives to increase involvement and 'ownership', communication, leadership development, developing a sense of excitement in the job, and developing various HR policy and practice initiatives designed to enhance the employee value proposition (what the organization has to offer that employees value and that persuades them that it is 'a great place to work'). As explained by Purcell et al (2003: 13), commitment will be increased if the organization's vision and values are 'embedded, collective, measured and managed'.

KEY LEARNING POINTS

Engagement defined

- Engagement happens when people are committed to their work and the organization and motivated to achieve high levels of performance.
- Engaged people at work are positive, interested in, and even excited about their jobs and are prepared to put discretionary effort into their work beyond the minimum to get it done.
- Job engagement can be distinguished from organizational engagement.

Importance of engagement

A considerable amount of research has indicated that higher levels of engagement produce a range of organizational benefits.

Discretionary behaviour

There is a close link between high levels of engagement and positive discretionary behaviour.

Factors affecting engagement

The factors affecting engagement are the work environment, the work itself, the quality of leadership and management, opportunities for personal growth, opportunities to contribute and commitment to the organization.

Developing engagement strategies

When developing engagement strategies the first step is to establish what is happening now, and in the light of that determine what strategies are required. Levels of engagement should be measured regularly in order to identify successes and failures and analyse any gaps between what is wanted and what is actually going on.

References

Balain, S and Sparrow, P (2009) *Engaged to Perform: A new perspective on employee engagement*, Lancaster University Management School, Lancaster

Boswell, W R (2006) Aligning employees with the organization's strategic objectives: out of 'line of sight', out of mind, *The International Journal of Human Resource Management*, **17** (9), pp 1489–511

CIPD (2007) *Working Life: Employee attitudes and engagement*, CIPD, London

Conference Board (2006) *Employee Engagement: A review of current research and its implications*, Conference Board, New York

Corporate Leadership Council (2004) *Driving Performance and Retention Through Employee Engagement*, Corporate Executive Board, Washington DC

Gallup (2006a) *Feeling Good Matters in the Workplace*, Gallup Inc, Washington DC

Gallup (2006b) *Engagement Predicts Earnings per Share*, Gallup Inc, Washington DC

Gallup (2009) *Workplace Audit*, Gallup Inc, Washington DC

Hackman, J R and Oldham, G R (1974) Motivation through the design of work: test of a theory, *Organizational Behaviour and Human Performance*, **16** (2), pp 250–79

IDS (2007) Building an engaged workforce, *HR Studies Update*, IDS, London

Kochan, T A and Dyer, L (1993) Managing transformational change: the role of human resource professionals, *International Journal of Human Resource Management*, **4** (3), pp 569–90

MacDuffie, J P (1995) Human resource bundles and manufacturing performance, *Industrial Relations Review*, **48** (2), pp 199–221

Macey, W H et al (2009) *Employee Engagement*, Wiley-Blackwell, Malden, MA

MacLeod, D and Clarke, N (2009) *Engaging for Success: Enhancing performance through employee engagement*, Department for Innovation, Business and Skills, London

Mowday, R, Porter, L and Steers, R (1982) *Employee-organization Linkages: The psychology of commitment, absenteeism and turnover*, Academic Press, London

Purcell, J (2001) The meaning of strategy in human resource management, in *Human Resource Management: A critical text*, second edition, (ed) J Storey, pp 59–77, Thompson Learning, London

Purcell, J et al (2003) *People and Performance: How people management impacts on organisational performance*, CIPD, London

Reilly, P and Brown, D (2008) Employee engagement: future focus or fashionable fad for reward management? *WorldatWork Journal*, **17** (4), pp 37–49

Reynolds, J (2004) *Helping People Learn*, CIPD, London

Saks, A M (2006) Antecedents and consequences of employee engagement, *Journal of Managerial Psychology*, **21** (6), pp 600–19

Sloman, M (2003) E-learning: stepping up the learning curve, *Impact*, CIPD, January, pp 16–17

Vance, R J (2006) *Effective Practice Guidelines: Employee engagement and commitment*, SHRM Foundation, Alexandria, VA

15

Knowledge management strategy

KEY CONCEPTS AND TERMS

Communities of practice
Explicit knowledge
Knowledge management
Tacit knowledge

LEARNING OUTCOMES

On completing this chapter you should be able to define the key concepts above. You should also understand about:

- the process of knowledge management;
- the sources and types of knowledge;
- the approaches to the development of knowledge management strategies;
- strategic knowledge management issues;
- the components of a knowledge management strategy.

Introduction

Knowledge management involves transforming knowledge resources within organizations by identifying relevant information and then disseminating it so that learning can take place. Knowledge management strategy aims to capture an organization's collective expertise and distribute it to where it can be best used. It ensures that knowledge is shared by linking people with people and by linking them to information so that they learn from documented experiences. This is in accordance with the resource-based view of the firm, which, as argued by Grant (1991), suggests that the source of competitive advantage lies within the firm (ie in its people and their knowledge), not in how it positions itself in the market. A successful company is a knowledge-creating company.

The process of knowledge management

Knowledge management is 'any process or practice of creating, acquiring, capturing, sharing and using knowledge, wherever it resides, to enhance learning and performance in organizations' (Scarborough et al, 1999: 1). They suggest that it focuses on the development of firm-specific knowledge and skills that are the result of organizational learning processes. Knowledge management is concerned with both stocks and flows of knowledge. Stocks include expertise and encoded knowledge in computer systems. Flows represent the ways in which knowledge is transferred from people to people or from people to a knowledge database.

The purpose of knowledge management is to transfer knowledge from those who have it to those who need it in order to improve organizational effectiveness. It is concerned with storing and sharing the wisdom and understanding accumulated in an organization about its processes, techniques and operations. It treats knowledge as a key resource. It can be argued that in the information age, knowledge rather than physical assets or financial resources is the key to competitiveness.

Knowledge management is as much if not more concerned with people and how they acquire, exchange and disseminate knowledge as it is about information technology. That is why it has become an important strategic HRM area. Scarborough et al (1999: 59) believe that HR specialists should have 'the ability to analyse the different types of knowledge deployed by the organization... [and] to relate such knowledge to issues of organizational design, career patterns and employment security'.

The concept of knowledge management is closely associated with intellectual capital theory in that it refers to the notions of human, social and organizational or structural capital. It is also linked to the concepts of organizational learning and the learning organization.

Sources and types of knowledge

Strategies for knowledge management should be founded on an understanding of the sources and types of knowledge to be found in organizations.

Knowledge can be stored in databanks and found in presentations, reports, libraries, policy documents and manuals. It can be moved around the organization through information systems and by traditional methods such as meetings, workshops, courses, 'master classes', written publications, disks and e-mails. The intranet provides an additional and very effective medium for communicating knowledge.

As argued by Nonaka (1991) and Nonaka and Takeuchi (1995), knowledge is either explicit or tacit. Explicit knowledge can be codified – it is recorded and available and is held in databases, in corporate intranets and in intellectual property portfolios. Tacit knowledge exists in people's minds. It is difficult to articulate in writing and is acquired through personal experience. Hansen et al (1999) suggested that it includes scientific or technological expertise, operational know-how, insights about an industry and business judgement. The main challenge in knowledge management is how to turn tacit knowledge into explicit knowledge.

Approaches to the development of knowledge management strategies

Two approaches to knowledge management have been identified by Hansen et al (1999):

1 The codification strategy – knowledge is carefully codified and stored in databases where it can be accessed and used easily by anyone in the organization. Knowledge is explicit and is codified using a 'people-to-document' approach. This strategy is therefore document driven. Knowledge is extracted from the person who developed it, made independent of that person and re-used for various purposes. It will be stored in some form of electronic repository for people to use and this allows many people to search for and retrieve codified knowledge without having to contact the person who originally developed it. This strategy relies largely on information technology to manage databases and also on the use of the intranet.

2 The personalization strategy – knowledge is closely tied to the person who has developed it and is shared mainly through direct person-to-person contacts. This is a 'person-to-person' approach that involves sharing tacit knowledge. The exchange is achieved by creating networks and encouraging face-to-face communication between individuals and teams by means of informal conferences, communities of practice, workshops, brainstorming and one-to-one sessions.

The research conducted by Hansen et al (1999) established that companies that use knowledge effectively pursue one strategy predominantly and use the second strategy to support the first. Those who try to excel at both strategies risk failing at both.

Strategic knowledge management issues

The following need to be addressed in developing knowledge management processes.

The pace of change

How can the strategy ensure that knowledge management processes keep up with the pace of change and identify what knowledge needs to be captured and shared?

Relating knowledge management strategy to business strategy

Hansen et al (1999: 109) contended that it is not knowledge per se but the way it is applied to strategic objectives that is the critical ingredient in competitiveness. 'A company's knowledge management strategy should reflect its competitive strategy: how it creates value for customers, how that value supports an economic model, and how the company's people deliver on the value and the economics.'

Technology and people

Technology is central to organizations adopting a codification strategy. But for those following a broader and potentially more productive personalization strategy, IT assumes more of a supportive role. As Hansen et al (1999: 113) commented: 'In the codification model, managers need to implement a system that is much like a traditional library – it must contain a large cache of documents and include search engines that allow people to find and use the documents they need. In the personalization model, it's more important to have a system that allows people to find other people.'

Scarborough et al (1999: 35) suggested that 'technology should be viewed more as a means of communication and less as a means of storing knowledge'. Knowledge management is more about people than technology. As research by Davenport (1996) established, managers get two-thirds of their information from face-to-face or telephone conversations. There is a limit to how much tacit knowledge can be codified. In organizations relying more on tacit than explicit knowledge, a person-to-person approach works best, and IT can only support this process; it cannot replace it.

The significance of process and social capital and culture

A preoccupation with technology may mean that too little attention is paid to the processes (social, technological and organizational) through which knowledge combines and interacts in different ways (Blackler, 1995). The key process is the interactions between people. This constitutes the social capital of an organization, ie the 'network of relationships [that] constitute a valuable resource for the conduct of social affairs' (Nahpiet and Ghoshal, 1998). Social networks can be particularly important to ensure that knowledge is shared. What is also required is another aspect of social capital, ie trust. People will not be willing to share knowledge with those whom they do not trust.

The culture of the company may inhibit knowledge sharing. The norm may be for people to keep knowledge to themselves as much as they can because 'knowledge is power'. An open culture will encourage people to share their ideas and knowledge.

Components of a knowledge management strategy

A knowledge management strategy could be concerned with organizational people management processes that help to develop an open culture. This will be one in which the values and norms emphasize the importance of sharing knowledge and facilitate knowledge sharing through networks. It might aim to encourage the development of communities of practice, defined by Wenger and Snyder (2000: 139) as 'groups of people informally bound together by shared expertise and a passion for joint enterprise'. The strategy could refer to methods of motivating people to share knowledge and rewarding those who do so. The development of processes of organizational and individual learning including the use of seminars and symposia, which will generate and assist in disseminating knowledge, could also be part of the strategy.

KEY LEARNING POINTS

Knowledge management defined

Knowledge management involves transforming knowledge resources within organizations by identifying relevant information and then disseminating it so that learning can take place. Knowledge management is 'any process or practice of creating, acquiring, capturing, sharing and using knowledge, wherever it resides, to enhance learning and performance in organizations' (Scarborough et al, 1999).

Purpose of knowledge management

The purpose of knowledge management is to transfer knowledge from those who have it to those who need it in order to improve organizational effectiveness. Knowledge can be stored in databanks and found in presentations, reports, libraries, policy documents and manuals. Knowledge is either explicit or tacit.

Knowledge management strategy defined

Knowledge management strategy aims to capture an organization's collective expertise and distribute it to where it can be best used. It ensures that knowledge is shared by linking people with people and by linking them to information so that they learn from documented experiences.

Approaches to knowledge management strategy

Two approaches to knowledge management: the codification strategy and the personalization strategy.

Strategic knowledge management issues

Issues include the pace of change, relating knowledge management strategy to business strategy, technology and people, and the significance of process and social capital and culture.

Components of a knowledge management strategy

A knowledge management strategy could be concerned with organizational people management processes that help to develop an open culture. It might aim to encourage the development of communities of practice.

References

Blackler, F (1995) Knowledge, knowledge work and experience, *Organization Studies*, **16** (6), pp 16–36

Davenport, T H (1996) Why re-engineering failed: the fad that forgot people, *Fast Company, Premier Issue*, pp 70–74

Grant, R M (1991) The resource-based theory of competitive advantage: implications for strategy formation, *California Management Review*, **33** (3), pp 14–35

Hansen, M T, Nohria, N and Tierney, T (1999) What's your strategy for managing knowledge? *Harvard Business Review*, March/April, pp 106–16

Nahpiet, J and Ghoshal, S (1998) Social capital, intellectual capital and the organizational advantage, *Academy of Management Review*, **23** (2), pp 242–66

Nonaka, I (1991) The knowledge creating company, *Harvard Business Review*, Nov/Dec, pp 96–104

Nonaka, I and Takeuchi, H (1995) *The Knowledge Creating Company*, Oxford University Press, New York

Scarborough, H, Swan, J and Preston, J (1999) *Knowledge Management: A literature review*, Institute of Personnel and Development, London

Wenger, E and Snyder, W M (2000) Communities of practice: the organizational frontier, *Harvard Business Review*, January/February, pp 139–45

Resourcing strategy

LEARNING OUTCOMES

On completing this chapter you should be able to define the key concepts above. You should also understand:

- the rationale for strategic resourcing;
- the strategic HRM approach to resourcing;
- the process of integrating business and resourcing strategies;
- the process of bundling resourcing strategies and activities;
- the components of employee resourcing strategy;
- what an employee value proposition does;
- how resource planning works;
- how to plan a retention strategy.

Introduction

Resourcing is what organizations do to ensure they have the people they need. Resourcing strategy is concerned with identifying how many and what sort of people are required and making plans to obtain and retain them and to employ them efficiently. Strategic resourcing is a key part of the strategic human resource management process, which is fundamentally about matching human resources to the strategic and operational needs of the organization and ensuring the full utilization of those resources. It is concerned not only with obtaining and keeping the number and quality of staff required but also with selecting and promoting people who 'fit' the culture and the strategic requirements of the organization.

The rationale for strategic resourcing

A rationale for developing a resourcing strategy flows from the suggestion by Keep (1989: 122) that HRM should make a significant effort towards: '... obtaining the right basic material in the form of a workforce endowed with the appropriate qualities, skills, knowledge and potential for future training. The selection and recruitment of workers best suited to meeting the needs of the organization ought to form a core activity upon which most other HRM policies geared towards development and motivation could be built.'

The concept that the strategic capability of a firm depends on its resource capability in the shape of people (the resource-based view) provides the rationale for resourcing strategy. The aim of this strategy is therefore to ensure that a firm achieves competitive advantage by employing more capable people than its rivals. These people will have a wider and deeper range of skills and will behave in ways that will maximize their contribution. The organization attracts such people by being 'the employer of choice'. It retains them by providing better opportunities and rewards than others and by developing a positive psychological contract that increases commitment and creates mutual trust. Furthermore, the organization deploys its people in ways that maximize the added value they supply.

The strategic HRM approach to resourcing

HRM places emphasis on finding people whose attitudes and behaviour are likely to be congruent with what management believes to be appropriate and conducive to success. In the words of Townley (1989: 92), organizations are concentrating more on 'the attitudinal and behavioural characteristics of employees'. This tendency has its dangers. Innovative and adaptive organizations need non-conformists, even mavericks, who can 'buck the system'. If managers recruit people 'in their own image' there is the risk of staffing the organization with conformist clones and of perpetuating a dysfunctional culture – one that may have been successful in the past but is no longer appropriate in the face of new challenges (as Pascale, 1990, put it: 'nothing fails like success').

The HRM approach to resourcing therefore emphasizes that matching resources to organizational requirements does not simply mean maintaining the status quo and perpetuating a moribund culture. It can and often does mean radical changes in thinking about the skills and behaviours required in the future to achieve sustainable growth and cultural change.

Integrating business and resourcing strategies

The philosophy behind the strategic HRM approach to resourcing is that it is people who implement the strategic plan. As Quinn Mills (1985) expressed it, the process is one of 'planning with people in mind'.

The integration of business and resourcing strategies is based on an understanding of the direction in which the organization is going and the determination of:

- the numbers of people required to meet business needs;
- the skills and behaviour required to support the achievement of business strategies;
- the impact of organizational restructuring as a result of rationalization, decentralization, delayering, acquisitions, mergers, product or market development, or the introduction of new technology – for example, cellular manufacturing;
- plans for changing the culture of the organization in such areas as ability to deliver, performance standards, quality, customer service, teamworking and flexibility, which indicate the need for people with different attitudes, beliefs and personal characteristics.

These factors will be strongly influenced by the type of business strategies adopted by the organization and the sort of business it is in. These may be expressed in such terms as Miles and Snow's (1978) typology of defender, prospector and analyser organizations.

Resourcing strategies exist to provide the people and skills required to support the business strategy, but they should also contribute to the formulation of that strategy. HR directors have an obligation to point out to their colleagues the human resource opportunities and constraints that will affect the achievement of strategic plans. In mergers or acquisitions, for example, the ability of management within the company to handle the new situation and the quality of management in the new business will be important considerations.

Bundling resourcing strategies and activities

Employee resourcing is not just about recruitment and selection. It is concerned with any means available to meet the needs of the firm for certain skills and behaviours. A strategy to enlarge the skill base may start with recruitment and selection but would also extend into learning and development to enhance skills and modify behaviours, and methods of rewarding people for the acquisition of extra skills. Performance management processes can be used to identify development needs (skill and behavioural) and motivate people to make the most effective use of their skills. Competency frameworks and profiles can be prepared to define the skills and behaviours required, and be used in selection, employee development and employee reward processes. The aim should be to develop a reinforcing bundle of strategies along these lines. Talent management is a 'bundling' process, which is an aspect of resourcing.

The components of employee resourcing strategy

The components of employee resourcing strategy as considered in this chapter are:

- Workforce planning – assessing future business needs and deciding on the numbers and types of people required.
- Developing the organization's employee value proposition and its employer brand.
- Resourcing plans – preparing plans for finding people from within the organization and/or for learning and development programmes to help people learn new skills. If needs cannot be satisfied from within the organization, it involves preparing longer-term plans for ensuring that recruitment and selection processes will satisfy them.
- Retention strategy – preparing plans for retaining the people the organization needs.
- Flexibility strategy – planning for increased flexibility in the use of human resources to enable the organization to make the best use of people and adapt swiftly to changing circumstances.
- Talent management strategy – ensuring that the organization has the talented people it requires to provide for management succession and meet present and future business needs (see Chapter 17).

Workforce planning

Workforce planning determines the human resources required by the organization to achieve its strategic goals and prepares and implements programmes for satisfying those requirements. It was defined by the CIPD (2010: 4) as: 'A core process of human resource management that is shaped by the organizational strategy and ensures the right number of people, with the right skills, in the right place and at the right time to deliver short- and long-term organizational objectives'.

Workforce planning (often called human resource planning) is based on the belief that people are an organization's most important strategic resource. It is generally concerned with matching resources to business needs in the longer term, although it will also be concerned with shorter-term requirements. It addresses people needs both in quantitative and qualitative terms. This means answering two basic questions: (1) How many people? and (2) What sort of people? Workforce planning also looks at broader issues relating to the ways in which people are employed and developed in order to improve organizational effectiveness. It can therefore play an important part in strategic human resource management.

Link to business planning

Workforce planning should be an integral part of business planning. The strategic planning process defines projected changes in the types of activities carried out by the organization and the scale of those activities. It identifies the core competences the organization needs to achieve its goals and therefore its skill and behavioural requirements.

Workforce planning interprets these plans in terms of people requirements. But it may influence the business strategy by drawing attention to ways in which people could be developed and deployed more effectively to further the achievement of business goals. It may also focus on any problems that might have to be resolved in order to ensure that the people required will be available and will be capable of making the necessary contribution. As Quinn Mills (1985: 105) indicated, human resource planning is 'a decision-making process that combines three important activities: (1) identifying and acquiring the right number of people with the proper skills, (2) motivating them to achieve high performance, and (3) creating interactive links between business objectives and people-planning activities'.

Hard and soft workforce planning

A distinction can be made between 'hard' and 'soft' workforce planning. The former is based on quantitative analysis in order to ensure that the right number of the right sort of people is available when needed. Soft planning is concerned with broader issues about the employment of people than the traditional quantitative approach is. But it also addresses those aspects of human resource management that are primarily about the organization's requirements for people from the viewpoint of numbers, skills and how they are deployed.

Limitations

However, it must be recognized that although the notion of workforce planning is well established in the HRM vocabulary, it does not seem to be embedded as a key HR activity. As Rothwell (1995: 175) commented about human resource planning: 'Apart from isolated examples, there has been little research evidence of increased use or of its success'. She explains the gap between theory and practice as arising from:

- the impact of change and the difficulty of predicting the future – 'the need for planning may be in inverse proportion to its feasibility';
- the 'shifting kaleidoscope' of policy priorities and strategies within organizations;
- the distrust displayed by many managers of theory or planning – they often prefer pragmatic adaptation to conceptualization;
- the lack of evidence that human resource planning works.

Research conducted by Cowling and Walters (1990) indicated that the only formal and regular activities carried out by respondents were the identification of future training needs, analysis of training costs and analysis of productivity. Fewer than half produced formal labour supply and demand forecasts, and less than 20 per cent formally monitored HR planning practices.

Summarizing the problem, Taylor (1998: 64–65) commented that: 'It would seem that employers, quite simply, prefer to wait until their view of the future environment clears sufficiently for them to see the whole picture before committing resources in preparation for its arrival. The perception is that the more complex and turbulent the environment, the more important it is to wait and see before acting.'

Be that as it may, it is difficult to reject out of hand the belief that some attempt should be made to determine broadly the future human resource requirements as a basis for strategic planning and action. And research conducted by the CIPD (2010) confirmed that some large organizations are taking a serious interest in it.

Approaches to workforce planning

Resourcing strategies show the way forward through the analysis of business strategies and demographic trends. They are converted into action plans based on the outcome of the following interrelated planning activities:

- Demand forecasting – estimate future needs for people and competences by reference to corporate and functional plans and forecasts of future activity levels.
- Supply forecasting – estimate the supply of people by reference to analyses of current resources and future availability, after allowing

for wastage. The forecast will also take account of labour market trends relating to the availability of skills and to demographics.

- Forecasting requirements – analyse the demand and supply forecasts to identify future deficits or surpluses with the help of models where appropriate.
- Action planning – prepare plans to deal with forecast deficits through internal promotion, training or external recruitment. If necessary, plan for unavoidable downsizing so as to avoid any compulsory redundancies, if that is possible. Develop retention and flexibility strategies.

Although these are described as separate areas they are closely interrelated and often overlap. For example, demand forecasts are estimates of future requirements, and these may be prepared on the basis of assumptions about the productivity of employees. But the supply forecast will also have to consider productivity trends and how they might affect the supply of people.

A flow chart of the process of workforce planning is shown in Figure 16.1, which represents an ideal deterministic model of how it should happen. It is useful to have such a model and the activities involved in mind, but it should be remembered that, in practice, organizations tend to do their workforce planning on the hoof, for the reasons given earlier. Some or all the activities represented on the model may take place, but not in a neat sequential sequence. As Mabey et al (1998: 520) commented: 'Much SHRM literature assumes a naive, over-rationalist view of organizational decision-making'. It ignores both the political realities and the inability of senior managers to make SHRM decisions. This applies as much if not more to workforce planning as to any other SHRM activity.

Employee value proposition

A resourcing strategy is concerned with shaping what the organization has to offer to people who join and stay with the organization. This can be done by developing and articulating an employee value proposition – a statement of what an organization will provide for people that they will value. It will include remuneration, which is important but can be over-emphasized compared with other elements. These non-financial factors may be crucial in attracting and retaining people, and include:

- the attractiveness of the organization;
- responsibility – corporate conduct and ethics;
- respect – diversity and inclusion;
- work–life balance;
- opportunities for personal and professional growth.

FIGURE 16.1   Workforce planning flow chart

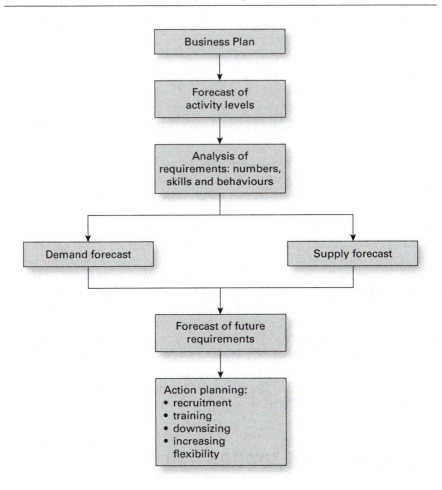

The employee value proposition can be expressed as an employer brand that defines what is special, even unique, about an organization, which will attract people to join it and encourage those already there to stay. Employer branding is the creation of a brand image of the organization for prospective employees. It will be influenced by the reputation of the organization as a business or provider of services, as well as by its reputation as an employer. To create an employer brand it is necessary to:

- analyse what ideal candidates need and want and take this into account in deciding what should be offered and how it should be offered;

- establish how far the core values of the organization support the creation of an attractive brand and ensure that these are incorporated in the presentation of the brand as long as they are 'values in use' (lived by members of the organization) rather than simply espoused;

- define the features of the brand on the basis of an examination and review of each of the areas that affect perceptions of people about the organization as 'a great place to work' – the way people are treated, the provision of a fair deal, opportunities for growth, work–life balance, leadership, the quality of management, involvement with colleagues, and how and why the organization is successful;
- benchmark the approaches of other organizations (the *Sunday Times* list of the 100 best companies to work for is useful) to obtain ideas about what can be done to enhance the brand;
- be honest and realistic.

Resourcing plans

The analysis of future requirements should indicate what steps need to be taken to appoint people from within the organization and what learning and development programmes should be planned. The analysis will also establish how many people will need to be recruited in the absence of qualified employees within the organization and if it is impossible to train people in the new skills in time.

Internal resourcing

Ideally, internal resourcing should be based on data already available about skills and potential. This should have been provided by regular skills audits and the analysis of the outcomes of performance management reviews. A 'trawl' can then be made to locate available talent, which can be accompanied by an internal advertising campaign.

External resourcing

External resourcing requirements can be met by developing a recruitment strategy. The aims of this strategy would be first to make the organization 'the employer of choice' in its particular field or for the people it wants to recruit (eg graduates). Secondly, the strategy should plan the best methods of defining precisely what is needed in terms of skills and competencies. Finally, the strategy should be concerned with planning to use the most effective methods of obtaining the number and type of people required. The strategy should be developed as follows:

1 Define skill and competency (behavioural) requirements – ideally this should be carried out by the use of systematic skill and competency analysis techniques. These can form the material upon which focused and structured interviews can take place and be used as criteria for

selection. They may also indicate where and how psychometric tests could be helpful.

2 Analyse the factors affecting decisions to join the organization – these include:

- the pay and total benefits package – this may have a considerable effect on decisions to join the organization but it is by no means the only factor; those set out below can be just as important and even more significant for some people;

- career opportunities;

- the opportunity to use existing skills or to acquire new skills;

- the opportunity to use the latest technology and equipment with which the organization is well supplied (of particular interest to research scientists and engineers);

- access to high level training;

- a responsible and intrinsically rewarding job;

- a belief that what the organization is doing is worthwhile;

- the reputation of the organization as an employer;

- the opportunity the job will provide to further the individual's career – for example, the scope to achieve and have achievements recognized, increase in employability, or a respected company name to put on a CV.

3 Competitive resourcing – this will start from an analysis of the basis upon which the organization competes with other firms for employees. The factors mentioned above should be covered and the aim would be to seek competitive advantage by exploiting those that are superior to those of rivals. One of the factors will be pay. This may not be the only one but it can be important. It is necessary to track market rates and make a policy decision on where the organization wants to be in relation to the market.

4 Alternative strategies for satisfying people requirements – these consist of outsourcing, re-engineering, increasing flexibility skills training, multiskilling and downsizing.

5 Recruitment and selection techniques – the strategy should explore methods not only of recruiting the number of people required, but also of finding staff who have the necessary skills and experience, who are likely to deliver the right sort of behaviour and who will fit into the organization's culture readily. These processes and techniques will include the use of:

- skills analysis;

- competency mapping;

- the internet and social networks for recruitment;

- biodata;
- structured interviews;
- psychometric testing;
- assessment centres.

The aim of the strategy is to develop the best mix of recruitment and selection tools. It has been demonstrated that a 'bundle' of selection techniques is likely to be more effective as a method of predicting the likely success of candidates than relying on a single method such as an interview.

Retention strategy

Retention strategies aim to ensure that key people stay with the organization and that wasteful and expensive levels of employee turnover are reduced. They will be based on an analysis of why people stay and why they leave.

The reasons why people remain with the organization can be established through attitude surveys. These could segment respondents according to their length of service and analyse the answers of longer-serving employees to establish if there are any common patterns. The survey results could be supplemented by focus groups that would discuss why people stay and identify any problems.

An analysis of why people leave through exit interviews may provide some information but they are unreliable – people rarely give the full reasons why they are going. A better method is to conduct attitude surveys at regular intervals. The retention plan should address each of the areas in which lack of commitment and dissatisfaction can arise. The actions to be considered under each heading are listed below.

Pay

Problems arise because of uncompetitive, inequitable or unfair pay systems. Possible actions include:

- reviewing pay levels on the basis of market surveys;
- introducing job evaluation or improving an existing scheme to provide for equitable grading decisions;
- ensuring that employees understand the link between performance and reward;
- reviewing performance-related pay schemes to ensure that they operate fairly;
- adapting payment-by-results systems to ensure that employees are not penalized when they are engaged only on short runs;

- tailoring benefits to individual requirements and preference;
- involving employees in developing and operating job evaluation and contingent pay systems.

Job design

Dissatisfaction results if jobs are unrewarding in themselves. Jobs should be designed to maximize skill variety, task significance, autonomy and feedback, and they should provide opportunities for learning and growth.

Performance

Employees can be demotivated if they are unclear about their responsibilities or performance standards, are uninformed about how well they are doing, or feel that their performance assessments are unfair. The following actions can be taken:

- express performance requirements in terms of hard but attainable goals;
- get employees and managers to agree on those goals and the steps required to achieve them;
- encourage managers to praise employees for good performance but also get them to provide regular, informative and easily interpreted feedback – performance problems should be discussed as they happen in order that immediate corrective action can be taken;
- train managers in performance review techniques such as counselling;
- brief employees on how the performance management system works and obtain feedback from them on how it has been applied.

Learning and development

Resignations and turnover can increase if people are not given opportunities for learning and development, or feel that demands are being made upon them that they cannot reasonably be expected to fulfil without proper training. New employees can go through an 'induction crisis' if they are not given adequate training when they join the organization. Learning and development programmes should be developed and introduced, which:

- give employees the competence and confidence to achieve expected performance standards;
- enhance existing skills and competencies;
- help people to acquire new skills and competencies so that they can make better use of their abilities, take on greater responsibilities,

undertake a greater variety of tasks and earn more under skill- and competency-based pay schemes;

- ensure that new employees quickly acquire and learn the basic skills and knowledge needed to make a good start in their jobs;
- increase employability, inside and outside the organization.

Career development

Dissatisfaction with career prospects is a major cause of turnover. To a certain extent, this has to be accepted. More and more people recognize that to develop their careers they need to move on, and there is little their employers can do about it, especially in today's flatter organizations where promotion prospects may be limited. These are the individuals who acquire a 'portfolio' of skills and may consciously change direction several times during their careers. To a certain degree, employers should welcome this tendency. The idea of providing 'cradle to grave' careers is no longer as relevant in the more changeable job markets of today, and this self-planned, multiskilling process provides for the availability of a greater number of qualified people. But there is still everything to be said in most organizations for maintaining a stable core workforce and in this situation employers should still plan to create career opportunities by:

- providing employees with wider experience;
- introducing more systematic procedures for identifying potential, such as assessment or development centres;
- encouraging promotion from within;
- developing more equitable promotion procedures;
- providing advice and guidance on career paths.

Commitment

This can be increased by:

- explaining the organization's mission, values and strategies and encouraging employees to discuss and comment on them;
- communicating with employees in a timely and candid way, with the emphasis on face-to-face communications through such means as briefing groups;
- constantly seeking and taking into account the views of people at work;
- providing opportunities for employees to contribute their ideas on improving work systems;
- introducing organization and job changes only after consultation and discussion.

Lack of group cohesion

Employees can feel isolated and unhappy if they are not part of a cohesive team or if they are bedevilled by disruptive power politics. Steps can be taken to tackle this problem through:

- teamwork – setting up self-managing or autonomous work groups or project teams;
- teambuilding – emphasizing the importance of teamwork as a key value, rewarding people for working effectively as members of teams and developing teamwork skills.

Dissatisfaction and conflict with managers and supervisors

A common reason for resignations is the feeling that management in general, or individual managers and team leaders in particular, are not providing the leadership they should, or are treating people unfairly or bullying their staff (not an uncommon situation). As the saying goes, people tend to leave their managers, not the organization. This problem should be remedied by:

- selecting managers and team leaders with well-developed leadership qualities;
- training them in leadership skills and in methods of resolving conflict and dealing with grievances;
- introducing better procedures for handling grievances and disciplinary problems, and training everyone in how to use them.

Recruitment, selection and promotion

Rapid turnover can result simply from poor selection or promotion decisions. It is essential to ensure that selection and promotion procedures match the capacities of individuals to the demands of the work they have to do.

Over-marketing

Creating unrealistic expectations about career development opportunities, tailored training programmes, increasing employability and varied and interesting work can, if not matched with reality, lead directly to dissatisfaction and early resignation. Care should be taken not to oversell the firm's employee development policies. This can be achieved by using realistic previews (telling people as it is) as part of the selection process.

Flexibility strategy

The aims of the flexibility strategy should be to provide for greater operational and role flexibility. The steps to be considered are:

- take a radical look at traditional employment patterns to find alternatives to full-time, permanent staff – this may take the form of segregating the workforce into a 'core group' and one or more peripheral groups;
- outsourcing – getting work done by external firms or individuals;
- multiskilling to increase the ability of people to switch jobs or carry out any of the tasks that have to be undertaken by their team.

KEY LEARNING POINTS

Resourcing defined

Resourcing is what organizations do to ensure that they have the people they need.

Resourcing strategy defined

Resourcing strategy is concerned with identifying how many and what sort of people are required and making plans to obtain and retain them and to employ them efficiently.

The rationale for strategic resourcing

The concept that the strategic capability of a firm depends on its resource capability in the shape of people (the resource-based view) provides the rationale for resourcing strategy. Resourcing strategies exist to provide the people and skills required to support the business strategy, but they should also contribute to the formulation of that strategy.

Workforce planning

Workforce planning determines the human resources required by the organization to achieve its strategic goals and prepares and implements programmes for satisfying those requirements. Although the notion of workforce planning is well established in the HRM vocabulary, it does not seem to be embedded as a key HR activity.

Resourcing strategies

Resourcing strategies show the way forward through the analysis of business strategies and demographic trends. They are converted into action plans based on the outcome of a number of interrelated planning activities.

Resourcing strategies are concerned with shaping what the organization has to offer to people who join and stay with the organization. This can be done by developing and articulating an employee value proposition. The employee value proposition can be expressed as an employer brand that defines what is special, even unique, about an organization, which will attract people to join it and encourage those already there to stay.

Resourcing plans

The analysis of future requirements should indicate what steps need to be taken to appoint people from within the organization and what learning and development programmes should be planned.

Retention strategies

Retention strategies aim to ensure that key people stay with the organization and that wasteful and expensive levels of employee turnover are reduced. They will be based on an analysis of why people stay and why they leave.

Flexibility strategies

Flexibility strategies aim to provide for greater operational and role flexibility.

References

CIPD (2010) *Workforce Planning*, Chartered Institute of Personnel and Development, London

Cowling, A and Walters, M (1990) Manpower planning: where are we today? *Personnel Review*, March, pp 9–15

Keep, E (1989) Corporate training strategies: the vital component? in *New Perspectives on Human Resource Management*, (ed) J Storey, pp 109–25, Routledge, London

Mabey, C, Salaman, G and Storey, J (1998) *Human Resource Management: A strategic introduction*, Blackwell, Oxford

Miles, R E and Snow, C C (1978) *Organizational Strategy: Structure and process*, McGraw Hill, New York

Pascale, R (1990) *Managing on the Edge*, Viking, London

Quinn Mills, D (1985) Planning with people in mind, *Harvard Business Review*, July/August, pp 139–45

Rothwell, S (1995) Human resource planning, in *Human Resource Management: A critical text*, (ed) J Storey, pp 167–202, Routledge, London

Taylor, S (1998) *Employee Resourcing*, IPD, London

Townley, B (1989) Selection and appraisal: reconstructing social relations? in *New Perspectives on Human Resource Management*, (ed) J Storey, pp 92–108, Routledge, London

Talent management strategy

Introduction

The concept of talent management as a process of ensuring that the organization gets, develops and keeps talented people only emerged in the late 1990s. The basis of talent management is the belief that those with the best people win. It has become recognized as a major resourcing activity, although its elements are all familiar. Talent management has been called a fad or a fashion, but David Guest argues that: '... talent management is an idea that has been around for a long time. It's been re-labelled, and that enables wise organisations to review what they are doing. It integrates some old ideas and gives them a freshness, and that is good' (quoted in Warren, 2006: 29).

The familiar elements in talent management are resource planning (predicting future needs for talented people and making provisions to obtain them), succession planning (to ensure a supply of people coming through who can take key roles in the future), performance management (to identify talented employees and their development needs), management development (to enhance skills and potential), reward management (to help attract, retain and motivate talent), and the crafting of an employee value proposition that makes the organization an attractive place in which to work. But the beauty of the concept of talent management is that it brings all these processes together so that an integrated and coherent approach can be used to find and develop talent. The talent management package is in effect a connected group of HR activities that is there to achieve the aims of 'bundling', ie linking several HR practices so that they are interrelated and reinforce and complement one another. Talent management is 'focused bundling' – it exists to do one thing: to provide the organization with the talent it needs by ensuring that all the constituent parts work together towards that end.

Talent management defined

Talent management is the process of identifying, developing, recruiting, retaining and deploying talented people. As defined by Baron and Armstrong (2007: 101), 'talent management is a comprehensive and integrated set of activities which ensure that the organization attracts, retains, motivates and develops the talented people it needs now and in the future'.

The term talent management may refer simply to management succession planning and management development activities, although this notion does not really add anything to these familiar processes except a new (but admittedly quite evocative) name. It is better to regard talent management as a more comprehensive and integrated bundle of activities, the aim of which is to secure the flow of talent in an organization, bearing in mind that talent is a major corporate resource.

Strategic talent management

Talent management is a strategic management process because, in the words of Johnson et al (2005: 6), it involves 'understanding the strategic position of an organization, making strategic choices for the future, and turning strategy into action'. Talent management concentrates on understanding and satisfying the requirements of the business to achieve organizational capability, growth and competitive advantage. It aligns its policies with the organization's strategic intent – its competitive strategy and operational goals.

What is talent?

If you are going to manage talent you have to understand what is meant by talent, ie who the talented people you are going to manage are. In general, talented people could be described as those who have the skills and ability to do something well. But it is necessary to be more specific about which talented people will be the concern of talent management. An elitist policy would be to limit talent management to people who possess exceptional ability and are going to go far. This would lead to a strategic talent management approach as described below by Collings and Mellahi (2009).

SOURCE REVIEW   Strategic talent management defined
                     – Collings and Mellahi (2009: 304)

Activities and processes that involve the systematic identification of key positions which differentially contribute to the organization's sustainable competitive advantage, the development of a talent pool of high potential and high performing incumbents to fill these roles, and the development of a differentiated human resource architecture to facilitate filling these positions with competent incumbents and to ensure their continued commitment to the organization.

A less elitist definition would be that talent is what any able person has who does well in their role and has growth potential. This is broadly in line with the following view expressed by the CIPD (2007: 8): 'Talent consists of those individuals who can make a difference to organizational performance, either through their immediate contribution or in the longer term by demonstrating the highest levels of potential'. These two approaches could be described as exclusive or inclusive.

There are different views about what talent means. Some follow the lead given by McKinsey & Company, who coined the phrase 'the war for talent' in 1997. A book on this subject by Michaels et al (2001) identified five imperatives that companies need to act on if they are going to win the war for managerial talent. These are:

1 Creating a winning employee value proposition that will make your company uniquely attractive to talent.

2 Moving beyond recruiting hype to build a long-term recruiting strategy.

3 Using job experience, coaching and mentoring to cultivate the potential in managers.

4 Strengthening your talent pool by investing in A players, developing B players and acting decisively on C players.

5 Central to this approach is a pervasive mind set – a deep conviction shared by leaders throughout the company that competitive advantage comes from having better talent at all levels.

The McKinsey prescription has often been misinterpreted to mean that talent management is only about obtaining, identifying and nurturing high flyers, ignoring the point they made that competitive advantage comes from having better talent at all levels.

Jeffrey Pfeffer has the following doubts about the war for talent concept, which he thinks is the wrong metaphor for organizational success.

SOURCE REVIEW Problems with the notion of 'the war for talent' – Pfeffer (2001: 252)

Fighting the war for talent itself can cause problems. Companies that adopt a talent war mind-set often wind up venerating outsiders and downplaying the talent already in the company. They frequently set up competitive zero-sum dynamics that make internal learning and knowledge transfer difficult, activate the self-fulfilling prophesy in the wrong direction (those labelled as less able become less able), and create an attitude of arrogance instead of an attitude of wisdom. For all these reasons, fighting the war for talent may be hazardous to an organization's health and detrimental to doing the things that will make it successful.

HR people also have different views. On the one hand they say that everyone has talent and it is not just about the favoured few, and on the other hand that you need to focus on the best. Some people believe that you must maximize the performance of your workforce as a whole if you are going to maximize the performance of the organization. Thorne and Pellant (2007: 9) wrote that: 'No organization should focus all its attention on development of only part of its human capital. What is important is recognizing the needs of different individuals within its community.' Others think that it is not helpful to confuse talent management with overall employee development – both are important but talent management is best kept clear and focused on those who are judged to have talent, bearing in mind what the organization needs. The general consensus seems to be that while talent management may focus on obtaining, identifying and developing people with high potential, this should not be at the expense of the development needs of people generally.

Organizations will tend to take a pragmatic view when formulating their talent management strategy. The CIPD (2007: 8) established from their research that: 'On the one hand there was an exclusive approach, in which talent is viewed on the basis of those destined for the top positions. On the other hand there was an inclusive approach, in which talent is defined as all the employees who work for the organization. The reality is that most organizations had a hybrid approach to talent, in which both exclusivity and inclusivity are accommodated and indeed driven by the changing needs of the workforce' (and, they could have added, the organization).

The process of talent management

Talent management takes the form of a 'bundle' of interrelated talent management processes that constitute the talent pipeline. These processes are all directed to creating and maintaining a pool of talented people with potential, as shown in Figure 17.1.

Talent management starts with the business strategy and what it signifies in terms of the talented people required by the organization. Ultimately, its aim is to develop and maintain a pool of talented people. The business strategy informs the HR strategy, which is concerned generally with each aspect of talent management and particularly with talent relationship management. The elements of the talent management pipeline are described below.

The resourcing strategy

The business plan provides the basis for workforce resource planning, which defines human capital requirements and leads to attraction and retention policies and programmes for internal resourcing (identifying talented people within the organization and developing and promoting them).

Attraction and retention policies and programmes

These policies and programmes describe the approach to ensuring that the organization both gets and keeps the talent it needs. Attraction policies lead to programmes for external resourcing (recruitment and selection of people from outside the organization). Retention policies are designed to ensure that people remain as committed members of the organization. The outcome of these policies is a talent flow that creates and maintains the talent pool.

FIGURE 17.1 The talent management pipeline

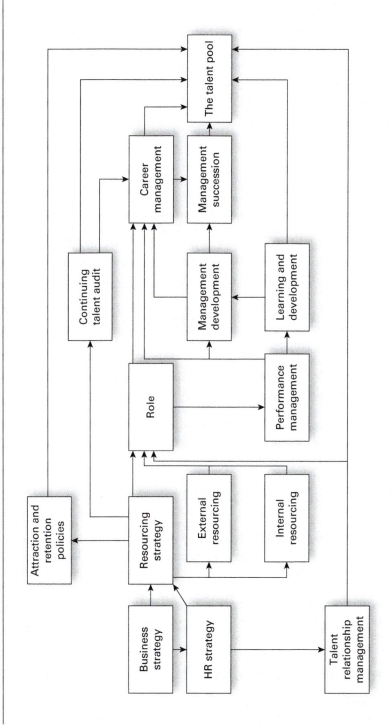

Talent audit

A talent audit identifies those with potential and provides the basis for career planning and development – ensuring that talented people have the sequence of experience supplemented by coaching and learning programmes that will fit them to carry out more demanding roles in the future. Talent audits can also be used to indicate the possible danger of talented people leaving (risk analysis) and what action may need to be taken to retain them.

Role

Talent management is concerned with the roles people carry out. This involves role design – ensuring that roles provide the responsibility, challenge and autonomy required to create role engagement and motivation. It also means taking steps to ensure that people have the opportunity and are given encouragement to learn and develop in their roles. Talent management policies focus on role flexibility – giving people the chance to develop their roles by making better and extended use of their talents.

Talent relationship management

Talent relationship management is the process of building effective relationships with people in their roles. It is concerned generally with creating a great place to work, but in particular it is about treating individual employees fairly, recognizing their value, giving them a voice and providing opportunities for growth. The aim is to achieve 'talent engagement', ensuring that people are committed to their work and the organization. It is always best to build on an existing relationship rather than try to create a new one when someone leaves.

Performance management

Performance management processes provide a means of building relationships with people, identifying talent and potential, planning learning and development activities, and making the most of the talent possessed by the organization. Line managers can be asked to carry out separate 'risk analyses' for any key staff to assess the likelihood of their leaving. Properly carried out, performance management is a means of increasing the engagement and motivation of people by providing positive feedback and recognition. This is part of a total reward system.

Learning and development

Learning and development policies and programmes are essential components in the process of talent management – ensuring that people acquire and enhance the skills and competencies they need. Policies should be formulated by reference to 'employee success profiles', which are described in terms of competencies and define the qualities that need to be developed. Employee success profiles can be incorporated into role profiles.

Career management

Career management consists of the processes of career planning and management succession. Career planning shapes the progression of individuals within an organization in accordance with assessments of organizational needs, defined employee success profiles, and the performance, potential and preferences of individual members of the enterprise. 'Destination jobs' can be identified for people with high potential, which are attainable only if they continue to perform, impress and demonstrate growth potential.

Management succession planning

Management succession planning takes place to ensure that, as far as possible, the organization has the managers it requires to meet future business needs.

The talent pool

The talent pool consists of all those employees who have been identified as talented and who have undergone or are undergoing the various processes of performance management, learning and development, management development, career management, and talent relationship management that constitute the talent management pipeline.

Developing a talent management strategy

A talent management strategy consists of a declaration of intent on how the processes described above should mesh together with an overall objective – to acquire and nurture talent wherever it is and wherever it is needed by using a number of interdependent policies and practices. Talent management is the notion of 'bundling' in action.

Components of a talent management strategy

A talent management strategy involves:

- defining who the talent management programme should cover;
- defining what is meant by talent in terms of competencies and potential;

- defining the future talent requirements of the organization;
- developing the organization as an 'employer of choice' – a 'great place to work';
- using selection and recruitment procedures which ensure that good quality people are recruited who are likely to thrive in the organization and stay with it for a reasonable length of time (but not necessarily for life);
- introducing and managing processes – talent audits and performance management – for identifying talented people and their development needs and assessing potential;
- designing jobs and developing roles that give people opportunities to apply and grow their skills and provide them with autonomy, interest and challenge;
- providing talented staff with opportunities for career development and growth;
- creating a working environment in which work processes and facilities enable rewarding (in the broadest sense) jobs and roles to be designed and developed, providing scope for achieving a reasonable balance between working in the organization and life outside work;
- developing a positive psychological contract;
- developing the leadership qualities of line managers;
- recognizing those with talent by rewarding excellence, enterprise and achievement;
- introducing management succession planning procedures that identify the talent available to meet future requirements and indicate what management development activities are required.

The qualities required

The development and implementation of a talent management strategy requires high-quality management and leadership from the top and from senior managers and the HR function. As suggested by Younger et al (2007), the approaches required involve emphasizing 'growth from within', regarding talent development as a key element of the business strategy, being clear about the competencies and qualities that matter, maintaining well-defined career paths, taking management development, coaching and mentoring very seriously, and demanding high performance.

KEY LEARNING POINTS

Talent management defined

Talent management is the process of identifying, developing, recruiting, retaining and deploying talented people.

Talent management is a strategic management process

Talent management is a strategic management process because in the words of Johnson et al (2005: 6), it involves 'understanding the strategic position of an organization, making strategic choices for the future, and turning strategy into action'.

The meaning of talent

Talented people are those who have the skills and ability to do something well.

The process of talent management

Talent management takes the form of a 'bundle' of interrelated talent management processes that constitute the talent pipeline.

Talent management strategy

A talent management strategy consists of a declaration of intent on how the processes in the talent pipeline should mesh together with an overall objective – to acquire and nurture talent wherever it is and wherever it is needed by using a number of interdependent policies and practices.

References

Baron, A and Armstrong, M (2007) *Human Capital Management: Achieving added value through people*, Kogan Page, London

Chartered Institute of Personnel and Development (2007) *Talent: Strategy, management, measurement*, CIPD, London

Collings, D G and Mellahi, K (2009) Strategic talent management: a review and research agenda, *Human Resource Management Review*, **19**, pp 304–13

Johnson, G, Scholes, K and Whittington, R (2005) *Explaining Corporate Strategy*, 7th edition, FTPrentice Hall, Harlow

Michaels, E G, Handfield-Jones, H and Axelrod, B (2001) *The War for Talent*, Harvard Business School Press, Boston, MA

Pfeffer, J (2001) Fighting the war for talent is hazardous to your organization's health, *Organizational Dynamics*, **29** (4), pp 248–59

Thorne, K and Pellant, A (2007) *The Essential Guide to Managing Talent*, Kogan Page, London

Warren, C (2006) Curtain call, *People Management*, 23 March, pp 24–29

Younger, J, Smallwood, N and Ulrich, D (2007) Developing your organization's brand as a talent developer, *Human Resource Planning*, **30** (2), pp 21–29

Learning and development strategy

KEY CONCEPTS AND TERMS

Development
Discretionary learning
Double-loop learning
Learning
Learning culture

Learning organization
Organizational learning
Single-loop learning
Strategic human resource development
Training

LEARNING OUTCOMES

On completing this chapter you should be able to define the key concepts above. You should also understand:

- the meaning, aims and philosophy of strategic HRD;
- the constituent parts of human resource development;
- how to develop a learning culture;
- the nature of organizational learning strategies;
- the nature of individual learning strategies.

Introduction

Learning and development strategies enable activities to be planned and implemented that ensure that the organization has the talented and skilled people it needs and that individuals are given the opportunity to enhance their knowledge and skills and levels of competency. They are the active components of an overall approach to strategic human resources development (strategic HRD) as described below. Learning and development strategies are concerned with developing a learning culture, promoting organizational learning, establishing a learning organization, and providing for individual learning, as also described in this chapter.

Strategic human resource development (SHRD)

Strategic HRD takes a broad and long-term view about how HRD policies and practices can support the achievement of business strategies. It is business-led and the learning and development strategies that are established as part of the overall SHRD approach flow from business strategies, although they have a positive role in helping to ensure that the business attains its goals.

Strategic HRD aims

Strategic HRD aims to produce a coherent and comprehensive framework for developing people through the creation of a learning culture and the formulation of organizational and individual learning strategies. Its objective is to enhance resource capability in accordance with the belief that a firm's human resources are a major source of competitive advantage. It is therefore about developing the intellectual capital required by the organization, as well as ensuring that the right quality of people are available to meet present and future needs. The main thrust of SHRD is to provide an environment in which people are encouraged to learn and develop. Although SHRD is business-led, its specific strategies have to take into account individual aspirations and needs. The importance of increasing employability outside as well as within the organization should be one of its concerns.

Strategic HRD policies are closely associated with that aspect of strategic HRM that is concerned with investing in people and developing the organization's human capital. As Keep (1989: 112) says: 'One of the primary objectives of HRM is the creation of conditions whereby the latent potential of employees will be realized and their commitment to the causes of the organization secured. This latent potential is taken to include, not merely the capacity to acquire and utilize new skills and knowledge, but also a hitherto untapped wealth of ideas about how the organization's operations might be better ordered.'

Human resource development philosophy

The philosophy underpinning strategic HRD is as follows:

- Human resource development makes a major contribution to the successful attainment of the organization's objectives and investment in it benefits all the stakeholders of the organization.
- Human resource development plans and programmes should be integrated with and support the achievement of business and human resource strategies.
- Human resource development should always be performance-related – designed to achieve specified improvements in corporate, functional, team and individual performance and make a major contribution to bottom-line results.
- Everyone in the organization should be encouraged and given the opportunity to learn – to develop their skills and knowledge to the maximum of their capacity.
- The framework for individual learning is provided by personal development plans that focus on self-managed learning and are supported by coaching, mentoring and formal training.
- The organization needs to invest in learning and development by providing appropriate learning opportunities and facilities, but the prime responsibility for learning and development rests with individuals, who will be given the guidance and support of their managers and, as necessary, members of the HR department.

This involves creating a learning culture, the characteristics of which are self-managed learning not instruction, long-term capacity-building not short-term fixes, and empowerment not supervision.

Elements of human resource development

The key elements of human resource development are:

- Learning – the process by which a person acquires and develops new knowledge, skills, capabilities, behaviours and attitudes.
- Training – the planned and systematic modification of behaviour through learning events, programmes and instruction that enables individuals to achieve the levels of knowledge, skill and competence needed to carry out their work effectively.
- Development – the growth or realization of a person's ability and potential through the provision of learning and educational experiences.

Learning should be distinguished from training: 'Learning is the process by which a person constructs new knowledge, skills and capabilities, whereas training is one of several responses an organization can undertake to promote learning' (Reynolds et al, 2002: 9).

Strategies for creating a learning culture

A fundamental aim of learning and development strategy is to create a learning culture. A learning culture is one in which learning is recognized by top management, line managers and employees generally as an essential organizational process to which they are committed and in which they engage continuously. It is described by Reynolds (2004: 21) as a 'growth medium' that will 'encourage employees to commit to a range of positive discretionary behaviours, including learning' and that has the following characteristics: empowerment not supervision, self-managed learning not instruction, and long-term capacity-building not short-term fixes. Discretionary learning, according to Sloman (2003), happens when individuals actively seek to acquire the knowledge and skills that promote the organization's objectives.

The steps required to create a learning culture as proposed by Reynolds (2004: 12–20) are:

1 Develop and share the vision – belief in a desired and emerging future.

2 Empower employees – provide 'supported autonomy'; freedom for employees to manage their work within certain boundaries (policies and expected behaviours) but with support available as required. Adopt a facilitative style of management in which responsibility for decision making is ceded as far as possible to employees.

3 Provide employees with a supportive learning environment where learning capabilities can be discovered and applied, eg peer networks, supportive policies and systems, and protected time for learning.

4 Use coaching techniques to draw out the talents of others by encouraging employees to identify options and seek their own solutions to problems.

5 Guide employees through their work challenges and provide them with time, resources and, crucially, feedback.

6 Recognize the importance of managers acting as role models.

7 Encourage networks – communities of practice.

8 Align systems to vision – get rid of bureaucratic systems that produce problems rather than facilitate work.

Organizational learning strategies

Organizations can be described as continuous learning systems, and organizational learning has been defined by Marsick (1994: 28) as a process of: 'Co-ordinated systems change, with mechanisms built in for individuals and groups to access, build and use organizational memory, structure and culture to develop long-term organizational capacity'.

Organizational learning strategy aims to develop a firm's resource-based capability. This is in accordance with one of the basic principles of human resource management, namely that it is necessary to invest in people in order to develop the human capital required by the organization and to increase its stock of knowledge and skills. As stated by Ehrenberg and Smith (1994: 279–80), human capital theory indicates that: 'The knowledge and skills a worker has – which comes from education and training, including the training that experience brings – generate a certain stock of productive capital'.

Five principles of organizational learning have been defined by Harrison (1997):

1 The need for a powerful and cohering vision of the organization to be communicated and maintained across the workforce in order to promote awareness of the need for strategic thinking at all levels.

2 The need to develop strategy in the context of a vision that is not only powerful but also open-ended and unambiguous. This will encourage a search for a wide rather than a narrow range of strategic options, will promote lateral thinking, and will orient the knowledge-creating activities of employees.

3 Within the framework of vision and goals, frequent dialogue, communication and conversations are major facilitators of organizational learning.

4 It is essential to challenge people continuously to re-examine what they take for granted.

5 It is essential to develop a climate that is conducive to learning and innovation.

Single- and double-loop learning

Argyris (1992) suggests that organizational learning occurs under two conditions: first when an organization achieves what is intended and second when a mismatch between intentions and outcomes is identified and corrected. But organizations do not perform the actions that produce the learning, it is individual members of the organization who behave in ways that lead to it, although organizations can create conditions that facilitate such learning.

Argyris distinguishes between single-loop and double-loop learning. Single-loop learning organizations define the 'governing variables', ie what they expect to achieve in terms of targets and standards. They then monitor and review achievements and take corrective action as necessary, thus completing the loop. Double-loop learning occurs when the monitoring process initiates action to redefine the 'governing variables' to meet the new situation, which may be imposed by the external environment. The organization has learned something new about what has to be achieved in the light of changed circumstances, and can then decide how this should be achieved.

Learning organization strategy

The process of organizational learning is related to the concept of a learning organization, which Senge (1990: 3) described as one 'where people continually expand their capacity to create the results they truly desire, where new and expansive patterns of thinking are nurtured, where collective aspiration is set free, and where people are continually learning how to learn together'. A learning organization was defined by Wick and Leon (1995: 299) as one that 'continually improves by rapidly creating and refining the capabilities required for future success', and by Pedler et al (1997: 3) as an organization that 'facilitates the learning of all its members and continually transforms itself'. As Burgoyne (1999) pointed out, learning organizations have to be able to adapt to their context and develop their people to match that context.

Garvin *et al* (1993) suggested that learning organizations are good at doing five things:

1 Systematic problem solving, which rests heavily on the philosophy and methods of the quality movement. Its underlying ideas include relying on scientific method rather than guesswork for diagnosing problems – what Deming (1986) calls the 'plan-do-check-act' cycle and others refer to as 'hypothesis-generating, hypothesis-testing' techniques. Data rather than assumptions are required as the background to decision making – what quality practitioners call 'fact-based management' – and simple statistical tools such as histograms, Pareto charts and cause-and-effect diagrams are used to organize data and draw inferences.

2 Experimentation – this activity involves the systematic search for and testing of new knowledge. Continuous improvement programmes – 'kaizen' – are an important feature of a learning organization.

3 Learning from past experience – learning organizations review their successes and failures, assess them systematically, and record the lessons learned in a way that employees find open and accessible. This process has been called the 'Santayana principle', quoting the philosopher George Santayana who coined the phrase: 'Those who cannot remember the past are condemned to repeat it'.

4 Learning from others – sometimes the most powerful insights come from looking outside one's immediate environment to gain a new perspective. This process has been called SIS (for 'steal ideas shamelessly'). Another more acceptable word for it is benchmarking – a disciplined process of identifying best practice organizations and analysing the extent to which what they are doing can be transferred, with suitable modifications, to one's own environment.

5 Transferring knowledge quickly and efficiently throughout the organization by seconding people with new expertise, or by

education and training programmes, as long as the latter are linked explicitly with implementation.

One approach, as advocated by Senge (1990), is to focus on collective problem solving within an organization. This is achieved using team learning and a 'soft systems' methodology whereby all the possible causes of a problem are considered in order to define more clearly those that can be dealt with and those that are insoluble.

A learning organization strategy will be based on the belief that learning is a continuous process rather than a set of discrete training activities (Sloman, 1999). It will incorporate strategies for organizational learning as described above and individual learning as discussed below.

Individual learning strategies

The individual learning strategies of an organization are driven by its human resource requirements, the latter being expressed in terms of the sort of skills and behaviours that will be required to achieve business goals. The starting point should be the approaches adopted to the provision of learning and development opportunities, bearing in mind the distinction between learning and development made by Pedler et al (1997), who see learning as being concerned with an increase in knowledge or a higher degree of an existing skill, whereas development is more towards a different state of being or functioning. Sloman (2003: 17) pointed out that:

> Interventions and activities which are intended to improve knowledge and skills will increasingly focus on the learner. Emphasis will shift to the individual learner (or team). And he or she will be encouraged to take more responsibility for his or her learning. Efforts will be made to develop a climate which supports effective and appropriate learning. Such interventions and activities will form part of an integrated approach to creating competitive advantage through people in the organization.

The learning strategy should cover:

- how learning needs will be identified;
- the role of personal development planning and self-managed learning;
- the support that should be provided for individual learning in the form of guidance, coaching, learning resource centres, mentoring, external courses designed to meet the particular needs of individuals, internal or external training programmes, and courses designed to meet the needs of groups of employees.

KEY LEARNING POINTS

Learning and development strategies defined

- Learning and development strategies enable activities to be planned and implemented that ensure that the organization has the talented and skilled people it needs and that individuals are given the opportunity to enhance their knowledge and skills and levels of competency.

- Learning and development strategies are concerned with developing a learning culture, promoting organizational learning, establishing a learning organization, and providing for individual learning.

Strategic HRD defined

- Strategic HRD takes a broad and long-term view about how HRD policies and practices can support the achievement of business strategies.

- Strategic HRD aims to produce a coherent and comprehensive framework for developing people through the creation of a learning culture and the formulation of organizational and individual learning strategies.

The key elements of human resource development

The key elements of human resource development are:

- Learning – the process by which a person acquires and develops new knowledge, skills, capabilities, behaviours and attitudes.

- Training – the planned and systematic modification of behaviour through learning events, programmes and instruction, which enable individuals to achieve the levels of knowledge, skill and competence needed to carry out their work effectively.

- Development – the growth or realization of a person's ability and potential through the provision of learning and educational experiences.

- Learning culture – a fundamental aim of learning and development strategy is to create a learning culture. A learning culture is one in which learning is recognized by top management, line managers and employees generally as an essential organizational process to which they are committed and in which they engage continuously.

- Organizational learning strategy – this aims to develop a firm's resource-based capability.

- Learning organization – the process of organizational learning is related to the concept of a learning organization, which Senge (1990) describes as: 'An organization that is continually expanding to create its future'.

- Individual learning strategies – these are driven by the organization's human resource requirements, which are expressed in terms of the sort of skills and behaviours that will be required to achieve business goals.

References

Argyris, C (1992) *On Organizational Learning*, Blackwell, Cambridge, MA

Burgoyne, J (1999) Design of the times, *People Management*, 3 June, pp 39–44

Deming, W E (1986) *Out of the Crisis*, Massachusetts Institute of Technology Centre for Advanced Engineering Studies, Cambridge, MA

Ehrenberg, R G and Smith, R S (1994) *Modern Labor Economics*, Harper Collins, New York

Garvin, D A, Edmonson, A C and Gino, F (2008) Is yours a learning organization? *Harvard Business Review*, March, pp 110–16

Harrison, R (1997) *Employee Development*, 1st edition, IPM, London

Keep, E (1989) Corporate training strategies: the vital component? in *New Perspectives on Human Resource Management*, (ed) J Storey, pp 109–25, Routledge, London

Marsick, V J (1994) Trends in managerial invention: creating a learning map, *Management Learning*, 25 (1), pp 11–33

Pedler, M, Burgoyne, J and Boydell, T (1997) *The Learning Company: A strategy for sustainable development*, 2nd edition, McGraw-Hill, Maidenhead

Reynolds, J (2004) *Helping People Learn*, CIPD, London

Reynolds, J, Caley, L and Mason, R (2002) *How Do People Learn?* CIPD, London

Senge, P (1990) *The Fifth Discipline: The art and practice of the learning organization*, Doubleday, London

Sloman, M (1999) Seize the day, *People Management*, 20 May, p 31

Sloman, M (2003) E-learning: stepping up the learning curve, *Impact*, January, pp 16–17

Wick, C W and Leon, L S (1995) Creating a learning organisation: from ideas to action, *Human Resource Management*, 34 (2), pp 299–311

Reward strategy

Introduction

Reward strategy is concerned with the policies and practices required to ensure that the value of people and the contribution they make to achieving organizational, departmental and team goals is recognized and rewarded. It is about planning and executing the design and implementation of reward systems (interrelated reward processes, practices and procedures) that aim to satisfy the needs of both the organization and its stakeholders and to operate fairly, equitably and consistently. These systems will include arrangements for assessing the value of jobs through job evaluation and market pricing, the design and management of grade and pay structures, performance management processes, schemes for rewarding and recognizing people according to their individual performance or contribution and/or team or organizational performance, and the provision of employee benefits.

Reward strategy defined

Reward strategy is a declaration of intent. It defines what an organization wants to do in the longer term to address critical reward issues and to develop and implement reward policies, practices and processes that will further the achievement of its business goals and meet the needs of its stakeholders. It starts from where the reward practices of the business are now and goes on to describe what they should become.

Reward strategy provides a sense of purpose and direction, a pathway that links the needs of the business and its people with the reward policies and practices of the organization and thereby communicates and explains these practices. It constitutes a framework for developing and putting into effect reward policies, practices and processes that ensure that people are rewarded for doing the things that increase the likelihood of the organization's business goals being achieved.

Reward strategy is underpinned by a reward philosophy. It is concerned not only with what should be done but how it should be done; with implementation as well as planning. It is based on an understanding of the culture of the organization and an appreciation of its needs and those of its people within the context in which the organization operates. This provides the basis upon which cultural fit is achieved and needs *are* satisfied.

Why have a reward strategy?

Overall, in the words of Duncan Brown (2001: 44), 'Reward strategy is ultimately a way of thinking that you can apply to any reward issue arising in your organization, to see how you can create value from it'. More specifically, there are four arguments for developing reward strategies:

1 You must have some idea where you are going, or how do you know how to get there, and how do you know that you have arrived (if you ever do)?

2 Pay costs in most organizations are by far the largest item of expense – they can be 60 per cent and often much more in labour-intensive organizations – so doesn't it make sense to think about how they should be managed and invested in the longer term?

3 There can be a positive relationship between rewards, in the broadest sense, and performance, so shouldn't we think about how we can strengthen that link?

4   As Cox and Purcell (1998: 65) wrote: 'The real benefit in reward strategies lies in complex linkages with other human resource management policies and practices'. Isn't this a good reason for developing a reward strategic framework that indicates how reward processes will be linked to HR processes so that they are coherent and mutually supportive?

Characteristics of reward strategies

Armstrong and Murlis (2004: 33) pointed out that: 'Reward strategy will be characterised by diversity and conditioned both by the legacy of the past and the realities of the future'. All reward strategies are different, just as all organizations are different. Of course, similar aspects of reward will be covered in the strategies of different organizations but they will be treated differently in accordance with variations between organizations in their contexts, strategies and cultures.

Reward strategists may have a clear idea of what needs to be done but they have to take account of the views of top management and be prepared to persuade them with convincing arguments that action needs to be taken. They have to take particular account of financial considerations – the concept of 'affordability' looms large in the minds of chief executives and financial directors, who will need to be convinced that an investment in rewards will pay off. They also have to convince employees and their representatives that the reward strategy will meet their needs as well as business needs.

The basis of reward strategy

Reward strategy should be based on a detailed analysis of the present arrangements for reward, which would include a statement of their strengths and weaknesses. This could take the form of a 'gap analysis', which compares what it is believed should be happening with what is actually happening and indicates which 'gaps' need to be filled. A format for the analysis is shown in Table 19.1.

TABLE 19.1

What should be happening	What is happening	What needs to be done
1 A total reward approach is adopted that emphasizes the significance of both financial and non-financial rewards.		
2 Reward policies and practices are developed within the framework of a well-articulated strategy that is designed to support the achievement of business objectives and meet the needs of stakeholders.		
3 A job evaluation scheme is used that properly reflects the values of the organization, is up to date with regard to the jobs it covers, and is non-discriminatory.		
4 Equal pay issues are given serious attention. This includes the conduct of equal pay reviews that lead to action.		
5 Market rates are tracked carefully so that a competitive pay structure exists that contributes to the attraction and retention of high-quality people.		
6 Grade and pay structures are based on job evaluation and market rate analysis, are appropriate to the characteristics and needs of the organization and its employees, facilitate the management of relativities, provide scope for rewarding contribution, clarify reward and career opportunities, are constructed logically, operate transparently, and are easy to manage and maintain.		

TABLE 19.1 *Continued*

What should be happening	What is happening	What needs to be done
7 Contingent pay schemes reward contribution fairly and consistently, support the motivation of staff and the development of a performance culture, deliver the right messages about the values of the organization, contain a clear 'line of sight' between contribution and reward, and are cost-effective.		
8 Performance management processes contribute to performance improvement, people development and the management of expectations, operate effectively throughout the organization and are supported by line managers and staff.		
9 Employee benefits and pension schemes meet the needs of stakeholders and are cost-effective.		
10 A flexible benefits approach is adopted.		
11 Reward management procedures exist that ensure that reward processes are managed effectively and that costs are controlled.		
12 Appropriate use is made of computers (software and spreadsheets) to assist in the process of reward management.		
13 Reward management aims and arrangements are transparent and communicated well to staff.		
14 Surveys are used to assess the opinions of staff about reward and action is taken on the outcomes.		
15 An appropriate amount of responsibility for reward is devolved to line managers.		

- the introduction of a new grade and pay structure, eg a broad-graded or career family structure;
- the replacement of an existing decayed job evaluation scheme with a scheme that more clearly reflects organizational values and is less bureaucratic;
- the improvement of performance management processes so that they provide better support for the development of a performance culture and more clearly identify development needs;
- the introduction of a formal recognition scheme;
- the development of a flexible benefits system;
- the conduct of equal pay reviews with the objective of ensuring that work of equal value is paid equally;
- communication programmes designed to inform everyone of the reward policies and practices of the organization;
- training, coaching and guidance programmes designed to increase line management capability (see also page 266).

Guiding principles

Guiding principles define the approach an organization takes to dealing with reward. They are the basis for reward policies and provide guidelines for the actions contained in the reward strategy. They express the reward philosophy of the organization – its values and beliefs about how people should be rewarded.

Members of the organization should be involved in the definition of guiding principles, which can then be communicated to everyone to increase understanding of what underpins reward policies and practices. However, employees will suspend their judgement of the principles until they experience how they are applied. What matters to them are not the philosophies themselves but the pay practices emanating from them and the messages about the employment 'deal' that they get as a consequence. It is the reality that is important, not the rhetoric.

Guiding principles should incorporate or be influenced by general beliefs about fairness, equity, consistency and transparency. They may be concerned with such specific matters as:

- developing reward policies and practices that support the achievement of business goals;
- providing rewards that attract, retain and motivate staff and help to develop a high performance culture;
- maintaining competitive rates of pay;
- rewarding people according to their contribution;

- recognizing the value of all staff who are making an effective contribution, not just the exceptional performers;
- allowing a reasonable degree of flexibility in the operation of reward processes and in the choice of benefits by employees;
- devolving more responsibility for reward decisions to line managers.

Developing reward strategy

The formulation of reward strategy can be described as a process for developing and defining a sense of direction. There are four key development phases:

1 The diagnosis phase, when reward goals are agreed, current policies and practices assessed against them, options for improvement considered and any changes agreed.
2 The detailed design phase, when improvements and changes are detailed and any changes tested (pilot testing is important).
3 The final testing and preparation phase.
4 The implementation phase, followed by ongoing review and modification.

A logical step-by-step model for doing this is illustrated in Figure 19.1. This incorporates ample provision for consultation, involvement and communication with stakeholders, who include senior managers as the ultimate decision-makers as well as employees and line managers.

In practice, however, the formulation of reward strategy is seldom as logical and linear a process as this. Reward strategies evolve; they have to respond to changes in organizational requirements that are happening all the time. They need to track emerging trends in reward management and may modify their views accordingly, as long as they do not leap too hastily on the latest bandwagon.

It may be helpful to set out reward strategies on paper for the record and as a basis for planning and communication. But this should be regarded as no more than a piece of paper that can be torn up when the needs of the organization change – as they will – not a tablet of stone.

Effective reward strategies

An effective reward strategy is one that provides clear guidance on development planning and implementation and achieves its objectives when implemented. Duncan Brown (2001: 14–15) has suggested that effective reward strategies have three components:

FIGURE 19.1 A model of the reward strategy development process

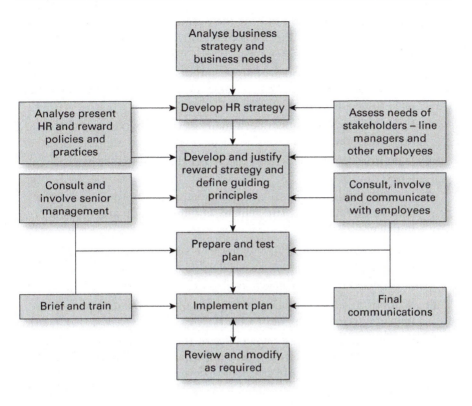

1 They have to have clearly-defined goals and a well-defined link to business objectives.

2 There have to be well-designed pay and reward programmes, tailored to the needs of the organization and its people, and consistent and integrated with one another.

3 Perhaps most important and most neglected, there needs to be effective and supportive HR and reward processes in place.

Criteria for effectiveness

The questions to be answered when assessing the effectiveness of a reward strategy as posed by Armstrong and Brown (2006) are:

1 Is it aligned with the organization's business strategy (vertical alignment or integration) and its HR strategies (horizontal alignment or integration)?

2 Will it support the achievement of business goals and reinforce organizational values? If so, how?

3 Are the objectives of the reward strategy clearly defined, including a convincing statement of how the business needs of the organization will be met and how the needs of employees and other stakeholders will be catered for?

4 Is it based on a thorough analysis and diagnosis of the internal and external environment of the organization and the reward issues that need to be addressed?

5 Has a realistic assessment been made of the resources required to implement the strategy and the costs involved?

6 Is it affordable in the sense that the benefits will exceed any costs?

7 Have steps been taken to ensure that supporting processes such as performance management, communication and training are in place?

8 Is the programme for implementation realistic?

9 Have steps been taken to ensure that the strategy is supported and understood by line managers and staff?

10 Will HR and line managers be capable of implementing and managing the strategy in practice?

11 Has accountability and ownership for the various reward policies and practices been clarified, defining what success looks like and how it will be measured? Are effective review mechanisms in place?

12 Is the reward strategy flexible in adjusting to take account of changes in the business and in the environment?

Reward strategy and line management capability

HR can initiate new reward policies and practices but it is the line manager that has the main responsibility for implementing them. The trend is, rightly, to devolve more responsibility for managing reward to line managers. Some will have the ability to respond to the challenge and opportunity; others will be incapable of carrying out this responsibility without close guidance from HR; some may never be able to cope. Managers may not always do what HR expects them to do, and if compelled to they may be half-hearted about it. This puts a tremendous onus on HR and reward specialists to develop line management capability, to initiate processes that can readily be implemented by line managers, to promote understanding by communicating what is happening, why it is happening and how it will affect everyone, to provide guidance and help where required, and to provide formal training as necessary.

The problem with the concept of reward strategy

To what extent can pay be strategic? This question was posed by Trevor (2009: 21) who noted that pay is seen as 'a means of aligning a company's most strategic asset – their employees – to the strategic direction of the organization' and that strategic pay theory is predicated on the notion of strategic choice. But he claimed that rationalism is limited and pointed out that pay systems tend to be selected for their legitimacy (best practice as advocated by institutions such as the CIPD and by management consultants) rather than for purely economic reasons. His research into the pay policies and practice of three large consumer goods organizations revealed a gap between intended and actual practice – intent does not necessarily lead to action. 'Irrespective of the strategic desire or the saliency of the design, ineffectual execution results in ineffectual pay practice which then reacts negatively upon the pay outcomes experienced as a result... Attempting to use strategic pay systems such as incentive pay, results often in unintended consequences and negative outcomes that destroy value rather than create it' (ibid: 34). The main implications of the findings from this research were that: 'Theory is out of step with reality and may represent a largely unattainable ideal in practice... an alternative approach for the use of pay systems in support of strategy is required: one that acknowledges the relative limits on the ability of companies to manage pay strategically' (ibid: 37). As Wright and Nishii (2006: 11) commented: 'Not all intended HR practices are actually implemented and those that are may often be implemented in ways that differ from the original intention'.

A similar point was made by Armstrong and Brown (2006) when they described 'the new reality' of strategic reward management as follows.

SOURCE REVIEW The reality of reward strategy – Armstrong and Brown (2006: 1–2)

When mostly North American concepts of strategic HRM and reward first entered into management thinking and practice in the UK we were both some of their most ardent advocates, writing and advising individual employers on the benefits of aligning their reward systems so as to drive business performance. We helped to articulate strategic plans and visions, and to design the pay and reward changes that would secure better alignment and performance.

Some twenty years later, we are a little older and a little wiser as a result of these experiences. We remain passionate proponents of a strategic approach to reward management. But in conducting and observing this work we have seen some of the risks as well as the opportunities in pursuing the reward strategy path: of an over-focus on planning at the expense of process and practice; on design rather than delivery; on the boardroom and the HR function rather than on first and front-line managers and employees; and on concept rather than communications.

At times there has been a tendency to over-ambition and optimism in terms of what could and couldn't be achieved by changing pay and reward arrangements, and how quickly real change could be delivered and business results secured. At times the focus on internal business fit led to narrow-minded reward determinism, and a lack of attention to the increasingly important external influences and constraints on reward, from the shifting tax and wider legislative, economic and social environment. And sometimes the focus on designs and desires meant that the requirements and skills of line and reward managers were insufficiently diagnosed and developed.

KEY LEARNING POINTS

Reward strategy defined

- Reward strategy is concerned with the policies and practices required to ensure that the value of people and the contribution they make to achieving organizational, departmental and team goals is recognized and rewarded.

- It is about planning and executing the design and implementation of reward systems (interrelated reward processes, practices and procedures) that aim to satisfy the needs of both the organization and its stakeholders and to operate fairly, equitably and consistently. Reward strategy is a declaration of intent.

- It defines what an organization wants to do in the longer term to address critical reward issues and to develop and implement reward policies, practices and processes that will further the achievement of its business goals and meet the needs of its stakeholders.

- It starts from where the reward practices of the business are now and goes on to describe what they should become.

Arguments for developing reward strategy

There are four arguments for developing reward strategy:

1 Reward strategy provides a sense of purpose and direction.

2 Pay costs in most organizations are by far the largest item of expense and reward strategy can help to manage them properly.

3 The relationship between rewards and performance will be strengthened.

4 A reward strategic framework will indicate how reward processes will be linked to HR processes so that they are coherent and mutually supportive.

The process of reward strategy formulation

Reward strategists may have a clear idea of what needs to be done but they have to:

● take account of the views of top management and be prepared to persuade them with convincing arguments that action needs to be taken;

● take particular account of financial considerations;

● convince employees and their representatives that the reward strategy will meet their needs as well as business needs.

Reward strategy should be based on a detailed analysis of the present arrangements for reward, which would include a statement of their strengths and weaknesses.

The content of reward strategy

Reward strategy may be a broad-brush affair, simply indicating the general direction in which it is thought reward management should go. Additionally, or alternatively, reward strategy may set out a list of specific intentions dealing with particular aspects of reward management.

Reward guiding principles

Guiding principles define the approach an organization takes to dealing with reward. They are the basis for reward policies and provide guidelines for the actions contained in the reward strategy. They express the reward philosophy of the organization – its values and beliefs about how people should be rewarded.

Effective reward strategies

An effective reward strategy is one that provides clear guidance on development planning and implementation and achieves its objectives when implemented.

The role of line management

HR can initiate new reward policies and practices but it is the line manager that has the main responsibility for implementing them. The trend is, rightly, to devolve more responsibility for managing reward to line managers.

Limitations

There are limitations to the impact of reward strategy. Intent does not necessarily lead to action.

References

Armstrong, M and Brown, D (2006) *Strategic Reward: Making it happen*, Kogan Page, London

Armstrong, M and Murlis, H (2004) *Reward Management*, 5th edition, Kogan Page, London

Brown, D (2001) *Reward Strategies: From intent to impact*, CIPD, London

Cox, A and Purcell, J (1998) Searching for leverage: pay systems, trust, motivation and commitment in SMEs, in *Trust, Motivation and Commitment: A reader*, (ed) S Perkins, pp 60–65, SRRC, Faringdon

Trevor, J (2009) Can pay be strategic? in *Rethinking Reward*, pp 21–46, (eds) S Corby, S Palmer and E Lindop, Palgrave Macmillan, Basingstoke

Wright, P M and Nishii, L H (2006) Strategic HRM and organizational behaviour: integrating multiple levels of analysis, Working Paper 06-05, Cornell University, Ithica, NY

Employee relations strategy

LEARNING OUTCOMES

On completing this chapter you should be able to define the key concepts above. You should also understand:

- the meaning of employee relations strategy;
- the concerns of employee relations strategy;
- the directions that strategies may follow;
- the approaches available in developing strategy;
- the nature of partnership agreements;
- the approach to formulating employee relations strategies.

Introduction

Employee relations are concerned generally with managing the employment relationship and developing a positive psychological contract. In particular they deal with terms and conditions of employment, issues arising from employment, providing employees with a voice, and communicating with employees. Employees are dealt with either directly or through collective agreements where trade unions are recognized. This is an area of HRM where a strategic approach is particularly appropriate. Organizations need to have a clear idea of the route they want to follow in developing a cooperative and productive employee relations climate, one in which the perceptions of management, employees and their representatives about how employee relations are conducted and how the various parties (managers, employees and trade unions) behave when dealing with one another are positive.

Employee relations strategy defined

Employee relations strategy defines the intentions of the organization about what needs to be done and what needs to be changed in the ways in which the organization manages its relationships with employees and their trade unions. Like all other aspects of HR strategy, employee relations strategy will take account of the business strategy and will aim to support it. Generally, support will be provided if employee relations operate in a spirit of mutuality and partnership, and if this results in high levels of trust, co-operation and, ultimately, productivity.

A more particular example: if the business strategy is concentrated on achieving competitive edge through innovation and the delivery of quality to its customers, the employee relations strategy may emphasize processes of involvement and participation, including the implementation of programmes for continuous improvement and total quality management. If, however, the strategy for competitive advantage, or even survival, is cost reduction, the employee relations strategy may concentrate on how this can be achieved by maximizing cooperation with the unions and employees and by minimizing detrimental effects on those employees and disruption to the organization.

Employee relations strategies should be distinguished from employee relations policies. Strategies are dynamic. They provide a sense of direction, and give an answer to the question 'How are we going to get from here to there?' Employee relations policies are more about the here and now. They express 'the way things are done around here' as far as dealing with unions and employees is concerned. Of course they will evolve but this may not be a result of a strategic choice. It is when a deliberate decision is made to change policies that a strategy for achieving this change has to be formulated. Thus if the policy is to increase commitment, the strategy could consider how this might be achieved by involvement and participation processes.

Concerns of employee relations strategy

Employee relations strategy may be concerned with matters such as how to:

- build stable and cooperative relationships with employees, which minimize conflict;
- achieve commitment through employee involvement and communications processes;
- develop mutuality – a common interest in achieving the organization's goals through the development of organizational cultures based on shared values between management and employees;
- encourage social partnership – the concept that the parties involved in employee relations should aim to work together to the greater good of all, which is based on the mutual gains theory of Kochan and Osterman (1994) that employers, employees and trade unions gain from cooperative forms of employment relationships.

Strategic directions

The intentions expressed by employee relations strategies may direct the organization towards any of the following:

- changing forms of recognition, including single union recognition, or de-recognition;
- changes in the form and content of procedural agreements;
- new bargaining structures, including decentralization or single-table bargaining;
- the achievement of increased levels of commitment through involvement or participation – giving employees a voice;
- deliberately bypassing trade union representatives to communicate directly with employees;
- increasing the extent to which management controls operations in such areas as flexibility;
- generally improving the employee relations climate in order to produce more harmonious and cooperative relationships;
- developing a 'partnership' with trade unions, recognizing that employees are stakeholders and that it is to the advantage of both parties to work together (this could be described as a unitarist strategy aiming at increasing mutual commitment).

The approaches to employee relations strategy

There are four approaches to employee relations strategy:

1 Adversarial: the organization decides what it wants to do and employees are expected to fit in. Employees only exercise power by refusing to cooperate.

2 Traditional: a good day-to-day working relationship, but management proposes and the workforce reacts through its elected representatives.

3 Partnership: the organization involves employees in the drawing up and execution of the organization's policies, but retains the right to manage.

4 Power sharing: employees are involved in both day-to-day and strategic decision making.

Adversarial approaches are much less common today than in the 1960s and 1970s. The traditional approach is still the most typical but more interest is being expressed in partnership as discussed later in this chapter. Power sharing is rare.

Against the background of a preference for one of the four approaches listed above, employee relations strategy will be based on the philosophy of the organization on what sort of relationships between management and employees and their unions are wanted, and how they should be handled. A partnership strategy will aim to develop and maintain a positive, productive, cooperative and trusting climate of employee relations.

Formulating employee relations strategies

Like other business and HR strategies, those concerned with employee relations can, in Mintzberg's (1987: 68) words, '... emerge in response to an evolving situation'. But it is still useful to spend time deliberately considering the way forward to the establishment of a shared agenda with employees and, if they have them, their representatives, which will communicate a common perspective on what needs to be done. This can be expressed in writing but it can also be clarified through involvement and communication processes. A partnership agreement may well be the best way of getting employee relations strategies into action.

Partnership agreements

Partnership agreements are based on the concept of social partnership as mentioned earlier. Both parties (management and the trade union) agree to collaborate to their mutual advantage and to achieve a climate of more cooperative and therefore less adversarial industrial relations. Management may offer job security linked to productivity and the union may agree to more flexible working.

The perceived benefits of partnership agreements are that management and unions will work together in a spirit of cooperation and mutuality, which is clearly preferable to an adversarial relationship. Provision is made for change to be introduced through discussion and agreement rather than by coercion or power. Guest and Peccei (2001) found that the balance of advantage in partnership arrangements commonly appears to favour employees. Furthermore, an analysis by Guest et al (2008) of evidence from the 2004 Workshop Employee Relations Survey suggested that partnership practice remains relatively undeveloped and that it is only weakly related to trust between management and employee representatives and to employees' trust in management. Direct forms of participation generally have a more positive association with trust than representative forms.

Employee voice strategies

The term 'employee voice' refers to the say employees have in matters of concern to them in their organization. It describes a forum of two-way dialogue that allows employees to influence events at work and includes the processes of involvement, participation, upward problem solving and upward communication.

Wilkinson et al (2010: 9) commented that research has shown (Dundon and Gollan, 2007; Gibbons and Woock, 2007) that 'an integrated approach to employee participation in which such participation is accompanied by related initiatives in employment security, selective employee hiring, variable compensation, extensive training and information sharing with employees is most likely to lead to higher levels of performance'.

The employee relations strategy has to determine what voice arrangements should be made, if any. These can take the form of representative participation (collective representation through trade unions or staff associations or joint consultation) and/or upward communication through established channels (consultative committees, grievance procedures, 'speak-up' programmes etc) or informally.

The employee voice strategy appropriate for an organization depends upon the values and attitudes of management and, if they exist, trade unions, and the current climate of employee relations. Strategic planning should be based on a review of the existing forms of voice, which would include discussions with stakeholders (line managers, employees and trade union representatives) on the effectiveness of existing arrangements and any improvements required. In the light of these discussions, new or revised approaches can be developed but it is necessary to brief and train those involved in the part they should play.

KEY LEARNING POINTS

Employee relations defined
Employee relations are concerned generally with managing the employment relationship and developing a positive psychological contract.

Employee relations strategy defined
Employee relations strategy defines the intentions of the organization about what needs to be done and what needs to be changed in how the organization manages its relationships with employees and their trade unions.

Employee relations strategy concerns
Employee relations strategy may be concerned with matters such as how to build stable and cooperative relationships with employees that minimize conflict, achieve commitment, develop mutuality and encourage social partnership.

Employee relations strategy intentions
The intentions expressed by employee relations strategies may direct the organization towards any of the following: changing forms of recognition, changes in the form and content of procedural agreements, new bargaining structures, giving employees a voice, deliberately bypassing trade union representatives to communicate directly with employees, increasing the extent to which management controls operations in such areas as flexibility, generally improving the employee relations climate in order to produce more harmonious and cooperative relationships, or developing a 'partnership' with trade unions.

Approaches to employee relations strategy
The four approaches are adversarial, traditional, partnership and power sharing.

Partnership agreements
In partnership agreements, both parties (management and the trade union) agree to collaborate to their mutual advantage and to achieve a climate of more cooperative and therefore less adversarial industrial relations.

Employee voice
The term 'employee voice' refers to the say employees have in matters of concern to them in their organization. The employee relations strategy has to determine what voice arrangements should be made, if any.

References

Dundon, T and Gollan, P J (2007) Re-conceptualising voice in the non-union workshop, *International Journal of Human Resource Management*, 18 (7), pp 1182–98

Gibbons, J and Woock, C (2007) *Evidence-based Human Resources*, The Conference Board, New York

Guest, D E and Peccei, R (2001) Partnership at work: mutuality and the balance of advantage, *British Journal of Industrial Relations*, 39 (2), pp 207–36

Guest, D E et al (2008) Does partnership at work increase trust? An analysis based on the 2004 Workplace Employment Relations Survey, *Industrial Relations Journal*, 39 (2), pp 124–52

Kochan, T A and Osterman, P (1994) *The Mutual Gains Enterprise: Forging a winning partnership among labor, management and government*, Harvard University Business Press, Boston, MA

Mintzberg, H (1987) Crafting strategy, *Harvard Business Review*, July/August, pp 66–74

Wilkinson, A, Gollan, P J, Marchington, M and Lewin, D (2010) Conceptualizing participation in organizations, in *The Oxford Handbook of Participation in Organizations*, (eds) A Wilkinson, P J Gollan, M Marchington and D Lewin, pp 3–25, Oxford University Press, Oxford

PART FOUR
The strategic HRM toolkit

The purpose of the toolkit is to provide the basis for conducting a strategic review of human resource management practices in order to develop and implement strategic human resource management. The individual tools can serve as checklists to analyse different aspects of HR strategy. They can also be used to involve people in the formulation of strategy by prompting discussions in workshops and focus groups. The kit consists of the following tools:

- *Tool 1*: Overall business analysis and HR implications;
- *Tool 2*: Analysis of competitive strategy and its implications;
- *Tool 3*: Analysis of business strategies and their implications;
- *Tool 4*: Analysis of fit between type of organization and HR strategy;
- *Tool 5*: 'Best practice' analysis;
- *Tool 6*: Overall analysis of HR strategic goals;
- *Tool 7*: Overall strategic HRM gap analysis;
- *Tool 8*: Integration of business and HR strategies;
- *Tool 9*: Bundling of HR activities;
- *Tool 10*: Analysis of high-performance goals;
- *Tool 11*: High-performance work system gap analysis;
- *Tool 12*: Analysis of engagement and commitment levels – survey;
- *Tool 13*: Analysis of employee engagement goals;
- *Tool 14*: Employee engagement gap analysis;
- *Tool 15*: Analysis of resourcing goals;
- *Tool 16*: Resourcing gap analysis;
- *Tool 17*: Analysis of talent management goals;
- *Tool 18*: Talent management gap analysis;
- *Tool 19*: Analysis of learning and development goals;
- *Tool 20*: Gap analysis of learning and development activities;
- *Tool 21*: Analysis of reward management goals;

- *Tool 22*:   Gap analysis of reward management activities;
- *Tool 23*:   Analysis of employee relations goals;
- *Tool 24*:   Gap analysis of employee relations activities.

TOOL 1   Overall business analysis and HR implications

Business Matters		Human Resource Implications	
What business are we in?		What sort of people do we need in the business?	
Where are we going?		What sort of organization do we need to get there?	
What are our strengths, weaknesses, opportunities and threats?		To what extent are these strengths and weaknesses related to our HR capability?	
		What opportunities have we got to develop and engage our people?	
		What are the threats with regard to skills shortages and retention of key people?	
What are the main strategic issues facing the business?		To what extent do these issues involve HR considerations?	
What are the drivers of performance in the business?		What contribution should our people make to drive performance?	

TOOL 2 Analysis of competitive strategy and its implications

Strategy	HR Area	Possible Actions	Proposed Actions
Achieve competitive advantage through innovation	Resourcing	Recruit and retain high-quality people with innovative skills and a good track record in innovation.	
	Learning and development	Develop strategic capability and provide encouragement and facilities for enhancing innovative skills and enhancing the intellectual capital of the organization.	
	Reward	Provide financial incentives and rewards and recognition for successful innovations.	
Achieve competitive advantage through quality	Resourcing	Use sophisticated selection procedures to recruit people who are likely to deliver quality and high levels of customer service.	
	Learning and development	Encourage the development of a learning organization, develop and implement knowledge management processes, and support total quality and customer care initiatives with focused training.	
	Reward	Link rewards to quality performance and the achievement of high standards of customer service.	

TOOL 2 *Continued*

Strategy	HR Area	Possible Actions	Proposed Actions
Achieve competitive advantage through cost leadership	Resourcing	Develop core and periphery employment structures; recruit people who are likely to add value; if unavoidable, plan and manage downsizing humanely.	
	Learning and development	Provide training designed to improve productivity; inaugurate just-in-time training that is closely linked to immediate business needs and can generate measurable improvements in cost-effectiveness.	
	Reward	Develop performance management processes that enable both financial and non-financial rewards to be related to competence and skills; ensure that pay levels are competitive.	

TOOL 3 Analysis of business strategies and their implications

Business Strategy	HR Implications			
	Performance	Resourcing	Learning and Development	Reward
Market Development				
Product Development				
New Technology				
Diversification				
Merger, Acquisition				

TOOL 4 Analysis of fit between type of organization and HR strategy

Miles and Snow Classification	Implications for HR Strategy			
	Performance	Resourcing	Learning and Development	Reward
Prospectors, which operate in an environment characterized by rapid and unpredictable changes				
Defenders, which operate in a more stable and predictable environment than prospectors and engage in more long-term planning				
Analysers, which are a combination of the prospector and defender types. They operate in stable environments like defenders and also in markets where new products are constantly required like prospectors				
Reactors, which are unstable organizations existing in what they believe to be an unpredictable environment. They lack consistent, well-articulated strategies and do not undertake long-range planning				

TOOL 5   'Best practice' analysis

Pfeffer's List of Seven 'Best Practices'	'Best Practice' Adopted by Similar Organizations	Extent to which 'Best Practice' Exists in Own Organization	Extent to Which 'Best Practice' Should or Can Be Adopted in Context of Own Organization
1. Employment security			
2. Selective hiring			
3. Self-managed teams			
4. High compensation contingent on performance			
5. Training to provide a skilled and motivated workforce			
6. Reduction of status differentials			
7. Sharing information			

TOOL 6   Overall analysis of HR strategic goals

Possible HR Strategic Goals	Importance*	Effectiveness*
Support the achievement of the organization's goals		
Meet needs of employees		
Develop a high-performance culture		
Create a powerful employee value proposition		
Ensure that the organization is seen as a 'great place to work'		
Increase engagement		
Recruit and retain talented people		
Reward people according to their contribution		
Provide employees with a voice		
Improve communications		
Provide a good working environment		

* Scale: 10 = high; 0 = low

TOOL 7   Overall strategic HRM gap analysis

Strategic HRM Area	What We Are Doing	What We Should Be Doing	How We Should Fill the Gap
Performance			
Engagement			
Organization Development			
Resourcing			
Talent Management			
Learning and Development			
Reward Management			
Employee Relations			
Working Environment			

TOOL 8   Integration of business and HR strategies

Business Strategy	Integrated HR Strategy
1.	
2.	
3.	
4.	
5.	
6.	

TOOL 9   Bundling of HR activities

Possible Areas in Which Bundling (ie Linking HR Activities) Could Take Place	Extent to Which Any Bundling Has Taken Place	Any Further Action Required
High-performance work system		
Performance management		
Use of competency framework		
Development of joined-up talent management processes		
Development of blended learning processes		
Development of career grade and pay structures		

TOOL 10 Analysis of high-performance goals

Characteristics of the Culture	Importance*	Effectiveness*
People know what's expected of them – they understand their goals and accountabilities.		
People feel that their job is worth doing, and there is a strong fit between the job and their capabilities.		
Management defines what it requires in the shape of performance improvements, sets goals for success and monitors performance to ensure that the goals are achieved.		
There is strong leadership from the top that engenders a shared belief in the importance of continuing improvement.		
There is a focus on promoting positive attitudes that result in an engaged, committed and motivated workforce.		
Performance management processes are aligned to business goals to ensure that people are engaged in achieving agreed objectives and standards.		
Capacities of people are developed through learning at all levels to support performance improvement and are provided with opportunities to make full use of their skills and abilities.		
People are valued and rewarded according to their contribution.		
A pool of talent ensures a continuous supply of high performers in key roles.		
There is a climate of trust and teamwork, aimed at delivering a distinctive service to the customer.		

* Scale: 10 = high; 0 = low

TOOL 11   High-performance work system gap analysis

Strategic HPWS Area	What We Are Doing	What We Should Be Doing	How We Should Fill the Gap
Performance drivers identified and govern development of HPWS practices.			
Corporate performance goals cascaded to all employees.			
Roles clarify and emphasize performance goals.			
Effective performance management system in place.			
Rewards related to performance and contribution.			
Learning and development activities focus on delivering performance improvements.			
Performance improvement recognized as key aspect of leadership.			

TOOL 12 Analysis of engagement and commitment levels – survey

Please circle the number that most closely matches your opinion.				
	Strongly Agree	**Disagree**	**Strongly Agree**	**Disagree**
Engagement:	1	2	3	4
1. I am very satisfied with the work I do.	1	2	3	4
2. My job is interesting.	1	2	3	4
3. I know exactly what I am expected to do.	1	2	3	4
4. I am prepared to put myself out to do my work.	1	2	3	4
5. My job is not very challenging.	1	2	3	4
6. I am given plenty of freedom to decide how to do my work.	1	2	3	4
7. I get plenty of opportunities to learn in this job.	1	2	3	4
8. The facilities/ equipment/tools provided are excellent.	1	2	3	4
9. I do not get adequate support from my boss.	1	2	3	4
10. My contribution is fully recognized.	1	2	3	4
11. The experience I am getting now will be a great help in advancing my future career.	1	2	3	4

TOOL 12   *Continued*

Please circle the number that most closely matches your opinion.				
	Strongly Agree	Disagree	Strongly Agree	Disagree
12. I find it difficult to keep up with the demands of my job.	1	2	3	4
13. I have no problems in achieving a balance between my work and my private life.	1	2	3	4
14. I like working for my boss.	1	2	3	4
15. I get on well with my work colleagues.	1	2	3	4
Commitment:	1	2	3	4
16. I think this organization is a great place in which to work.	1	2	3	4
17. I believe I have a good future in this organization.	1	2	3	4
18. I intend to go on working for this organization.	1	2	3	4
19. I am not happy about the values of this organization – the ways in which it conducts its business.	1	2	3	4
20. I believe that the products/services provided by this organization are excellent.	1	2	3	4

TOOL 13   Analysis of employee engagement goals

Engagement Goals – Enhance Engagement by:	Importance*	Effectiveness*
Providing interesting and challenging work, responsibility (feeling that the work is important and having control over one's own resources), autonomy (freedom to act), scope to use and develop skills and abilities, the availability of the resources required to carry out the work, and opportunities for advancement.		
Establishing an enabling, supportive and inspirational work environment.		
Ensuring that leaders increase engagement through the ways in which they design jobs, allocate work, delegate and provide autonomy.		
Providing people with opportunities to grow and develop.		
Enabling people to feed their ideas and views upwards and feel they are making a contribution.		

* Scale: 10 = high; 0 = low

TOOL 14   Employee engagement gap analysis

Engagement Activity	What We Are Doing	What We Should Be Doing	How We Should Fill the Gap
Job Design			
Performance Management			
Total Reward System			
Leadership Development			
Skills and Career Development Opportunities			

TOOL 15 Analysis of resourcing goals

Resourcing Goals	Importance*	Effectiveness*
Match people resources to business requirements.		
Avoid unexpected deficits or surpluses of staff.		
Achieve human capital advantage by employing higher-quality people than competitors.		
Attract and recruit high-quality candidates.		
Minimize recruitment costs.		
Maximize 'recruitment intensity', ie high numbers of applicants per vacancy.		
Increase predictive validity, ie the extent to which predictions of performance and overall suitability made when recruiting people are achieved.		
Increase retention rates.		
Reduce cost of labour turnover.		
Achieve the required degree of flexibility in the use of people.		

* Scale: 10 = high; 0 = low

TOOL 16   Resourcing gap analysis

Resourcing Activity	What We Are Doing	What We Should Be Doing	How We Should Fill the Gap
Workforce planning based on thorough analysis of demand and supply forecasts.			
Take action to align resourcing plans to strategic business plans.			
Attractive employment brand developed to obtain good candidates.			
Speedy action taken to deal with forecast surpluses or deficits of staff.			
Use of a variety of potentially valuable sources of candidates.			
Role analysis uses competency framework and forms basis for structured interviews.			
Line managers trained in interviewing techniques.			
Interviews supplemented by batteries of valid and reliable tests.			
Causes of labour turnover analysed and action taken to reduce losses.			
Costs of labour turnover known and used to deliver message on the need to improve retention rates.			
Risk analysis carried out to identify potential losses and take preventative action.			
Effectiveness of resourcing activities regularly reviewed and corrective action taken as necessary.			

TOOL 17 Analysis of talent management goals

Talent Management Goals	Importance*	Effectiveness*
Define what is meant by talent in terms of competencies and potential.		
Ensure that talent is treated as a key corporate resource.		
Develop a pool of talent that will provide a guaranteed supply of high-quality people to meet future requirements.		
Provide for management succession.		
Rely primarily on growth from within while recognizing the need to bring in fresh blood from time to time.		
Identify those with talent and potential.		
Institute programmes to develop talent.		
Create a compelling 'employee value proposition'.		
Develop the organization as 'an employer of choice'.		

* Scale: 10 = high; 0 = low

TOOL 18   Talent management gap analysis

Talent Management Activity	What We Are Doing	What We Should Be Doing	How We Should Fill the Gap
Define organization's talent requirements.			
Conduct talent audits to identify talent.			
Identify sources of talent from within and outside the organization.			
Provide talented people with opportunities for career development and growth.			
Design jobs that provide talented people with the opportunity to develop their skills and potential.			
Define career paths and career 'aiming points' or 'destination jobs'.			
Apply systematic policies to improve retention rates.			
Create management succession plans.			
Recognize those with talent through the reward system.			

TOOL 19 Analysis of learning and development goals

Learning and Development Goals	Importance*	Effectiveness*
Create human capital advantage by ensuring that the organization has more skilled and competent people than its competitors.		
Improve individual, team and organizational performance.		
Attract and retain high-quality people by offering them learning and development opportunities.		
Extend the skills base of the organization.		
Improve organizational flexibility by multiskilling.		
Provide additional non-financial rewards to people in the form of growth and career opportunities.		
Reduce the length of learning curves and thus minimize learning costs.		
Ensure that talented people are developed to achieve their maximum potential.		
Provide line managers with the skills required to lead and develop their people.		

* Scale: 10 = high; 0 = low

TOOL 20   Gap analysis of learning and development activities

Learning and Development Activity	What We Are Doing	What We Should Be Doing	How We Should Fill the Gap
Encourage organizational learning.			
Develop the business as a learning organization.			
Identify learning needs.			
Introduce blended learning and development programmes to meet identified needs.			
Make good use of e-learning.			
Introduce systematic coaching.			
Develop a mentoring programme.			
Evaluate the outcome of learning and development programmes.			

TOOL 21 Analysis of reward management goals

Reward Management Goals	Importance*	Effectiveness*
Reinforce the achievement of organizational goals.		
Recruit and retain staff of the required calibre.		
Facilitate staff mobility.		
Achieve strong relationship between pay and performance.		
Reinforce organizational values.		
Engage and motivate employees.		
Cost-effective.		
Well communicated and understood by employees.		
Managed effectively in practice by line managers.		

* Scale: 10 = high; 0 = low

TOOL 22   Gap analysis of reward management activities

Reward Management Activity	What We Are Doing	What We Should Be Doing	How We Should Fill the Gap
Develop total reward processes.			
Use systematic processes for valuing roles and achieving internal equity.			
Regularly survey market rates to ensure pay levels are competitive.			
Develop and maintain grade and pay structures that provide a good framework for managing gradings and pay progression.			
Reward people for their contribution.			
Develop recognition programmes.			
Introduce flexible benefits.			
Manage general and individual pay reviews.			

TOOL 23 Analysis of employee relations goals

Employee Relations Goals	Importance*	Effectiveness*
Build stable and cooperative relationships with employees and their trade unions.		
Operate on a partnership basis with trade unions.		
Achieve engagement through employee involvement and communication processes.		
Minimize conflict with employees and their unions.		
Adopt a high-commitment approach that develops mutuality.		
Maintain bargaining structures and negotiating procedures that enable agreements to be reached smoothly.		

* Scale: 10 = high; 0 = low

TOOL 24 Gap analysis of employee relations activities

Employee Relations Activity	What We Are Doing	What We Should Be Doing	How We Should Fill the Gap
Recognize unions.			
Develop partnership agreements.			
Maintain effective industrial relations procedures.			
Resolve disputes.			
Negotiate terms and conditions.			
Communicate.			
Provide employees with a voice (involvement and participation).			

AUTHOR INDEX

SUBJECT INDEX

With over 1,000 titles in printed and digital format, **Kogan Page** offers affordable, sound business advice

www.koganpage.com

KoganPage

CPSIA information can be obtained
at www.ICGtesting.com
Printed in the USA
LVOW04s0051210116

471539LV00033B/231/P